Play, Death, and Heroism in Shakespeare

Play, Death, and Heroism in
SHAKESPEARE

By Kirby Farrell

The University of North Carolina Press
Chapel Hill and London

Library of Congress Cataloging-in-Publication Data

Farrell, Kirby, 1942–
    Play, death, and heroism in Shakespeare / by Kirby
Farrell.
    p.   cm.
    Includes index.
    ISBN 0-8078-1840-2 (alk. paper)
    1. Shakespeare, William, 1564–1616—Criticism and
interpretation. 2. Shakespeare, William, 1564–1616—
Characters—Heroes. 3. Death in literature. 4. Heroes in
literature. 5. Denial (Psychology) in literature. 6. Immortality
in literature. I. Title.
PR3069.D42F37 1989
822.3′3—dc 19   88-28346
                                                            CIP

The paper in this book meets the guidelines for permanence
and durability of the Committee on Production Guidelines for
Book Longevity of the Council on Library Resources.

Printed in the United States of America

93 92 91 90 89 5 4 3 2 1

For Helena and Vanessa

Ex oribus infantium . . .

My Shakespeare, rise; I will not lodge thee by
   Chaucer, or Spenser, or bid Beaumont lye
A little further, to make thee a roome;
   Thou art a Moniment, without a tombe,
And art alive still, while thy booke doth live,
   And we have wits to read, and praise to give.

                        —Ben Jonson

Contents

Preface

This book began as a series of papers and articles about the many characters in Shakespeare who play dead. From the start I was interested not only in the curious theatrical convention of play-death but also in the fantasies it implied. The subject began to open up for me when I realized that the rituals of self-effacement commonly practiced by children in Renaissance English society amounted to play-deaths followed by resurrections into adulthood. The same pattern appeared elsewhere in the structures of deference and dominance that shaped English society as a whole. Gradually I began to trace out other analogues of play-death and deliverance in imagery of death and rebirth, and self-sacrifice and heroic apotheosis.

Still, I only recognized the fantasy which governs many of these variations on play-death one day in a used bookstore when I happened on a copy of Ernest Becker's *The Denial of Death*. Skimming a few passages I felt a pang of discovery. Becker argues that "the idea of death, the fear of it, haunts the human animal like nothing else; it is a mainspring of human activity—activity designed largely to avoid the fatality of death, to overcome it by denying in some way that it is the final destiny for man." That death-denying activity is humankind's creation of heroic significance. Play-death, I saw, not only tested fears of annihilation, it dramatized possibilities of heroic deliverance from death.

Becker's book provided a powerful lens through which to look at art and culture. But not only that. As I was reading I was stunned to realize that I had already been through the book, eight or nine years before, when it had first appeared. Thanks to my own powers of denial, Becker's disturbing vision had disappeared without a trace under the magician's handkerchief of repression. Even as I struggled to ex-

plain away the lapse, I had a painfully comic sense of my own crea-
turely compulsion. After all, in my denial I had lately been rediscover-
ing death in a safely disguised form: play-death in Shakespeare. In
effect, I had been playing dead myself in order to transform a deeply
disturbing vision of life into an academic analysis which I could manage with heroic aplomb. The present book is the outcome of that
recognition.

Acknowledgments

For encouragement and wholesome scolding I am grateful to Rick Abrams, John Blanpied, Arthur Kinney, Mimi Sprengnether, and Jim Calderwood, who has himself lately begun to explore the crooked passages beneath the cloud-capped towers of heroism (*Shakespeare and the Denial of Death*, 1987). Some of this book was written while I was teaching at the University of Freiburg, aided by a grant from the Max Kade Foundation. The Graduate Research Council at the University of Massachusetts assisted me on several occasions, and the English Department has been unfailingly supportive.

In other forms Chapter 2 appears in *Shakespeare Studies* 16 (1984): 75–99, while Chapter 9 appears in *Shakespeare Studies* 19 (1987): 17–40 (reprinted by permission of the editors). Chapter 8, "Love, Death, and Patriarchy in *Romeo and Juliet*," also appears in *Shakespeare's Personality*, edited by Sidney Homan, Norman Holland, and Bernard Paris (Berkeley, Cal.: University of California Press, 1989).

Some of the book's arguments originated as papers presented before the New England Renaissance Society (1977); the 1978 MLA session on "Marriage and the Family in Shakespeare"; the 1983 and 1984 Themes in Drama Conferences at the University of California at Riverside; the 1985 conference on "Shakespeare's Personality" at the University of Florida, Gainesville; the International Shakespeare Society (1986); the 1988 Buffalo Symposium on Language and Literature; and the Fifth European-American Conference on Literature and Psychoanalysis (1988).

Part One

In the realm of fiction we discover
that plurality of lives for which we
crave. We die in the person of a
given hero, yet we survive him, and
are ready to die again with the
next hero, just as safely.

—Freud, "Reflections upon War and Death"

But death is the one concept you can't
deconstruct. Work back from there and
you end up with the old idea of an
autonomous self. I can die, therefore
I am.

—David Lodge, *Small World*

Chapter 1

Introduction

One afternoon as I was musing over Juliet's play-death and botched resurrection in *Romeo and Juliet*, I heard my three-year-old daughter Helena and her friend outside the window rescuing one another. With gusto one of them would clutch her breast, cry out "Help, I'm dy-y-y-ing," then expire in the grass. The other would spring to her side, make scrabbling "nurse" motions with her hands, and then pull the victim to her feet and back to life. Although they took turns dying, each ritualistic replay culminated in heroic deliverance. As the excitement of the game mounted, the "nurse" was inspired to telephone her late grandmother in heaven. The phone call seemed to get through to heaven all right, but was poignantly inconclusive. After saying hello, the heroine gawked at the invisible telephone she held in her fist, unable to go on. She assumed that somehow the silent grandmother was only playing dead, but she had no myth by which to recover her: no account of Persephone or Eurydice, no Renaissance frescos of the elect ranked across the face of heaven in a corporate portrait of eternal bliss. In that moment the child stumbled upon the problem Aeneas discovered during his famous excursion into the underworld:

> . . . facilis descensus Averno;
> noctes atque dies patet atri ianua Ditis;
> sed revocare gradum superasque evadere ad auras,
> hoc opus, hic labor est.

To descend into death is easy: to return, difficult.

As I thought about the girls rescuing each other from play-deaths, I recalled Romeo's dream that Juliet's kiss had brought him back to life and made him an emperor, and his heroic vow to preserve her from the "monster" death by joining her in the grave (5.3.104). The friar also promises heroic deliverance, since he would put Juliet through a mock death and then, like God, personally resurrect her. But then, Juliet herself is fascinated by the thought of playing dead as the way to union with Romeo. Rather than marry Paris, she cries,

> . . . hide me nightly in a charnel-house,
> O'ercover'd quite with dead men's rattling bones,
> With reeky shanks and yellow chapless skulls;
> Or bid me go into a new-made grave,
> And hide me with a dead man in his shroud
> Things that, to hear them told, have made me tremble
> And I will do it without fear or doubt,
> To live an unstain'd wife to my sweet love.
>
> [4.1.81–88][1]

Rushing toward forbidden independence, Juliet envisions playing dead as an initiation rite that will purge her guilt and fear of annihilation. The ordeal would climax in a resurrection that would validate her love.

Not every play-death acts out love and rescue; some mimic murder. In battle-games such as "king of the hill," children explore fantasies of aggression and sacrifice, supremacy and submission, loss and recovery, usually at an age when all doom seems reversible and the slain, like Falstaff at Shrewsbury, are expected to hop to their feet again.[2] Renaissance children played martial games even as their parents did. A week of wedding entertainments for King James's daughter Elizabeth in 1613, for example, climaxed in a simulation of the naval battle between the Turks and Venetians. The players, including five hundred Thames watermen and a thousand militiamen, wrought so many real casualties that the king had to call a halt to the festive hostilities.[3] This sort of play-death colors Shakespeare's conception of warfare in the histories. At the battle of Shrewsbury King Henry fields decoys who are his "counterfeits" or "shadows" (*1H4* 5.4.35, 30). Slaughtering these histrionic surrogates, Douglas finds death dissolving in play and the king a Hydra ever springing back to life (25).

An astonishing range of characters in Shakespeare undergo a simulation of death, including Falstaff, Cleopatra, *Much Ado's* Hero, King Lear and Gloucester, the much-afflicted Pericles and his wife Thaisa, Imogen, and Queen Hermione and her daughter Perdita. The Duke of Vienna and *All's Well's* Helena let themselves appear dead in order to act personally yet invisibly in the world. It could be argued that the plot of *The Tempest* dramatizes Prospero's triumphant recovery from a long play-death.[4]

Common to all of these examples is a rhythm of play-death and resurrection or heroic apotheosis. Uncannily returned to life, the degraded Queen Hermione and Perdita deliver Sicilia from death's shadow as if ransoming all the world (*WT* 5.2.15). Even actual death may seem to be a fictive experience—in effect, another form of play-death—as when Romeo dies elaborating an afterlife in which he will gloriously defend Juliet from violence such as he has known in Verona. Hearing of Cleopatra's suicide, Antony vows to plunge into the underworld to join her in paradise,

> Where souls do couch on flowers, we'll hand in hand,
> And with our sprightly port make the ghosts gaze.
> Dido and her Aeneas shall want troops,
> And all the haunt be ours.
>
> [4.14.50–53]

As if death is but a momentary interruption of routine, Antony projects himself and Cleopatra into the afterlife as celebrities—sublimely meretricious demigods who will forever outshine the great.

II

The following chapters explore a pattern of imaginative behavior that embraces all of the fantasies sketched above. In different ways the pattern is present in Antony's strolling apotheosis and in the anxious game of the two children outside my window. Throughout this book I mean to evoke both play-death, the most literal form of the pattern, in which characters explicitly feign a demise, and the more encompassing interrelationship of play, death, and heroic significance, which produces cultural forms that serve to tame real death. By "play" I mean imaginative behavior that is suppositional, improvisatory, and heuristic: behavior that manipulates and explores the limits of cultural conventions. Theater is play, as are jokes; but so is a state of mind open to questions about unsettling subjects such as death and love and authority. In any particular circumstance play can be destructive as well as creative; it can be subversive or recuperative or escapist—or for that matter can combine those possibilities and more. Above all, play is a crucial part of the symbolizing process by which we go about substantiating ourselves in the world: which is why such a slippery concept is necessary in a book about the cultural construction of death and heroic values.

Shakespeare dominates my argument because the pattern I want to unfold appears profoundly and accessibly in his art. I began with the girls' game not only to put the Shakespearean text in a context of ongoing human concerns, but also to make clear at the outset that imaginative responses to death are inherently cultural processes. We are not born with conceptions of death; they have to be learned and invented. And because the subject is so menacing, we may learn less by formal instruction than by indirect means, internalizing attitudes around us—repression included—or thinking about the unthinkable in the mediating forms of play. Invariably we learn to contain death: to measure it, locate it, invest it with meaning and some predictability. By playing at dying, as the girls did, we may also be trying it out, taming it, even trying to preempt it. At the same time, as I argue beginning in Chapter 3, we transform the pressure of death into heroic forms, so that dread becomes not only endurable but a source of creative energy.

Play-death is an explicit instance of culture's use of fictions to engage death. Expiring on the lawn outside my window, my daughter and her friend were improvising a drama, even as the melodramatic forms they borrowed from television and elsewhere were reciprocally shaping the girls' identities, providing them roles and putting words in their mouths.[5] Since the roles made victim and rescuer alike larger than life, each flirtation with doom became an affirmation of self and of solidarity. Their play enabled the girls to think out loud in public, despite taboos, about their discovery of mortality and, crucially important, to make something of it. Something similar takes place when audiences identify with a character who perishes in a film or in a Shakespearean tragedy: they are vicariously participating in symbolic constructions of death that help to make life supportable.

Culture, says Clifford Geertz, is "a set of symbolic devices for controlling behavior, extrasomatic sources of information" analogous to genetic codes. "Our ideas, our values, our acts, even our emotions are, like our nervous system itself, cultural products—products manufactured, indeed, out of tendencies, capacities, and dispositions with which we were born, but manufactured nonetheless."[6] Playing at heroic deliverance, my daughter and her friend were ontologically substantiating themselves: not just solving problems (or fulfilling needs), and not merely acting to control panic, but also, more basically, forming themselves out of some of the symbolic materials, including adventure stories, which their society offered them. Energized by danger, they assumed historically conditioned roles (medical nurse/mother) that led them to adaptive cooperation rather than to competitive aggression.

One distant source of those controlling materials is of course Shakespeare, whose vision continues to influence us even though the culture it originally served has long since disappeared. Since this book aspires to look through Shakespeare to that now-lost culture, let me turn to some of the fantasies of play-death and heroism in action there. To begin with a global perspective, consider the idea of a renaissance, which the age used to define itself. "The Renaissance," says Thomas Greene, "chose to open a polemic against what it called the Dark Ages. The ubiquitous imagery of disinterment, resurrection, and renascence needed a death and burial to justify itself; without the myth of medieval entombment, its imagery, which is to say its self-understanding, had no force. The creation of this myth . . . expressed a belief in change and loss, . . . loss of a remote, prestigious past that might nonetheless be resuscitated."[7] Regret for lost glory, that is, went hand in hand with a belief that imaginative striving could undo death. The myth enabled Renaissance Europeans to project a vision of human greatness into the past, beyond criticism, from whence it could be gloriously recovered.

In England the Renaissance play at loss and renewal reinforced a crucial political myth. As Queen Elizabeth aged, the nation turned her Accession Day rite into a forthright public fantasy of rebirth. The celebration "helped to establish the myth that the Elizabethan age was different—a different era, a new beginning, a *renovatio* of ancient purity long lost. And it helped to create the 'uniqueness' of the reign . . . while it was actually being lived. In its cyclical view of history, Elizabethans were taught to view their Queen's reign as a rebirth."[8] The myth presupposed that new vitality may come out of decay. But it did more than console: it invested the queen with ancient authority and encouraged the nation to believe it was special, a chosen people.

Like the Accession Day rites, Elizabeth's motto, "Semper eadem," and her emblem, the reborn phoenix, functioned as propaganda. Yet like the popular fancy that the eagle scorches itself in the sun and then plunges into water to be reborn, the royal propaganda also expressed widely held assumptions about the natural world. Shakespeare echoes those assumptions in wordplay on "womb" and "tomb" that dissolves a seemingly fatal opposition by making its terms interchangeable. The idea of rebirth served the Crown by signifying both conservative continuity and purifying change, while claiming for the queen mysterious powers of survival.

Less exalted folk also used such imagery to serve their own ends. Like the conviction that ghosts return to redress injustice, fantasies of death and rebirth could give voice to social conflicts ordinarily too dangerous to contemplate. Take the belief that the fox plays dead to catch birds. In a highly authoritarian culture such a belief may tacitly recommend—or express anxiety about—feigned deference. Where the regal lion is free to pounce, the lowly fox thrives by playing the victim, using self-effacement rather than confrontation to get his way.

In *A Dialogue against the Pestilence* (1573) William Bullein presents a beggar who celebrates the mortality of the rich in plague time: "[W]e poor people have mickle good. Their loss is our luck; when they do become naked, we then are clothed against their wills; . . . their sickness is our health, their death our life."[9] In this monologue the rich man's tomb becomes the womb for a beggar and inverts the social order. Not rebellious anger or Christian charity but inscrutable death helps the meek to inherit. For the beggar, the revenge and needy opportunism latent in this scenario help to reduce its menace. The decorous equations—their loss, our luck; their death, our life—euphemize the beggar's ruthless will to live. As in the games of war I mentioned earlier, an adversary's fall strengthens the survivor's grip on life.

For the privileged, by contrast, the fantasy of prosperity gleaned from death may dramatize the horror of social decay, as when the failing Timon of Athens curses Alcibiades' mistresses: "thatch your poor thin roofs / With burthens of the dead—some that were hang'd, / No matter; wear them, betray with them" (*TA* 4.3.145–47). Timon envisions whores disguising the ravages of syphilis with wigs made from the hair of executed criminals. While protesting the violation of the dead, he also makes the grave the wellspring of pollution and anarchy. Stripped of his "immortal" gold, his identity now as perishable as his body, Timon inverts William Bullein's aggression in a rage for survival.

In a pamphlet produced during the epidemic that closed the theaters in 1593, Simon Kellway can also be seen using the idea of play-death to manage anxiety. Reporting that children sometimes "flock together in companies, and [feigning] one of their members to be dead, solemnize the burying in mournful sort," Kellway claims that such behavior foretells plague.[10] The adult Simon Kellway registers the mysterious aura of significance surrounding the children's play, convinced that their rites uncannily presage, and thereby provide some control over, real death.

Even without catastrophic disease, the mortality rates of the early modern period provided impressive models of funeral behavior. In playing at burials the children joined together to emulate the "solemnizing" roles of parents and priests, "feigning" to be heroic agents of the heavenly order. Presumably the children were seeking to strengthen themselves against traumatic loss, seeking mastery that was in some measure confirmed by the "deceased's" revival at the game's end.

But anxiety alone makes much too narrow an explanation for play-death. Like the queen, William Bullein's beggar uses the idea of rebirth as a source of vitality and self-justification. Attempting to turn the anarchic horror of plague into a blessing, Bullein the writer is himself seeking power. For him the vitality of the rich is recreated, as in play-death, in the poor. His fantasy is a way of reconceiving a society that systematically nullifies its poor. The force of Bullein's vignette comes from its revelation of the meaning of that social death. Compare the beggar, excluded on all sides, with this description of Ashanti life: "No problems of identity arise for the Ashanti, whose name and birthday and family taboos relate him to a richly textured web of forces; he recognizes sins by thought and deed, but guilt does not oppress him, since purification is at hand; he can virtually slough off his errant, unintended weaknesses and start afresh."[11] In this light fantasies of play-death are tools evolved to produce a sense of "starting afresh" by giving imagination leverage to budge burdensome social forms.

III

Fantasies of play-death give shape to ineffable ultimates—death, divinity—yet the forms are implicated in everyday social life. Meanings devised to control death turn out to be at the core of cultural production. *Antony and Cleopatra*, where heaven and earth, myth and diplomacy, intermingle, is a case in point. Enobarbus jokes that Cleopatra "dies instantly" on a taste of bad news: "I do think there is mettle in death, which commits some loving act upon her, she hath such a celerity in dying" (1.2.142–44). He must mean that she has used fainting or a feigned collapse to get her way long before she fools Antony into suicide: "go tell him that I have slain myself" (4.13.7). This pretended self-slaughter is a personal fantasy of expiation and punishment and a political strategy as well. Playing possum for Antony's benefit, pretending to kill herself in contrition, Cleopatra uses sham deference to maintain her power. Implicitly she casts Antony as her murderer, manipulating his guilt and affection.

When Cleopatra does finally take her own life "for real," as it were, her visionary demise, like the one Antony entertains (4.14.50–54), is also a form of play. In her last moments she takes the roles of wife and mother, monarch and rebel, among others, and finishes as a huntress in a cunning semblance of sleep, "As she would catch another Antony in her / strong toil of grace" (5.2.347–48). In her theatricality she uses her body as a sign to send the message that "great Caesar" is an "ass / Unpolicied" (307–8) and that she herself is triumphant. Nevertheless, in all her wiles there is something obsessively earnest too, since her physician reports "She hath pursued conclusions infinite / Of easy ways to die" (354–56). Even Cleopatra's final leave-taking is both a personal negotiation of destiny and a form of social behavior.

Any represented death—a noble suicide, say—reflects the values through which a particular group projects itself into and, however reluctantly, out of the world. For the dramatist, actors, and audience, Cleopatra's self-sacrifice focussed a myriad of overlapping and historically layered assumptions about life. For my purposes, the guiding thread in this labyrinth is the premise that in constructing an illusion of death in the theater people were collaborating, as they did in other areas of their lives, to convert the threat of pollution, instability, and nothingness into a source of fertility or productiveness: to make death yield heroic meaning that could sustain society.

To unfold the cultural logic implied by such complex imaginative behavior I use a combination of anthropological and psychoanalytic criticism. My effort has been to integrate the symbolical analysis the Shakespearean text invites with sociological and historical investigation. Like a series of core samples, the following chapters build up a fragmentary, highly inferential picture of things ordinarily inaccessible. With some unavoidable repetition my argument crisscrosses unexplored terrain, testing it from different points on a grid, and refining the interpretation that emerges. Initially I focus on play-death in Shakespeare because its relative concreteness makes it a useful paradigm. As the book proceeds, however, the concept of play-death quickly expands into a range of associations that lead beyond theater. Chapter 2, for instance, considers the social implications of play-death, relating it to the belief pervasive in Shakespeare's England that through self-effacement an individual may become autonomous. The chapter analyzes that belief as it operates in Renaissance social dynamics, family structure, and in the transaction of theater itself.

Chapter 3 explores play-death and heroism as responses to real death. Whatever the form, fantasies of play-death subordinate death to life. Imagination acts to attenuate the reality of annihilation and to control the sound and fury of existence. Such fantasies convert the ultimate revelation of human helplessness into an assertion of humankind's primary value. The conversion is a form of cognitive substitution that replaces one mental set with another. The resulting overestimation of humankind is often tantamount to apotheosis. Taking *Antony and Cleopatra* and *Twelfth Night* as its primary examples, Chapter 3 follows Ernest Becker in arguing that the dread of annihilation inspires the essential cultural project of creating heroic significance.

Chapter 4 synthesizes earlier chapters by showing how the threat of traumatic loss may produce a social system based on heroism and hero worship, with people bound into postures of dominance and submission, self-effacement and apotheosis. As illustrated by Shakespeare's early histories, such a system promises to be symbiotic, with hero-worshippers fulfilled through the hero, yet it proves unstable. The source of that instability lies in the inherent ambivalence of heroism—which is evident in the children's games of rescue and aggression sketched above. At its close Chapter 4 posits affirmative and negative forms of heroism that entail antithetical projection and incorporation of selves, bestowing immortality on, or consuming, other lives. Chapter 5 explores connections between play-death, the quest of the archetypal hero, and ritual sacrifice. The argument comes to focus on the hero's mission as a release from entombment, as in the New Testament resurrection of Lazarus. Examination of the tomb as a controlling boundary between life and death leads to the subject of Chapter 6, spatial representations of death and renewal in Shakespeare.

Part Two uses heroic fantasy to read individual works in their original cultural context. In *Venus and Adonis* (Chapter 7) Adonis's problematical apotheosis suggests that Shakespeare is responding to intolerable contradictions in the conception of heroism, especially as those stresses affected courtiers such as his patron Southampton in his relations with the queen. Chapter 8 interprets Renaissance patriarchy as a system of heroic immortality that is breaking down in the Verona of *Romeo and Juliet*. The lovers attempt to find heroic significance in love. They negate themselves in "invisible" night and in the simulated death the friar contrives for Juliet. Attempting to transcend the violence endemic to patriarchal fantasy, they aspire to a "resurrection" that could redeem Verona, yet are themselves tragically captive to the patriarchal vision.

Chapter 9 turns to *Richard III* and the *Henriad*, where it unfolds opposed fantasies of heroic apotheosis based on uses of prophecy. The essay takes prophecy to be a strategy of self-effacement that displaces the self into a messianic political future. Chapter 10 recapitulates earlier themes in a psychoanalytic examination of the relationship between fantasies of play-death and individuation in the early *Midsummer Night's Dream* and the last romances. It concludes by asking to what extent Prospero's farewell represents his effort to take responsibility for his own death.

The Epilogue glances at the fortunes of play-death and heroism after Shakespeare, closing with some examples of the pattern in contemporary American culture.

Chapter 2

Play-Death, Self-Effacement, and Autonomy

To show how fantasies of play-death shape social behavior in Shakespeare and his culture, I want to relate the pattern of play-death and apotheosis to a pattern of self-effacement and autonomy. In both, a radical loss of identity leads to compensatory self-aggrandizement. By effacing themselves individuals may fulfill themselves. By nullifying or appearing to nullify their own wills, they may free themselves to act with greater personal force. For simplicity's sake I begin with examples of this fantasy that directly dramatize a sequence of death and resurrection or strongly imply it. After surveying the fantasy in the plays, I examine it in the context of contemporary family and social dynamics, and then in relation to the imaginative process of theater itself.

In many of the plays a crisis of autonomy clearly leads to self-effacement. Playing dead then becomes a means of circumventing oppression. When Juliet resists an arranged marriage, her father threatens either deathlike rejection—"hang, beg, starve, die in the streets" (3.5.192)—or deathlike submission that would negate her will. Faking death according to the friar's plan, Juliet preempts her parents' control and aspires to a liberating rebirth in her lover's arms. Banished from Verona, socially destroyed, Romeo dreams that he died and then Juliet "breathed such life with kisses in my lips / That I revived and was an emperor" (5.1.8–9).

Given the formidably hierarchical and competitive social world projected in most Shakespearean drama, self-effacement is at least in part a submissive gesture. As in the England Shakespeare himself knew, authority in the plays is palpably personal. However prominent the cultural and metaphysical apparatus of power, in action power is the king's will or the father's. In addition, there is no imaginative model of reasoned resistance to authority in the plays, any more than there was in Elizabethan England. Challenged by an angry ruler, minions in Shakespeare routinely protest their eagerness to die, thereby hoping to prove their loyalty and preempt death. Antigonus offers to sacrifice himself to save the infant Perdita from her despotic father (*WT* 2.3.166–67). When Pericles plays tyrant, his lieutenant Helicanus promptly offers to die: "I have ground the axe myself" (*Per.* 1.2.58). In a literal fulfillment of the wish Romeo dreams, Pericles suddenly rewards the self-effacing Helicanus by making him ruler of Tyre in his stead.

Pericles himself undergoes a figurative play-death. Cowed by a despotic father figure, "the great Antiochus, / Gainst whom I am too little to contend" (1.2.17–18), Pericles abandons his princely identity and flees. Shipwrecked, he reacts as if appeasing an angry father, begging the elements to "remember, earthly man / . . . must yield to you; / And I . . . do obey you." Straightaway he finds "Nothing to think on but ensuing death" (2.1.2–7). Overwhelmed by adversity, the prince enters a deathlike paralysis. When his daughter Marina restores him to himself, purged of his self-disabling anxieties, his recovery is explicitly a rebirth: "Thou . . . beget'st him that did thee beget" (5.1.195).

Where comedy or tragicomedy prevails in the plays, fantasies of self-effacement usually lead to wish fulfillment. Like Pericles' flight from Antiochus, Falstaff's fake death at the feet of Douglas is escapism. Yet as Pericles' eventual revival seems magically to undo the original threat by confirming him a strong, benign father himself, so Falstaff's resurrection brings him to the wish-fulfilling role of warrior-hero. Similarly, Marina escapes a murderous stepmother and apparent doom— "She is not dead . . . as she should have been" (*Per.* 5.1.215)—to find her rightful identity and parents.

At its most wishful, the fantasy of self-effacement promises to resolve conflicts with authority in a world where self assertion may appear inherently rebellious. In *A Midsummer Night's Dream*, Hermia can choose a husband only by defying Egeus, Theseus, and the state itself. Rebelling, Hermia and Lysander abandon their Athenian identities, "losing themselves" in the wood. Undergoing a "death-counterfeiting sleep" (3.2.364), the lovers awake to find themselves transformed. They seem to have achieved a new autonomy that the play dramatizes when Theseus gratuitously invites them into his own privileged circle.

The same dynamics, however, also served the Renaissance state as a means of violent control over its subjects. Not uncommonly condemned criminals were pardoned at the last moment, in the presence of the executioner, to the applause of spectators who were apt to be the protagonist's friends. Officially rehearsed for death, pledging eternal loyalty to the punishing crown, the condemned might suddenly find his life restored. In this scenario play-death amounts to traumatic dissociation. Shaken from its claims on life, the (criminal) self is effaced and then reconstituted as a penitent self publically grateful to the merciful ruler.[1] Presumably this fantasy motivates *Measure for Measure's* Duke Vincentio when, playing friar, he counsels the condemned Claudio to "Be absolute for death" (3.1.5), and Claudio replies, "I humbly thank you. / To sue to live, I find I seek to die, / And seeking death, find life. Let it come on" (41–43). In theory at least, such a play-death may reorganize personality, inducing a conversion experience.

In *The Winter's Tale*, by contrast, unyielding integrity is treated as insubordination, and self-effacement becomes self-sacrifice or martyrdom. Paulina uses the illusory loss of Hermione and Perdita to drive a long-suffering Leontes to penance and renewed feeling. The supposed deaths transform the king and his kingdom as well. The play's fantasy of efficacious martyrdom gives form to rebellious energies that might otherwise be perverted or remain repressed, with damaging consequences.

Hermione's return from the grave makes vivid some associations that are often latent in other examples of the self-effacement fantasy. As in the language of the oracle that calls for the recovery of Perdita, requiring "that which is lost" to be "found" (3.2.135), Hermione's resurrection draws on the complex of ideas at the core of the Christian myth, where the meek shall inherit and individuals must lose themselves to find themselves. When the statue comes alive in Paulina's chapel, the play insists that the change is in the eye of the beholder, a spiritual transformation. Like the golden statues of Romeo and Juliet, the image of Hermione is the public apotheosis of redemptive love.

Restored to life, Hermione possesses a new spiritual force sufficient to awe her once-dominating husband and king. The same spiritual power emanates from the ascendant Marina, Perdita, and *All's Well's* Helena, among others. Whether characters are expressly aware of the fantasy or it is subsumed in the structure of the play, its dynamics are constant. By passing through a tacit death, an eclipse of identity in the eyes of the world, characters acquire—or dream of acquiring—autonomy. The process promises to transform painful subservience into personal authority that can challenge and perhaps transcend the social hierarchy.

Psychologically, the wish for autonomy expresses a need to ground identity on something more profound than customary social and theatrical roles. In this way the fantasy of self-effacement relates to other symbolic modes by which character is realized in Shakespeare, especially disguise.[2] In *1 Henry IV* Hal's plan to keep himself in eclipse while his father rules the land allows him to preserve his integrity by resisting the roles his father would impose on him. In effect, Hal has assumed a disguise, and he describes it in terms that suggest a play-death and resurrection. He will imitate the sun, allowing clouds to "smother" him so that he "may be more wond'red at" when he finally breaks through the mists that seem "to strangle him" (1.2.201–7). His metaphors depict murderous oppression from which, at the last moment, the victim will miraculously revive and flourish.

Shakespeare repeatedly associates disguise with this rhythm of self-effacement and triumphant revival. Shipwrecked and presumed drowned, *Twelfth Night*'s Viola in effect plays dead, assuming a new identity, until at last she emerges to claim a fulfilling role. Her destiny is a variant of Hermione's: from "an eunuch," an impotent servant, a nobody (1.2.56), she transforms herself into her "master's mistress" (5.1.326). To act in the patriarchal world of Venice, Portia too hides herself, appearing in court as the authoritative "Balthasar." If we are meant to sense new depths and resources in Portia after her return to Belmont, as some critics argue, then we might see the self-effacement fantasy at work, confirming in her the autonomy she has pined for since her will was "curbed by the will of a dead father" (*MV* 1.2.24–25). Likewise the disguising of Rosalind and Celia in *As You Like It*. The same fantasy is also at work in the so-called bed tricks by which *Measure for Measure*'s Mariana and *All's Well*'s Helena efface themselves in order to be free to act and thereby claim longed-for, legitimate roles as wives.

In all of the examples above fantasies of self-effacement depend on the social world for corroboration. In *Much Ado* the friar construes Hero's play-death in social terms. Out of her "travail" he looks "for greater birth." Dying, she "Shall be lamented, pitied, and excused / Of every hearer" (4.1.213–17). In the friar's prescription as in the explicit martyrdom of Hermione, everything depends on the responsiveness of the beholder.

As Hero's restoration illustrates, self-effacement may be fruitless. Society may be corrupt and unresponsive, as in many of the tragedies. Edgar providentially turns his blind father's suicide into a play-death that enables Gloucester to bear his suffering. Lear, by contrast, tries to manipulate his daughters by conspicuously sacrificing his power, only to have them betray him. Relinquishing his royal identity, Lear would "Unburthened crawl toward death" (1.1.41). Trying to use death to win pity and become the model of the secure, beloved father, Lear falsifies his relations with his daughters. In turn his self-effacement exposes him to his daughters' depredations and to a death-counterfeiting sleep of harrowing profundity. "You are wrong to take me out of the grave," he cries to Cordelia. "Thou art a soul in bliss; But I am bound / Upon a wheel of fire," as if in the underworld (4.7.44–46).

If the comedies celebrate the self-effacement fantasy, the tragedies emphasize its perils. Romeo's dream of being revived as an emperor proves to be a compensatory and doomed solution to his exiled impotence. Juliet's play-death is similarly escapist and self-defeating. As she ominously goes through the motions of suicide in drinking the potion, so the lovers' evasion of communication with the social world ominously prefigures their mutual miscommunication and suicides in the graveyard.

One danger of the fantasy is that it may serve not only self-fulfilling wishes but also aggressive ends. Like Lear invoking a pathetic crawl toward death, Cleopatra manipulates pity to demand love. Inadvertently provoking Antony's suicide, her impulse to play dead expresses her ambivalence toward her lover. Self-destruction is more overtly aggressive in Antony's fantasy of striking at Caesar by slaying himself. Ordering Eros to kill him, he vows: "Thou strik'st not me; 'tis Caesar thou defeat'st" (4.15.68).

In Juliet's apparent demise self-effacement implies inwardly directed aggression that may finally result in suicide. Yet when her supposed death is discovered, the fantasy reveals its complexity. Like magical curses, her father's earlier death threats against her (3.5.192) suddenly appear borne out. In turn, Juliet's play-death symbolically kills him. Identifying himself with his daughter, the old man cries: "O child! My soul and not my child! / Dead art thou—alack my child is dead, / And with my child my joys are burie'd" (4.5.62–64). Given old Capulet's harsh authority and selfish grief, Juliet unwittingly accomplishes a gratifying revenge by her apparent death. Finally "All are punished" by the lovers' deaths (5.3.295). In this context the play acts out a fantasy in which, as in Freud's early theory of suicide, self-destruction is transposed murder.[3] In part, the proposed statues objectify the lovers' devious triumph over patriarchal Verona.

As gold statues Romeo and Juliet would achieve autonomy but only in art, their apotheosis a form of play-death, ideal and yet abstract, hypothetical. But then, the lovers have consistently blurred the boundaries between life and death, thought and reality, as if imagination can leap over such fatal distinctions. In *Othello* the fantasy brings unmitigated catastrophe. Othello behaves as if he can purify Desdemona by forcing her through a death and transfiguration. Kissing his sleeping wife he vows: "Be thus when thou art dead, and I will kill thee, / And love thee after" (5.2.18). Wishing to kill without truly destroying her, Othello fantasizes ultimate control over a woman who causes him soul-shaking pleasure and pain. Imagining her suspended between life and death, seeing her as "monumental alabaster" (5), a funerary statue of herself, he acts out a tragic version of the resurrection that idealizes Hermione and restores autonomy in *The Winter's Tale*.

One of the abiding problems of criticism has been how to evaluate the resurrections implied by the fantasy of playing dead. Does Lear, for example, succumb believing Cordelia is coming to life in his arms? Does he, that is, resort to the fantasy of play-death and resurrection to make this last catastrophe bearable? And if so, does he "die of joy" as R. W. Chambers claims, or does he expire more deluded than ever?[4] Or would the fantasy make such simple judgments seem inadequate? These questions also apply to Cleopatra. Is her suicide a victorious apotheosis or one last tricky evasion? "I am again for Cydnus," she cries, "To meet Mark Antony" (5.2.228–29). And again: "I have / Immortal longings in me" (280–81). How are we to take this vision and the divinization—the ultimate autonomy—implied in "immortal longings"? Or again, in Othello's nearly hallucinatory final speeches self-effacement more than once turns into self-aggrandizement, and in a context of death and afterlife. To Gratiano he brags one moment, then cries "O vain boast" and, relinquishing all his power, virtually invites his own murder: "Man but a rush against Othello's breast, / And he retires" (5.2.261, 267–68). Almost immediately he projects himself past death into a hell of spectacular horror, where he is at once nullified, a "curséd, curséd slave," and yet also a tormented evildoer of heroic proportions: "Whip me, ye devils, / From the possession of this heavenly sight! / Blow me about in winds! roast me in sulphur! / Wash me in steep-down gulfs of liquid fire!" (274–77). What we are beholding is an imagination that tries to survive onrushing annihilation by role-playing. Othello draws on the dynamics of the self-effacement fantasy, projecting a nullifying play-death and the eschatological suffering of a mythic, tragic Othello who may live on in the minds of men.

II

There are many ways of looking at the imaginative pattern I have been describing. To open it up more fully I want to draw together some characteristics of Renaissance English society, the family, and the theater, beginning with Tudor society's official conception of itself.

Although the ideology based on the great chain of being was pro-mulgated to justify the unprecedented absolutism of Tudor govern-ment and therefore was never wholly in touch with the social reality it pretended to describe, it presupposes a static world that is accordingly selfless. In theory, as a chain of being ordered the universe, so a hierar-chy of obedience ordered the family and society. Dependent persons were "subsumed" into the personalities of their fathers and masters.[5] Havoc resulted from self-assertion, whether in the present or, myth-ically dissociated, in the violation of the Tree of Knowledge and origi-nal sin. Week after week, as prescribed by law, preachers warned that any resistance to authority was an evil madness and meant damnation. According to the official "Homily on Obedience (1559)," even Christ himself and his Apostles "received many and diverse injuries of the un-faithfull and wicked menne in auctoritie," yet "they paciently suffered death itself obedientlye." Threatened by Pilate, "Jesus aunswered: Thou couldst have no power at all againste me except it were given thee from above." Christ's rebuke signifies not the power of individual faith and suffering in the face of persecution, but "plainly, that even the wicked rulers have their power and auctoritie from God."[6]

The doctrine of the chain of being so polarized the concept of obedience that it permitted virtually no autonomy in the modern sense. In theology, since God was absolute and unmoved, judgment was merely metaphorical. The soul's actions automatically determined its fate. Sin was death, a direct rejection of God "in which the soul becomes a negative image to its previous capacity for union with God. Sin is the anti-matter to God's reality."[7] In its social form this opposi-tion between obedience and nullity tended to minimize or deny the autonomy of those who served, thereby aggrandizing authority figures such as the father and the king. Since obedience means identification with the will of a superior, absolute obedience entails self-effacement. Like sin, disobedience is nullity. Tudor authorities commonly dehumanized and nullified the disobedient, labeling them beasts, blaming their behavior on magical charms (as Shakespeare's despotic fathers do with willful daughters), branding their bodies, or making them outright slaves to be treated, in the famous futile 1547 statute on vagabonds, for example, like "movable goods or cattle."[8] In the hierarchy derived from the chain of being the only truly autonomous person is the king. Such a system makes personal autonomy a function of absolute authority: a sort of apotheosis beyond the scale of ordinary life. It presupposes a radical polarity between self-negation and self-assertion.

Similarly, in the popular mind the Christian myth of salvation placed the believer in a cosmic family structured by the polarities of dominance and submission, all and nothing. By submitting to the Father, the Christian could hope to pass through death to a triumphant rebirth that parallels the child's achievement of adulthood and identification with the father, on the one hand, and the entrance into the ranks of the elect, on the other.[9] Through abnegation the figurative child could be elevated in a union with the Lord that was also both an individual eschatological triumph and a rise above the intervening ranks of society.

In these secular and religious paradigms the polarity of relationships resembles the structure of the self-effacement fantasy in Shakespeare. But the internal dynamics are similar too insofar as individuals must surrender themselves in order to identify with powerful authority. What complicates matters, in Shakespeare and in his culture, is emergent individualism. However rigid their social roles, the English seem to have been complexly individualistic, even as dramatic characters such as Iago or Falstaff may appear highly particularized while revealing typological origins or lineaments.[10]

On one level, for example, Hermione's resurrection implies the paradigm of Christ's sacrifice. The scene of her rebirth echoes the words of Christ the Redeemer, "I am the resurrection and the life; he that believeth in me, though he were dead, yet shall he live." For Paulina has bidden Leontes to "awake your faith," and commands: "Bequeath to death your numbness, for from him / Dear life redeems you" (*WT* 5.3.95, 102–03). If Paulina is addressing Leontes, or Leontes as well as Hermione—which is plausible since Leontes has been numb with remorse for sixteen years—then the redemptive "Dear life" is Hermione. Once despised and slandered, the now revered queen evokes the archetypal Christian paradox that—in Augustine's words— "God humbled Himself in order to be exalted."[11]

Although her actions are "Holy" (5.3.104), Hermione is far from an allegorical figure. At the outset she is strikingly individualized and matches wits with Polixenes precisely on the subject of autonomy, asserting that "a lady's 'Verily' is / As potent as a lord's" (1.2.50–51). She detects the disquiet that would lead Polixenes to "say / Your queen and I are devils" as if he fears that women may be treacherously insubordinate and subvert men's self-control (81–86). When Hermione pretends to be dead, her alter ego Paulina takes over that mocking, rebellious voice and might be said to speak for her. For the resurrected Hermione is so idealized that her autonomy can be consummated in a mute identification with authority as she embraces the king (5.3.111), while her potentially threatening aspect—her uncompromising individuality—is displaced onto the outspoken Paulina.

Self-effacement fantasies frequently culminate in a style of autonomy that holds in suspension conflicting desires to merge with a powerful authority figure and also to become fully an individual. When Rosalind and Portia emerge from disguise to assume new identities in *As You Like It* and *The Merchant of Venice*, for example, their behavior dramatizes this need to balance wishes for union and independence. At once Rosalind pledges herself wholly to her father ("for I am yours") and to Orlando ("for I am yours"), by her wit implying that she is also wholly herself (*AYLI* 5.4.116–17).

Clearly this doubleness reflects the authoritarian and yet incipiently individualistic nature of Elizabethan culture. A deeper explanation might look to the specific role of judgment in the self-effacement pattern and in the culture. The church and the nation rewarded subjects who accepted authority figures, internalizing them as conscience to combat the sinful—usually instinctual—parts of their own nature. Shakespeare's characters often play dead in reaction to an overwhelming judgment of guilt. *Much Ado's* Hero expires "the instant she was accused," and looks to be "excused / Of every hearer" (4.1.214–16). The friar expects that on her return to life she will be wholly loved. Vindication means overcoming rejection and uniting with a formidable judge. While Falstaff's collapse in battle is a survival tactic, it also comments ironically on the role of judgment in the warrior code, which moves men to sacrifice themselves for reputation and glory. After playing possum Falstaff rises to identify with the slain Hotspur, the model warrior, then equates his resurrection with a new, elevated social identity: "I look to be either earl or duke, I can assure you" (5.4.142–43).

Falstaff's change from abnegation to dominance is in fact a reversal of role. Its suddenness calls attention to an aspect of contemporary society that further illuminates the wish to identify with authority. In ordinary social rituals deference required its complement, mastery, and in an authoritarian society mastery is apt to take violent forms. "The key symbols of Tudor and Early Stuart society were the hat and the whip. The former was [used] to emphasize the complex hierarchy of ranks and authorities [and] the principle of subordination. . . . Physical punishment was used, as it never had been used before, as the prime means of enforcing obedience." The whip was a "mark of dignity, a prerequisite of property," and its use extended from the Crown down to the flogged child at the bottom of the social scale (Stone 1967, pp. 34–35). As the symbols of hat and whip suggest, the social order demanded that individuals be capable not only of self-effacement but also of self-aggrandizement insofar as they had to act out their dominance on their own inferiors.[12] People had to play contradictory roles, submitting to their betters one moment, dominating those below them the next. Only the rigidity of social categories and the static absoluteness of the ideology, it would seem, stood between individuals and an unsettling awareness of conflict in their roles and in turn their identity. The steeper the hierarchy, the more wrenching may be the change from submission to mastery.

Part of the shock of Lear's decline, for example, is in the way even the first slight changes in his status prove to be violent reversals. "Thou mad'st thy daughters thy mothers," the Fool protests, for "thou gav'st them the rod and put down thine own breeches" (1.4.173–74). Having yielded supreme authority, the king is suddenly a child subject to scourging or even to annihilation. Given the deep conflict between mastery and effacement in social behavior, to relinquish one is to risk falling into the other.

The more imaginative sympathy people allow themselves, the more destabilizing is the conflict between dominant and submissive phases of a social role. Outside the court, exposed and alienated, Lear can identify with a victimized whore and protest against the beadle's hypocritical "lust" to whip her (4.6.162–65). Lear recognizes that the heart is susceptible to secret degradation that makes a vicious mockery of the social order.

Even in a static world, then, a highly stratified society could be a source of stress as well as security. In fact, however, there was considerable social mobility in Shakespeare's England. His own family had experienced fairly drastic shifts in status. His father had risen to a position of civic eminence in Stratford, then declined into debt. Grandson of a tenant farmer, Shakespeare reversed the family's fortunes and, in a tragicomic fulfillment, made himself a member of the gentry.

Change created a crisis of the aristocracy and also an ongoing crisis of dispossession and vagrancy that the poor laws tried to control. From one perspective the extensive migrations to the New World were a deliberate flight from the confines of the old society in search of greater autonomy.[13] As sumptuary legislation reveals, mobility was a persistent threat to the rituals on which class divisions depended. If clothes make the man, which is one assumption behind the sumptuary laws, then a beholder may be tempted to see an element of theatricality, as wishful and manipulable as theater itself, in the assertive costuming of rank. To pursue the metaphor, courtesy books were simultaneously supplying scripts that anyone with money could use to stage his or her pretensions to status. For many people an elite identity "was a mode of being that could be acquired[,] . . . a commodity . . . that could be *bought*, by means of courtesy books."[14] Courtesy books came to serve those they were originally intended to exclude. Like the failure of sumptuary legislation, the success of Castiglione witnesses how potent the desire for change must have been.

In some unexpected ways the fantasy of self-effacement dramatizes the irrationality associated with change. For one thing, "the fairy stories of the time are full of stories about changelings whose real identity had been concealed by an exchange carried out by the wetnurse" (Stone 1977, p. 100). Not only do changeling fantasies express uncertainty about one's identity: they also can be used to rationalize an unsatisfactory position in life ("if I was exchanged in the cradle, I could in truth be the noble person I sense myself to be"). Perdita's destiny plays out just this wish. "This," says the Shepherd who finds the abandoned baby, "is some changeling" (3.3.118).

A more fundamental sign of belief in the irrationality of change is the wheel of fortune. As in fairy stories, the wheel of fortune actually controls the threats of chance and change to an extent by structuring them, specifically by polarizing the extremes of fortune and the rising or falling dynamics that connect them. What falls will eventually rise. It seems to me likely that the self-effacement fantasy presupposes a superstitious belief that by making oneself nothing, one places oneself in fortune's upward path. There seems to be an echo of this belief in *The Merchant of Venice* when Bassanio, whose "state was nothing," makes his fortune by choosing not gold or silver but base lead. Since Bassanio risks all on lead (unlike his self-inflated rivals) and goes from "nothing" to a position of mastery, his success bears a strong resemblance to the self-effacement pattern.[15]

Although it threatens to undermine the static, official social doctrine, belief in a wheel of fortune as a model of change may be either conservative or nihilistic. One of the many abandoned children who begged their way around England is reported to have said that "if ever he should attain to be a King, he would have a brest of mutton with a pudding in it, and lodge every night up to his eares in dry straw."[16] As in the self-effacement pattern in Shakespeare, the boy dreams not of some small, realistic change of status, but of identification with the supremely autonomous, paternal role of king. While he can envision a reversal of roles, he envisions no rebellion. By contrast, Hamlet could be said to share the beggar child's sense of the contingency of roles but with a despairing twist when he jokes that a king may go a progress through the guts of a beggar. More evenly ambivalent is the way *Lear* plays out a version of the child's wish in the fall and rise of Edgar as the beggar Poor Tom and later king.

In Shakespeare self-effacement promises to minimize or even preempt direct social conflict. By contrast, here is Nashe's account of the strife to be seen in London around 1593: "From the rich to the poor ... there is ambition, or swelling above theyr states. ... The Auncients, they oppose themselves against the younger, and suppresse them and keepe them doune all that they may. The young men, they call them dotards, and swel and rage, and, with many others sweare ... they will not be kept under by such cullions, but goe good and neere to out-shoulder them."[17] Even at court this tension made itself felt. As Professor Esler has demonstrated, the queen's generation tended to consolidate its position after early years of struggle by adopting conservative policies and blocking the advancement of younger courtiers.[18] Elizabeth and the "Auncients" around her tried to "keep doune" the restive younger men. In turn, courtiers such as Essex and Ralegh sacrificed themselves and their more realistic interests by conspicuously risking death and striving for recognition and compensatory glory. Forced into submissive roles, feeling themselves belittled and nullified by authority, they reacted by courting destruction as if only by braving nothingness could they demonstrate their loyalty and command validating admiration. In different ways, but with haunting self-destructiveness, Essex and Ralegh went to the scaffold and died in personal dramas of fatal self-assertion. It is tempting to see in this behavior an aristocratic variation on the Shakespearean pattern of abnegation with aspiration to a phoenix-like rebirth.[19]

III

While the social background makes a useful explanatory context, I want to consider the fantasy of self-effacement more intimately by relating it to contemporary family structure and the formation of individual identity. For one thing, "it is impossible," Professor Stone warns, "to stress too heavily the impermanence of the Early Modern Family. . . . None could reasonably expect to remain together for very long, a fact which fundamentally affected all human relationships" (Stone 1977, p. 81). In this context play-deaths and resurrections are a means of controlling people's fear of their own deaths and also the deaths of their loved ones. Such play is a way of standing up to the terrifying contingency of life. That said, let me focus on family structure itself.

Following Aristotle's *Politics* 1:12, Elizabethan theorists likened the father to a king. As in the official social ideology, this model of the family assigned all power and autonomy to the ruler, and implicitly preempted the will of the governed. In theory at least the ideal child substituted the patriarchal will for his or her own.[20] In his obedience a boy became a model of his father's desires. Just as in school the prescribed memorization of rhetorical models virtually made the student an actor through whom venerable authorities might seem to speak,[21] so in the family the boy might be said to enact the father. While emulating her mother, a girl had to regard her as a husband's shadow, and herself as the shadow of a shadow. Only by deference could a boy or girl hope to pass from nonentity to adult autonomy. As in the Shakespearean fantasy of playing dead, children aspired to a transfiguring identity by acting as if they had no lives of their own. Such a transition would proceed not by self-actualizing growth, but rather by role reversal when a son at last inherits his father's role, or by an act of benevolent paternal creation when, as in the opening of *King Lear*, the father at last formally grants his daughters' independence.

In practice the authoritarian family must have experienced some deep conflicts. For unlike the lowest members of a social hierarchy, children are destined to be kings or queens themselves one day. Sooner or later, all children replace their parents in the world. Patriarchal authority can only postpone or deny the inevitable reversal of roles in which the child, like Prince Hal trying on his father's crown, comes to witness time's negation of the parent. By destiny, all children are usurpers, and all growth is potentially rebellious. Psychologically, self-effacement may preempt Oedipal antagonism, since the children deflect their aggression against themselves in hopes of winning love and living harmoniously through their parents.

When King Henry discovers his son trying on his crown, for instance, he construes the act as parricide: "This part of his conjoins with my disease / And helps to end me" (*2H4* 4.5.63–64). Fathers like himself "are murdered for our pains" (77); his son wishes for his death (92). Like Lear, Henry fears that his child's "life did manifest thou lov'dst me not" (104). To answer this accusation the prince professes "obedience" (146) and duty (147), not love.[22] Tacitly Hal plays dead, denying all personal interest in the crown, his destiny. Tellingly he links his father's death to his own: "thinking you dead, / And dead almost, my liege, to think you were, / I spake" (155–57). Even if Hal is only excusing himself with piety, his words acknowledge his own identity to be in part a function of his father's. Repeatedly he denies all desire to assume his ordained role as king. If he has any wish for the crown, he pleads, "Let God . . . make me as the poorest vassal is / That doth with awe and terror kneel to it" (174–76). If he aspires to autonomy, that is, let him be reduced to the condition of a child again, abject and socially inferior.

If Henry had been able to command absolute deference from his son, he might have been able to relinquish power willingly, for then he would have been replacing himself with a model of himself.[23] This is presumably the ideal fulfillment of the patriarchal system. Fathers such as Egeus, Old Capulet, Brabantio, and Lear behave as if they can dominate their daughters so completely that they may then choose a husband and make a marriage for them, becoming so profoundly a part of the resulting union that both the loss of the child and the potential rivalry with the younger male cease to be threatening. Cordelia's measured protest dramatizes her precarious balance—very similar to Prince Hal's—between patriarchal preemption of her identity and terrible mutiny: "Sure I shall never marry like my sisters, / To love my father all" (1.1.103–4).

So, too, Juliet's play-death suspends her between intolerable alternatives: submission to her father or revolt, each of which jeopardizes her identity. Drugging herself, Juliet symbolically takes her own life, forestalling the compulsion to actual suicide that she revealed earlier (4.1.52–54). That compulsion plays itself out in her hallucinatory terror of going mad in the family tomb and literally effacing herself by dashing out her brain with "some great kinsman's bone" (4.3.53), the grotesque objectification of patriarchal authority. For Juliet, that is, play-death acts out self-hatred. Deviously asserting her independence through the sleeping potion, she fears she will wake up engulfed by the family (the tomb) and smash her own brain, guiltily punishing her urge to think for herself. Her guilt internalizes the rage her father ("hang, beg, starve, die in the streets") and her mother ("I would the fool were married to her grave!") have directed at her (3.5.192, 140). At the same time her guilt redirects against herself the anger she could be expected to feel toward her parents.

Playing dead, that is, may act out latent aggression between parent and child. Not all play-deaths in Shakespeare involve a literal parent and child, of course. Yet as Freud would say, all adults are apt to construe their situation in the light of crucial childhood experience, and especially when, as in the fantasy of self-effacement, the dynamics of the situation recall the relationship between parent and child.

Historical evidence points to sharp ambivalence toward the young in the world Shakespeare knew. One sign of this conflict is the opposition between an Augustinian view of the infant as inherently contaminated by original sin, and a more optimistic view, based on the imagery of the infant Jesus as well as on traditional ideas of the unworldly, infantile fool, which identified infancy with innocence and human perfectibility. Didactic writers saw the "natural child" as bestial, excremental, and appetitive. To overcome original sin they called for severe discipline. As a fantasy about radical innocence, the contrasting view held that children embody an ideal past lost to adults. By the seventeenth century this attitude became associated with Anglican nostalgia for a pastoral England gone by, to which the child provided a symbolic link.[24] In actual families, presumably, contradictory feelings came together in complex combinations. Puritan child-rearing, for example, strove both to break children's sinful wills and make them selfless, and also to provide exemplary education and nurture since children were the hope of a better future.

From the sleeping princes in *Richard III* to the infant Perdita, Shakespeare attributes to children an idealized innocence that sets them apart from the world of adults. In *The Winter's Tale*, for instance, Polixenes sentimentalizes children as lambs who exchange "innocence for innocence," not knowing the "doctrine of ill-doing" (1.2.67–75). The child becomes an adult through a fall from grace (77). As in many examples of the self-effacement pattern, aspiration to autonomy produces a crisis. Just as Hermione challenges Polixenes to clarify his feelings about the fall from childish innocence (82–83), Leontes interrupts her. A moment later Leontes erupts in rage at the suspicion of "fallen" sin between his wife and friend.

In the symbolic logic of the scene Polixenes' anxious fantasy about the fall from childhood produces an overwhelming, dissociated guilt and anger expressed in the madness of his double, the "twin lamb" Leontes (67). The idealized image of lambs denies the anxieties of actual children as well as the anxieties children may cause adults. Polixenes' wish-fulfilling fantasy implies an unspoken opposite that surfaces in Leontes' murderous fury against the infant Perdita. And the solution to parental ambivalence which Perdita represents is of course her long abandonment and loss of identity in Bohemia.

To appreciate the intensity of this ambivalence we need to remember that in the world outside of the Globe Theater the young were a source of great pain and dread as well as hope and pleasure. As the motherless families in the plays may suggest, childbirth routinely brought death. In *Pericles*, Marina's birth aboard ship is figuratively a storm that kills her mother and so threatens the survivors that they cast the dead woman overboard to ward off the threat (3.1.48–49). The repudiated mother is replaced by—in effect, turns into—the malicious stepmother Dionyza, who plots Marina's murder.

Once born, the young were themselves appallingly likely to die before maturity.[25] As Peter Laslett cautions, it takes "an effort of the mind to remember all the time that children were always present in such numbers in the traditional world, nearly half the whole community living in a condition of semi-obliteration, many of them never destined to become persons at all." In the best of times economic pressures made children a drain on scarce resources. In fact, as Laslett goes on to observe, "the authoritarianism of traditional social life and educational practise becomes a little easier to understand when the youthfulness of so much of the community is borne in mind. A very high proportion of dependent bodies, mouths to feed and clothes and fuel to find, energy to summon up for the heavy work of rearing children, weights down the active members of society" (Laslett, p. 111). As a result parental attitudes seem to have ranged from indifference or hostility to an attachment so intense that a child's death might derange the mother.[26]

Historically the most primitive defense against the anxiety children cause has been to wish away the child. If the Essex Quarter Sessions Records are any indication, "infanticide was woefully common, and there were probably many other violent deaths by smothering or bruising which were concealed from the coroner."[27] In Shakespeare death wishes against children appear fairly often and with dramatic moral urgency. In *Pericles* during a famine mothers who "to nuzzle up their babes, / Thought nought too curious, are ready now / To eat those little darlings whom they loved" (1.4.42–44). A jealous stepmother would have Marina murdered. In *The Two Noble Kinsmen* the Amazonian Hippolyta protests, "We have been soldiers, and we cannot weep" at accounts of "babes broach'd on the lance, or women / That have sod their infants in (and after eat them) / The brine they wept at killing 'em" (1.3.18–22). Lady Macbeth can muse "How tender 'tis to love the babe that milks [her]" and yet envision dashing out its brains (1.7.54–59). Lear fantasizes about a savage "that makes his generation messes / To gorge his appetite" (1.1.117–18). Leontes wishes to destroy Perdita, while Richard III and Macbeth scheme to murder all the young who might inherit their power.

With its analogy to Herod's massacre of the innocents, Macbeth's slaughter recalls the central role of the sacrificed child in Christianity. Whatever its actual incidence in English society, infanticide was a crucial religious theme. While the Son of God ransomed all of the Father's children by his own cruel death, the threat of righteous paternal wrath gave meaning to God's mercy and must have influenced the believers' sense of identity. As Thomas Becon expostulated in a commentary on Luke 6.36–42 (1656), "we can not deny but GOD hath given us good measure. For if he would have given us after our desertes, he might have plagued us with wrathe, plague, pestilence, and all evill, and put us to death, assone as we were borne."[28] For Becon, a sinful human being is akin to an infant, potentially the object of its father's just violence but miraculously spared.

More common than physical denial of the child is psychological denial. The child is wished away by imaginative distortion or negation of its identity.[29] "Who sees a child sees nothing," says a proverb Elizabethans knew. Original sin served to justify an adult's projection of his own unacceptable feeling onto the child, yet even Polixenes' idealization of "twinned lambs" substitutes adult wishes for the reality of childhood. Fathers such as Egeus and Brabantio discount their daughters' wills by imagining that demonic or magical influences cause their rebellion. Fantasies of cannibalizing one's young, as in the examples from *Pericles* and *King Lear* above, reveal a wish to reincorporate a child whose independent existence threatens to exhaust or kill the parent by taking all the parent's love and sustenance.[30]

The ambivalent complement to denial is a reversal reaction in which adults project a parental role onto the child to serve their own needs. In Shakespeare wise daughters often guide and comfort parents. Pericles conceives of his daughter Marina as "Thou that beget'st him that did thee beget" (5.1.195), a wish-fulfilling version of the fantasy by which Lear made his daughters his mothers (1.4.173). As Bradley noticed, however, sons such as little Macduff and Mamillius tend to be "pathetic figures," too wise for this world, noble but doomed.[31]

It seems plausible, though I know of no way to prove it, that the self-effacement fantasy originates in this matrix of ambivalent projections. To be the object of other people's projections is to have one's identity altered or nullified, creating a disjunction between one's public and private selves. Fantasies of self-effacement take forms that dramatize this sense of simultaneously being oneself and not oneself, present and not present, as when Portia and Rosalind assume disguises or Falstaff or Juliet plays dead. The sense of doubleness is unmistakable in *Comedy of Errors* when the ostensibly dead Antipholus of Syracuse has the identity and life of his twin imposed on him in Ephesus. His experience in Ephesus is akin to the experience of living in a web of intensely projective relationships.

More specifically, self-effacement makes sense as a reaction to the parental attitudes described above: a reaction by which a child seeks to fulfill parental fantasies of denial or negation in order to avoid actual conflict and rejection. He tries to suspend his identity to protect it. Analogously, projective reversal permits the child a form of power and autonomy, however distorted, as does the resurrection that usually follows a play-death in Shakespeare. The dynamics of the relationships fantasized in art and in the culture, that is, seem to match.

Given the ambivalence between parents and children in Shakespeare and the world he knew, the pattern of loss and reunion in the plays must have been powerfully moving to his audiences. By projective distortions or outright aggression parent figures in the plays may deny their offspring during the most anxious years the way Egeus would be "as a god" to his daughter, free to change or destroy her identity as if it were wax (*MND* 1.1.47–51). Once past the critical transition to adulthood, the child may be resurrected in an idealized and untroubling form. As the old shepherd in *The Winter's Tale* complains, "I would there were no age between ten and three-and-twenty, or that youth would sleep out the rest" (3.3.59–61), for in that oblivion all youthful rebellion could be dissolved. If the young efface themselves, adults may then confidently grant them freedom as Prospero does Ariel and Ferdinand. This, after all, is the plot of *A Midsummer Night's Dream* and other Shakespearean comedies: young lovers flee a judgmental authority, become figuratively invisible and purged of disobedience, then rejoin society as honored members. As sleep transforms youth in a wood outside of Athens, so Perdita goes from helpless babe to queen as if, says Time, "you had slept between" (4.1.17).

In its cultural context the effacement that so often symbolically separates childhood from adulthood in Shakespeare appears to express not only adult denial of childhood, but also the child's denial (and the denial of the child in every once-vulnerable adult) of his own disturbing condition. As each maturing generation sought compensation for its own years of inferiority and impotence in projective demands on its young, presumably it unwittingly tended to perpetuate the cycle of insecurity.[32] Coming of age, some individuals must have repressed or redirected feelings of hurt, dread, and anger from their early lives. This process may be reflected in the "blackout" of self-effacement. In the theater the fantasy may have allowed spectators to rediscover vicariously, in a safely disguised form, disturbing formative experiences, with the possibility of integrating them more fully. The play would be bringing to new life or resurrecting material that has the potential to enhance self-awareness and in turn autonomy.

IV

The analogy between the fantasy of self-effacement and the imaginative process of theater itself brings this chapter to its final phase. As the fantasy in the plays is conditioned by historical, social, and familial structures, so those same relationships are implicated in Shakespeare's relation to his audience and to his art. In its psychological dynamics, for example, the fantasy bears a resemblance to the process of sublimation in the artist's experience. By giving up gratification in the world of action, the artist may create substitute worlds, projecting himself into or, colloquially, living through his art. Effacing himself, he aspires to transfiguring imaginative resurrection.

Since Shakespeare was a dramatist, this is not as abstractly figurative a connection as it might appear. For sublimation has a palpable analogue in the experience of the actor-playwright who is in a position every day of his working life to suspend his identity in order to live onstage in the character he plays in the heightened reality of the drama. For such an artist resurrection would be ambiguously real insofar as he was living out his own creation, watching it come to life around him, personages and place alike, in performance. What is more, in the theater all deaths are ultimately play-deaths.

The analogy does not necessarily stop here. Shakespeare participated in a system of artistic patronage that made deference a condition of recognition and reward. As prologues and epilogues insist, the artist lived by pleasing.[33] As patron, "Mr. W. H." would be "the only begetter" of the poems, a symbolic father with whom the poet submissively identifies himself, as if the patron creates through the artist as the patriarchal father works his will through an obedient, seemingly transparent son.

Titles such as *As You Like It* and *What You Will* similarly profess that the audience is the true creator. Moreover, in the theater, audiences, and especially aristocratic audiences, were inclined to dramatize themselves by disrupting the performance, forcing the playwright to devise strategies for accommodating their self-assertion.[34] Usually Shakespeare preempts resistance to the play by a mixture of flattery and self-deprecation, as when the actor Prospero begs the "indulgence" of the spectators to set him free. Despite the sly ironies—the dramatist has had the audience under his spell as Prospero has bewitched those within the play—the epilogue feigns total deference.[35]

Shakespeare's humility as an artist disguises striving for autonomy. If he is Puck, he is also Oberon; if he is the entreating servant, he is also Prospero the master magician. The extremes of the artist's role parallel the ambivalent valuation of art in the Renaissance. In the world-as-stage trope the play may express the essential nullity of man's earthly existence or, alternatively, man's power to shape himself and his world. Like the artist, art is nothing and yet supreme:

> Elizabethan public theaters like the Globe were, by a symbolism inherent in their very structure, models of the world. As scholars have observed, they represented emblematically the hierarchial order of the universe, as conceived by late-medieval thought. Still more significant . . . is their *ambivalence* as emblems. They may imply that life is no more real than a play, that 'the great globe itself' will dissolve . . . and leave not a rack behind. But they may also point to the immense, godlike power of human creativity.
>
> [Greenblatt 1973, p. 45]

Immediately self-effacing, the dramatist may nevertheless be "godlike" in the larger transaction that is the play.

Authorities in the real world made it risky for Shakespeare to assert the artist's potency too boldly. Fears of blasphemy and sedition clearly affected the content and production of plays. Not surprisingly, Shakespeare repeatedly mocks himself and his art even as his art asserts disturbing truth about the world. Had he not been so disarming about his claims—his artistic will—he might well have provoked retaliation, as the playing of *Richard II* nearly did during the rebellion of Essex. *The Winter's Tale* he mocks as "an old tale," disqualifying it as a criticism of life. Autolycus, the comic figure of the artist as low-life impersonator and trickster, provides the crucial disguise or fiction that allows Perdita to fulfill the oracle and resolve the play. "Though I am not naturally honest," he quips, "I am so sometimes by chance" (4.4.716–17). Also protected as well as undercut by irony is the play's comic apotheosis of the artist as godlike creator, Julio Romano. In the play of course there is no actual Julio Romano, and yet tacitly the illusory statue of the queen does defy death and "beguile Nature of her custom" (5.2.106–7). For by indirections Shakespeare asserts the power of imagination, himself creating the living illusion of Hermione and thereby holding momentary sway over an assenting audience in every enactment or resurrection of the play in the theater.

Ultimately a play is an event, an interaction of the dramatist's, the actors', and the spectators' imaginations. As such, the play's integrity depends on consensual goodwill, the will to understand, which Theseus illustrates by his empathetic openness to the performance of *Pyramus* in *A Midsummer Night's Dream*. Puck's epilogue mocks our experience of the play as an empty hallucination even as he insinuates it has the authority of Oberon's spell, and invites us to appreciate the imaginative community we have shared in the enactment. If, as C. L. Barber maintains, the plays bring to new life or resurrect repressed material that may enhance self-awareness, then the process of clarification and release depends for its efficacy on the willingness of everyone in the theater to overcome the divisions of hierarchy and share in the drama.[36] By responding to *Pyramus*, with its inadvertently wise parody of their own self-involved and destructive infatuation in the wood, the Athenian lovers share in a comic purgation analogous to the spectators' experience of the play as a whole. The last act moves toward a moment of vicarious insight and identity, a marriage of minds: "The dramatic experience in which playwright, actors, and audience all participate . . . becomes a kind of secular ritual of communion, with the play itself the focal illusion whose existence and significance are created by a collective imaginative act and whose value lies partly in the fact that it enables a sharing of inner experience otherwise inaccessible. The play and the audience imaginatively unite and mutually transform each other in the act of knowledge."[37] Insofar as this model of vicarious mutuality allows the artist to achieve autonomy even as he honors the bonds of community, it complements his self-effacement with a mode of action and mastery that represents a solution to conflicts at the heart of English life.

It goes without saying that Shakespeare the dramatist was both child and father to his culture, shaped by and himself reshaping its imaginative forms.[38] Like other artists, in idealizing or satirizing or simply entertaining alternatives to what exists, he must have risked alienation. Many of his plots get their energy from a motion away from an intolerable normative society—to a wood outside Athens, a stormy heath, to Eastcheap, dazzling Egypt, or an enchanted island. This motion is akin to the artist's imaginative disengagement from his culture, a means to perspective and a source of creativity. The more authoritarian the society, the more the artist must disguise or efface signs of alienation in himself and his art. As a form related to the core ideas of the fantasy of self-effacement, the model of dramatic communion described above seems to have been for Shakespeare a means of reconciling in art conflicting imperatives of submission and autonomy, community and individuality, and stasis and growth. Other plays, especially the tragedies, are by no means so sanguine about the possibility of community. And even in *A Midsummer Night's Dream* Puck is too much like a mischievous child or a Plautine servant ("As I am an honest Puck") to inspire enduring confidence. Still, in the context outlined in this essay, the play's projected marriage of minds makes the theater itself one solution, however provisional or ultimately illusory, to the alienation of art from culture and, given the force of historical change in Shakespeare's own lifetime, of culture from itself.[39]

Chapter 3

Play, Death, and Apotheosis

We cannot look directly at either the sun or death, says La Rochefoucauld. If we could not blink at death as we do at the sun, it would blind us. Let that saving reflex begin to lag, and anxiety emerges: in Kierkegaard's unforgettable phrase, the sickness unto death. A reflex makes a useful analogy for behavior that can be ambiguously conscious and unconscious, automatic yet sometimes overridden. This is the context in which Ernest Becker places heroism as "first and foremost a reflex of the terror of death."[1] In this chapter I want to examine play-death as one expression of that essential blinking reflex, not only because play-death enables the mortal mind to acknowledge death while shutting it out, but more specifically because it is a special instance of the universal process Becker describes, in which imagination generates heroism in order to master the prospect of its own annihilation.

It is difficult to think about death. Because death is nothingness and nature abhors a vacuum, imagination has to construe it vicariously, through symbolic equivalents. In life no less than art death is a complex symbol that varies from one individual and culture to another, and reflects the values of living imaginations. The dead sleep, go to their reward, lay down their burden, and so on. This cognitive peculiarity reinforces "the almost universal human recourse to magic and irrationality" in handling anxiety about mortality, and helps to explain the persistent belief that "death is a fictive experience"[2]—that is, a kind of play-death.

Let me make this subject less alien by evoking a particular child's concrete experience. One summer evening when my daughter Vanessa was nearly four years old she asked me with an uneasy stammer if I was going to die. When I answered yes, someday, she asked if she too would die. On the spot I offered her abridged versions of venerable consolations, putting as natural and reasonable a face on the problem as I could. The next evening I overheard her singing under her breath—too loudly to be ignored, too softly to be questioned—"My name's Vanessa, and I'm never going to die, never going to die. . . . " Listening without contradicting her, as she intended me to, I was participating in an impromptu ceremony that corroborated her wishful immortality. Like Sir Toby singing "But I will never die" (*TN* 2.3.106), she wanted company to celebrate a wishful defiance of reality.

A day or two later Vanessa demanded: Was it really true, what people had been telling her, that after you die you go to heaven? Many people, I answered, believed that it was true, although no one had come back from heaven to prove it. After a moment's thought, the not-quite-four year old countered: "But after you go to heaven, then where do you go?" Where indeed? Who moves the prime mover? The child's question leads directly into the traditional labyrinths of speculative eschatology. It points out the inherent inadequacy of the categories through which we approach the ultimate framework of thought.

As it happened, we were in a vast supermarket—even for a jaded adult an impressive storehouse of biological and cultural vitality—and all at once Vanessa began pushing the grocery cart. Bragging how strong she was, she climactically puffed herself up to boast: "I could pick up this whole building, all these people, with one hand!"

The moment seemed to offer a glimpse into the formation of heroic claims out of the self's discovery of its incomprehensible groundlessness. Commanding a storehouse of food-energy, promising (or threatening) to hoist the world in one hand, she was unwittingly evoking ancient archetypes. I am not trying to regerminate Western culture out of one anecdote or claiming that a supermarket epiphany explains the origins of Attic corn goddesses, Atlas, or the medieval image of God cupping the great globe in his hand. Rather, I want to make vivid the fundamental dynamic of under- and overestimation that accompanies our engagement of reality: the reflex by which we minimize death and maximize the self. My daughter was not merely repressing dread but also converting it into idealizing energy. And as she must have known perfectly well, she was falsifying reality. Her act was also an "act" before an audience happy to sanction a bit of escapist madness as child's play. Like the song she had chanted under her breath ("I'm never going to die, never going to die"), her boast was part—ordinarily a forgotten, "unconscious" part—of a lifelong process of creating a conviction of immortality.

Insofar as Vanessa's boast emulated storybook and television heroes, it was not only the survival wish of one person but also the cry of a particular culture.[3] In fact, both of us, parent and child, were engaged in culturally determined acts of creative denial. For in my blandly consoling role as Wise Old Professor I too was appealing to heroic authority in order to counter the spectre intruding on us.

While this view of human development may seem morbid, it does not mean that all experience is simply escapism or reducible to anxiety. As a rule the creation of heroic significance out of dread is an adaptive strategy, a means of releasing and channeling creative energy:

> as man cannot perform efficiently in the absence of a fairly high degree of reasonably persistent emotional activation, cultural mechanisms assuring the ready availability of the continually varying sort of sensory experience that can sustain such activities are equally essential. Institutionalized regulations against the open display of corpses outside of well-defined contexts (funerals, etc.) protect a peculiarly high-strung animal against the fears aroused by death and bodily destruction; watching or participating in automobile races (not all of which take place at tracks) deliciously stimulates the same fears.[4]

If play-death and heroism, too, "deliciously stimulate" fears, they become a means of optimizing excitement: crucial means by which culture turns a source of numbing paralysis into an enabling force.

Sometimes we can better appreciate our own embeddedness in culture if we look to the past. In Siena there is a painting by Simone Martini (1284–1344) in which a mother and four passersby watch in horror as a child falls from a loggia toward the stone street below, and Saint Augustine Novello (d. 1309) swoops down from heaven trailing a plume of cloud, exactly like Superman, to effect a midair rescue at the point of death.[5] The picture deploys a patriarchal hero not only to counter fears—most obviously maternal fears—for the imperiled child, but also to recreate and to transcend the traumatic childhood discovery of death. For the spectator may identify with the infant who has innocently plummeted out of its mother's protection into the knowledge of annihilation, causing the saint to reveal himself.

Simone Martini's painting is a culture-specific style of blinking at the unthinkable horror. The painter reinterprets the human family to

Simone Martini, *Miracle of Beato Agostino*. Siena, St. Agostino.
Courtesy of ALINARI / Art Resource, New York, New York.

illustrate orthodox medieval Christian doctrine, so that the loving if
careless mother (who, like fallen Eve, can give only mortal life) is
superseded by a supernatural father who can bestow a second, symbolic birth on the child. It could be argued that when my own daughter took her conceptual plunge toward mortality, I unconsciously
played out a twentieth-century middle-class American version of Augustine's patriarchal rescue, offering consolation in exchange for her
agreement to believe in the authority I mediated.

Every society, Ernest Becker contends, can be understood as "a symbolic action system, a structure of statuses and roles, customs and rules
for behavior, designed to serve as a vehicle for earthly heroism"
(Becker 1973, pp. 4–5). Each script is unique. Yet despite this diversity,

it doesn't matter whether the cultural hero-system is frankly magical, religious, and primitive or secular, scientific, and civilized. It is still a mythical hero system in which people serve in order to earn a feeling of primary value, of cosmic specialness, of ultimate usefulness to creation, of unshakable meaning. They earn this feeling by carving out a place in nature, by building an edifice that reflects human value: a temple, a cathedral, a totem pole, a skyscraper, a family that spans three generations. The hope and belief is that the things that man creates in society are of lasting worth and meaning, that they outshine death and decay, that man and his products count. [p. 5]

Beaten by his enemies, Brutus seems willingly to choose death until we realize that he is dreaming of personal transcendence: "I shall have glory by this losing day / More than Octavius and Mark Antony / By this vile conquest shall attain unto" (*JC* 5.5.36–38). Death is less real to him than the cultural code that transfixes him in noble, competitive, and vindictive triumph.

Denial is the inescapable condition of humanity. For as a creature whose consciousness is a function of symbolism and therefore potentially limitless, man is godlike and yet trapped in the body of an animal doomed to rot in the ground and disappear forever. Mind may contemplate symbolic perfection, yet the body lives by killing and chewing other creatures, digesting them into foul-smelling waste. From that appalling dilemma springs the effort to construct a world that can withstand engulfing reality:

Babies are occasionally born with gills and tails, but this is . . . hushed up.[6] Who wants to face up fully to the creatures we are, clawing and grasping for breath in a universe beyond our ken? I think such events illustrate the meaning of Pascal's chilling reflection: "Men are so necessarily mad that not to be mad would amount to another form of madness". . . . *Mad* because . . . everything that man does in his symbolic world is an attempt to deny and overcome his grotesque fate. He literally drives himself into a blind obliviousness with social games, psychological tricks, personal preoccupations so far removed from the reality of his situation that they are forms of madness—agreed madness, shared madness, disguised and dignified madness, but madness all the same.

[Becker 1973, p. 27]

Most people forget the sort of dissonance that first reveals our madness—if it was ever really allowed to sink in. For example, we give children cuddly stuffed animals to play with, animals usually proportioned to represent the young. Then one day at dinner the child thinks to ask what we are eating, and the tribal elders answer with blandly violent dissociation that we are eating a steak. And what is a steak? Not what but *who*: the moocow or Porky Pig; old friends, versions of ourselves. A host of inventions, from manners to culinary nomenclature, disguises the truth that we live by killing, in quotidian madness.

It needs to be emphasized that for Becker heroism means not merely particular conventional roles but individual and cultural value systems. Heroism is whatever produces a conviction of importance and worth, from religious texts to crass propaganda, from ownership to war. Moreover, elements of a given system are apt to be highly integrated and imply some transcendent ground. Dr. Dee, for instance, celebrated number for its "strange participation between things supernatural, unmortal, sensible, compounded and divisible" even as he was urging the military need for mathematics in the ordering of ranks, citing "Northumberland's young heir, with his addiction to arithmetic on the field of war: he kept the rules in a gold case round his neck."[7] "Number" here interacts with other sources of potency: religion, astrology, science, social privilege (the admirable heir of Northumberland), economic symbolism (the amulet-like gold case), law and, not least, the technology of violent conquest.

In my daughter's reaction to the discovery of her death the urge to heroic denial is plain. Yet her denial was a creative act. Making up a naive ditty ("I'm never going to die"), she was using art to substantiate a troubling wish. In her Herculean posture she turned role-player. So far I have been emphasizing the terror that vanishes with repression. But heroism is value-making activity, and the denial of death can be turned inside out to focus on the creativity that makes denial possible.

Let me use these categories to suggest the historical context into which Shakespeare's fantasies of play-death emerged. In Simone Martini's painting death has empowered rather than destroyed Saint Augustine. As a demigod, he mediates between heaven and earth. He not only promises eternal life to the faithful, his rescue of the child represents the arrival of a sense of security, even immortality, in everyday life. The great medieval churches tried to substantiate such supernatural security by impressively boxing the personal relics of saints on their premises. Yet the abiding contradiction between immortal spirit and a few odds and ends of bone and hair expressed cognitive dissonance that in time the Reformation explosively resolved by discrediting relics in the name of pure faith. This is the tension Huizinga found in "the dominant thought" of the medieval period, that it "hardly knew anything with regard to death but these two extremes: lamentation about the briefness of earthly glory, and jubilation over the salvation of the soul. All that lay between—pity, resignation, longing, consolation—remained unexpressed and was . . . absorbed by the . . . too vivid representation of Death hideous and threatening. Living emotion stiffens among the abused imagery of skeletons and worms."[8]

Among other things, it seems to me, a votive scene like Simone Martini's attempts to reconcile contradictory attitudes toward death by dramatizing its story of play-death and rescue. Where doctrine and empirical fact tend to be static and incontestable, the painting keeps ideas in play. It tries to visualize eschatological power in active human form. While it remains predominantly wishful, it does seek to incorporate elements of the mortal world in the family roles and mundane street it depicts.

By analogy, English dramatists beginning with Marlowe reconceived the problem of death in secular, tragic terms over the course of several decades. In a way, as Professor Spencer recognized, the dramatists rediscovered death.[9] Their tragic heroes played out emerging contradictions between medieval and humanistic attitudes toward death. In Becker's terms, they improvised new systems of symbolic immortality as old habits and categories lost their persuasiveness. Like the mediating Augustinian superman, they enabled imagination to explore what Huizinga calls the living emotion that lay between the conceptual extremes of dust and glory. It is in this historical context, with its unprecedented innovations in artistic and heroic forms, that Shakespeare's responses to death crystallized.

II

Cleopatra's final moments vividly illustrate some of the processes that generate symbolic immortality. The play is justly famous for its rhetoric of heroism. It celebrates the queen "Whom every thing becomes" (1.1.49) as an infinite source of value. The lovers' rhapsodies pitch from peak to peak of praise. In the play greatness is primarily a command over other people's imaginations. . . . At the lowest level, it is style, effective self-dramatization; at the highest, it is a means of overcoming time, death, and the world. . . . The audience for greatness in *Antony and Cleopatra* is multiple: it is, first, the small group of people on stage at any time; second, the entire known world to whom Antony and Cleopatra play and which seems always to regard them with fascination; it is also a timeless, superhuman audience, the heroes of history and legend and the gods themselves; finally, it is the audience of posterity, of whom we in the theater are a part.[10]

So plain is this preoccupation with value and value-making that for the moment I want to bypass it in order to concentrate on play: the dramatist's means of creating the cognitive conditions—the state of mind—that make a sense of immortality possible.

"Rebirth," Jung concedes, "is not a process that we can in any way observe. We can neither measure nor weigh nor photograph it."[11] Be that as it may (the stricture scarcely silenced Jung), criticism can analyze the cognitive conditions in cultural production that prompt people to speak of ineffable reality. It is instructive, for example, to watch Shakespeare's Cleopatra dissolve her worldly identity in order to project one less perishable, whether we call the result mystification or mystic rebirth.

Cleopatra's transformation works by momentarily merging conceptual categories that are as a rule fatally distinct. The text of her leave-taking is a bewildering interplay of mental worlds or mind-sets. Conceptually, Shakespeare's fundamental procedure is to generate such a wealth of meanings and affect that the mind registers all the nuances, transcendent claims included, without having time to analyze them.[12] The queen is playful yet earnest too. As jokes about the fatal phallic worm breed among her "immortal longings" (5.2.281), the mind-boggling wordplay and fertile associations produce multiple perspectives. Undertaking her death onstage, the woman's action is clear enough, even riveting, yet the overtones of her behavior are potently elusive.

As meanings proliferate, so do Cleopatra's roles. At once she is queen, lover, priestess, wife, mother, and more. Her own identity becomes a kind of pun, a ripple of meanings that she could expand infinitely the way the Clown would endlessly develop his jest upon the worm if her insistent farewells did not stop him. The expansion of cognitive space in the spectator is accompanied by a commensurate expansion of the queen's identity. She sublimates the "baser life" of a conventional self into the "fire and air" (289–90) of an expanded identity. She "plays" the impalpable elements, so to speak, while proclaiming herself "marble-constant" (240). "What *becomes* of Antony and Cleopatra flows from their *becomingness.* . . . They act on each other and on their audiences. They act on and act out their becomingness, striving even in death to become themselves, in both senses of the phrase" (Goldman, p. 126).

As Plotinus reasoned, role-playing is a reassuring model of rebirth: "[I]f dying is but changing a body as the actor changes a costume, or even an exit from the body like the exit of an actor from the boards when he has no more to say or do—though he will still return to act on another occasion—what is there so very dreadful in this transformation of living beings one into another?"[13] In such a reincarnation existence matters more than any particular identity, though of course the theater metaphor implies a controlling dramatist. Since personality is always richer than conventional social forms can express, role-playing can be creatively truthful as well as escapist. The dramatist stabilizes this dizzying equivocation by calling Cleopatra's end a sleep, one more—perhaps not even the last—of her "conclusions infinite / Of easy ways to die" (354–55).

Dissolving the boundaries of identity, Cleopatra also blurs conventional reality itself. In addition to wordplay, allusion, and irony, her farewell uses the inherent multiplicity of symbolism and paradoxical ideas to achieve her supralogical fecundity of meaning. Given the usual wordplay on "dying" and orgasm, "the pretty worm of Nilus" (243) joins killing and sexual regeneration in a way that suggests cyclical renewal in nature. "Age cannot wither" the woman herself, for "she makes hungry / Where most she satisfies" (2.2.234–37), echoing the paradox of vitality in exhaustion. Such imagery opens toward the ideas of Renaissance scientists like Paracelsus, who taught the interdependence of life and death, following Aristotle in his view that "decay is the beginning of all birth. . . . It brings about the birth and rebirth of forms a thousand times improved. . . . And this is the highest and greatest mysterium of God."[14] As Friar Lawrence formulates it in *Romeo and Juliet*, "The earth that's nature's mother is her tomb; / What is her burying grave, that is her womb" (2.3.9–10).

Shakespeare creates the impression of transformed vitality, then, partly by expanding some basic conceptual categories. A related device is suddenly to shift focus, as in the trick of perspective that awes the lovers who awaken from a "death-counterfeiting" midsummer night's sleep to find the "things" of conventional reality suddenly seeming "small and indistinguishable, / Like far-off mountains turned into clouds" (*MND* 3.2.364, 4.1.187–88). In Cleopatra's farewell the shape-shifting "far-off mountains" are the archetypes latent in the text: ideas distinct yet too remote to be empirically interrogated. The asp, say, implies not only the eternal serpent that bites its own tail but also the tempter of Eden, who raises behind Cleopatra the shadow of Eve. As the "baby at my breast, / That sucks the nurse asleep" (5.2.309–10), the poisonous killer becomes the symbol of new life, insinuating the queen into the role of mother-goddess, the paradox removed from close scrutiny into a mystified background, a conceptual "beyond."

One way of understanding the effects of Cleopatra's rhetoric is to consider the way it mimics primordial or mythic thought in which time is construed as an eternal present or an "eternal return." Mythic thought lacks the concept "nevermore" or takes it to be illusory. It does not attribute radical—and fatal—individuality to personality. Hence "the growth of ego-consciousness, the development of death as a problem, and the actualization of the linear time that unfolds in past, present, and future belong together."[15] F. M. Cornford could have been characterizing play-death when he described the essence of reincarnation as the belief "that the one life of the group or tribe extends continuously through the dead members as well as through the living; the dead are still part of the group, in the same sense as the living. This life, which is perpetually renewed, is reborn out of the opposite state, called 'death,' into which, at the other end of the arc, it passes again." Out of the group's collective soul or "Daemon" the king and the hero apparently emerged as the first individual souls. The soul of the king or hero is nonetheless immortal "primarily because it is, in a way, still the super-individual soul of the group, which outlives every generation of its members."[16]

Vestigial forms of these ideas appear in Renaissance ghost lore and theories of monarchy such as "the king's two bodies," in which the monarch is simultaneously a corporeal person and the supernatural spirit of his subjects.[17] The ghosts who ply Shakespeare's stage perpetuate the forms of life in death and seek to influence the living. The many reflexive jokes in the plays imply that life and death mingle backstage, and that every prologue marks a rebirth. Cleopatra envisions "Some squeaking Cleopatra boy[ing] my greatness" in the future (220), even as a boy-actor was impersonating her onstage in London: an utterance which is at once a sophisticated metadramatic joke and a primitive intuition that the present somehow contains the future and, from the spectator's vantage point in a London which was consciously replaying the glories of Rome[18] and shimmering Egypt, that the present preserves the past as well.

Art itself "lives" by appearing to transcend the flawed categories of conventional experience. Shakespeare's plays, for instance, are aggressively ordered and yet vitally irreducible. They are ideal forms full of brawling ambiguities. Just as Egyptian funeral arts transform the king's corpse into a mummy, which is both a real person and a static representation of life, the plays exploit the ambiguous status of the actor. They demonstrate the power of formal perfection over transitoriness in ways far more elemental and profound than trivial neoclassicism can appreciate. Criticism rarely makes much of the spellbinding energies that relate drama to primitive forms of immortalizing art such as the polished copper mirror, whose glow the ancient world identified with the sun, and whose reflection of the human image became associated with vitality, generation, and regeneration. Given its customary handle in the shape of a papyrus stalk and its solar glow, the mirror embodied the energy of seasonal death and renewal. The reflected image is a self apart, as the soul was thought to be and an actor is, and the mirror dramatizes the ability of an artistic object to capture dynamic vitality.

Among other things, *Antony and Cleopatra* is itself a vicarious form of funeral art. It invites spectators to mourn and celebrate the deaths of heroes. Like Charmian, who cries "Your crown's awry, / I'll mend it, and then play" (5.2.318–19), the play's emphasis on formal perfection integrates dissolution into life and makes play possible—indeed, *is* play. Hence the image of death as sleep which, like mummification, suspends rather than terminates life, allowing the symbolized value accumulated in the heroic figure to be at once relinquished and conserved. A timeless sleep evokes the teasing promise of immortalizing art, as does the "statue" of Hermione in *The Winter's Tale*, which, again like a mummy, is at once a real person and an artifact, as well as a state of mind in the beholder. When Caesar invokes the "sleeping" Cleopatra—"As she would catch another Antony / In her strong toil of grace" (5.2.347–8)—the play seems to be consoling its spectators by depicting an immortal image of her rather as Giotto and Fra Angelico painted the escaping soul as a naturalistic miniature of the dying person.

Dramatizing Cleopatra's end, Shakespeare combines deflation and reverence, dispassionate objectivity and a mystified wishfulness. As in the "natural perspective" created by Sebastian's return from "his watery tomb" in *Twelfth Night* (5.1.217, 234), death both is and is not. The mythic and objective modes of thought somehow coexist. The natural perspective gives form to the equivocation by which people ordinarily protect themselves from the terror of death. Cleopatra's end objectifies and tests the equivocal mentality of spectators in the theater. Our denial of death, says Robert Jay Lifton, "is indeed formidable. . . . But that denial can never be total; we are never fully ignorant of the fact that we die. Rather we go about life with a kind of 'middle knowledge' of death, a partial awareness of it side by side with expressions and actions that belie that awareness."[19]

Robert Jay Lifton stresses that we symbolize death and immortality through equivalents. He speaks of a sense of immortality as "the individual's experience of participation in some form of collective life-continuity," a "compelling and universal inner quest for continuous symbolic relationship to what has gone before and what will continue after our finite individual lives" (Lifton, p. 17). He means that people imagine themselves connected to the world that will survive them, through biology, posterity, significant deeds, and nature, for example. Defined this way, the post-Freudian psychiatrist's "sense of immortality" begins to resemble the archaic mentality Cornford describes, which also emphasized the indestructible connectedness of all living things. True, Lifton means his concept of immortality to be frankly symbolic and tacit, coexisting with awareness of annihilation, where the archaic imagination presumably made no clear distinction. But there is always some question about how far people are capable of separating the literal and the symbolic in a subject as ultimate as immortality. A "middle knowledge" of death depends in part on leaving certain categories undifferentiated. Even Lifton's modern social-scientific "sense of immortality" is ambiguous in ways that bring it closer to the mentality of play-death than objectivity warrants.[20]

III

Antony and Cleopatra does more than attenuate the reality of death: it celebrates the personages it destroys onstage. Again and again, as if by reflex, the play invests death with significance, whether we think of it as Aristotelian dignity, ritual sacrifice, or some deconstructible rhetorical chimera.[21] Sensing the compensatory nature of the lovers' grandeur, for example, one critic contends that a "bedrock of nihilism underlying the mountainous passion of Antony and Cleopatra is . . . finally exposed."[22] Yet no matter how nihilistic the play may seem to be, it insinuates that death is finally play-death—and by using the consoling metaphor "bedrock nihilism," the critic naively supports the characters' aspirations to superhuman permanence. The play's heroes may be abject shadows yet they cannot be nothing.

Just as the play achieves its climactic significance by ending itself, so Cleopatra disintegrates her conventional identity in order to sublimate herself in a plethora of roles, in fire and air and of course the words the spectators take out of the theater in memory. Insofar as her death consists of withdrawal and symbolic substitution, it is a form of play-death.

To some extent human behavior is always sublimated and compensatory. Every cognitive structure excludes other possibilities. Repression constricts imagination so it can function in the wondrous flux engulfing it. We restrict awareness even as, by idealizing, we inflate ourselves in an effort to stand up to the overwhelming forces around us. So fundamental is this process of self-diminishment and self-aggrandizement that ordinarily it goes unremarked. Yet the dynamic of withdrawal and symbolic substitution is a basic source of the fantasy of play-death and immortality. In this section I would like to look at Olivia's withdrawal into a house of mourning in *Twelfth Night* as an example of that dynamic.

Olivia's withdrawal is an act of identification with the structure that shelters her. A house may symbolically enlarge and substantiate the self it encloses, becoming a carapace more durable and imposing than the human body, so that a recluse may feel invulnerable. The process of identification begins in childhood, in the creation of defenses that allow a child to feel a sense of self-worth and control. In culture the process becomes transparently ideological, as when metonomy equates a queen and her palace. The "house" of a patriarch may encapsulate his ancestors and posterity as well as a present household. A single play may present a sequence of analogous dwellings or shells. The ship torn apart on Illyria's coast figuratively resurfaces as Olivia's battened-down house, becoming in time Malvolio's cell, a tomb, and a wedding chapel.

In *Twelfth Night* we hear that Olivia is the daughter of a count

That died some twelvemonth since, then leaving her
In the protection of his son, her brother,
Who shortly also died; for whose dear love,
They say, she hath abjur'd the company
And sight of men.

[1.3.36–41]

Twice stung by death, Olivia has withdrawn into her house not only to fortify herself like a snail in its shell, but also to "season" or preserve "A brother's dead love, which she would keep fresh / And lasting in her sad remembrance" (1.1.29–31). Playing dead, bequeathing her beauty to the world (1.5.244–49), she would create an imperishable imaginative space where she can keep her brother's love, and its validation of her, alive.[23]

Critics regularly deplore Olivia's delusions the way Gertrude and Claudius scold Hamlet for his morbidity. Yet death has shocked Olivia, and her obsession merely exaggerates the ordinary process by which people may restrict and harden themselves in order to preserve in memory childhood bonds on which identity is based. Whether it signifies mad fixation or loyalty to the highest human ideals, obsession provides some of the essential continuity and purposefulness that make character possible. In her grief Olivia counterfeits death in order to preempt it. If her alternative is to feel annihilated, her tears are creative inasmuch as they support a saving illusion of rescuing her brother from doom. With its roots in guilt and dread, her immobility comes close to what Lifton calls "a mimetic death," a form of numbing in which the "survivor 'undergoes a reversible form of symbolic death in order to avoid a permanent physical or psychic death'" (Lifton, p. 180). In this way Olivia's focus on the dead resembles Juliet's urge to be hidden in a charnel house "with a dead man in his shroud" (*RJ* 4.1.86) before magically undoing death with the vitality of Romeo's love.

Olivia's mourning is at once a fantasy of self-sacrifice and heroic rescue. With its connotation of tear-salted meat, her "seasoning" of her brother's love is a grotesque form of mummification. She would preserve him in memory like a nun meditating upon (in effect, immortalizing) the Savior. This scenario answered to complex cultural needs. It fulfilled patriarchal wishes for surrogate immortality, capturing a child/woman who would perpetuate a departed master's will. Olivia's situation caricatures the Renaissance conviction that to be remembered is to escape annihilation: "[T]he blankness of being forgotten was of all thoughts the most tormenting" (Spencer, p. 135).[24] The obsessed house becomes a funeral monument.

The role of grieving votary is often gender-determined—consider the Princess of France at the close of *Love's Labor's Lost* or the sea-nymphs hourly tolling the lost father in Ferdinand's lament (*Tem.* 1.2.397–405). But the role also parodies the old religion's chantries. For Olivia grief is a form of employment, and not without its rewards. Mourning enables her to play godlike guarantor of immortality while also insuring her independence. It enables her to subordinate her male kinsmen, living (Sir Toby) and dead, and to resist the gentle yoke of marriage. Which is to say that Olivia's play-death is also a means to autonomy.

Olivia's alter ego is "drowned Viola" (5.1.241), who also keeps a brother alive in imagination (1.2.19–21). At first Viola is drawn to Olivia as if her tomblike mourning house could be a mother's sheltering womb: "O that I serv'd that lady / And might not be delivered to the world / Till I had made mine own occasion mellow / What mine estate is" (42–44). Compromising with her wish for perfect autonomy, she recreates herself in her brother's image, enabled by this narcissistic emulation to establish a bond with the duke. Where Olivia remains in a shell until a "resurrected" brother reanimates her feelings, Viola frees herself to act by taking shelter in the role of "Cesario," a comic form of Caesar. As Viola/Sebastian, she is both the burlesque warrior-hero Sir Toby mocks and the puissant stranger who in fact puts Toby to rout. Once "Cesario" is strong enough, Viola can marry Orsino. Analogously, narcissism stirs Olivia to infatuation with the girlish boy Cesario, who can become the more fully masculine and alien Sebastian once Olivia has subdued her dread and herself played the masculine part of wooer.

The anagrammatic pair Olivia and Viola complement one another. They are two possible responses to annihilation, two modes of assuming form. Although obsession and the vicariousness of play are different modes, the play insinuates that they are interdependent. After all, Viola spends most of the play psyching out Olivia. Olivia's mourning prepares her to love Sebastian even as Viola's transformation allows her to reach out to share the autonomy and power of the duke. Together, that is, the women act out the process of withdrawal and substitution by which play-death in Shakespeare evokes symbolic immortality.[25] The outcome is the astonishing return of a lost brother from his "watery tomb" (5.1.234)—compare "house of tears"—and the nuptial promise of undying posterity.

Twelfth Night projects two Renaissance solutions to the problem of death and explores the conflict between them. The play challenges the idea that mourning insures immortality because mourning blocks marriage, the immortality rite that perpetuates society. Ecstatic love opens Olivia's house and draws her back into life, and love tacitly compensates her for accepting mortality. Yet the play is deeply equivocal about these ideologies. Implicitly it argues for the efficacy of mourning as a means to immortality by insinuating that the mourners' devotion contributes to the resurrection of the lost brother. Correspondingly the play jokes that Olivia's ecstatic love is so capriciously overpowering that it amounts to mad self-loss. Seen from this angle, *Twelfth Night*'s comedy indulges wishes ("what you will") while unfolding a dilemma.

IV

Although the term may seem extravagant and obsolete, I call the ultimate goal of play-death apotheosis. The word can mean "ascension to glory, departure or release from earthly life; resurrection" (*OED* 4). But its primary meaning is "transformation into a god, deification; divine status" (*OED* 1). If unconsciously we believe ourselves immortal, as Freud maintained, then we live continually on the verge of apotheosis. Since identity is a symbolic process, and imagination seemingly perfectible and unbounded, human experience is always incipiently godlike.

The drive toward apotheosis may prove benevolent, as in the rescue fantasies of the late romances, or vicious, as in the exterminating fury played out by Tamburlaine and Macbeth. It may be the foundation of political order, as in the rites that celebrated "the rather complete apotheosis of [Queen] Elizabeth, variously regarded as Deborah,

Phoebe, the Fairie Queen, Chastity, Peace or the Fortress of Perfect Beauty. Mythological gods and goddesses surrender their claims on deity in her presence, the one who seemingly embodies all virtue."[26] When Bolingbroke proves merciful, the Duchess of York prostrates herself: "A god on earth thou art" (*R2* 5.3.136). On the other hand, Julius Caesar's celestial ambitions fatally antagonize crucial followers.

Apotheosis takes its force from triumph over death. In the Renaissance at every turn the eye met doom and glory juxtaposed in Christian imagery. The transfigured Christ serenely displayed his mortal wounds. In apocalyptic lore the risen Savior was to become a warrior-lord smiting Antichrist, crushing death. Saints faced their last agonies with superhuman indifference. In a painting by the Venetian Vittore Carpaccio (1465–1526), the *Crucifixion and Apotheoses of the Ten Thousand Martyrs of Mount Ararat*, a multitude of semi-nude, athletic warriors are suffering crucifixion in fantastic trees while their heathen enemies fail to notice in the sky behind them the celestial spheres: a multiringed formation exactly resembling a flying saucer, from which angels are emerging to receive the souls of the expiring martyrs gathered on the mountain.[27]

A competitive female version of this apotheosis appears—even including the ten thousand martyrs—in a letter Arbella Stuart wrote to her uncle Gilbert (8 December 1603) vowing that women as a sex are more virtuous than men: "Ours shall still be the purer and more innocent kinde. Theare went 10000 Virgins to heauen in one day, look but in the Almanack and you shall finde that glorious day."[28]

In Shakespeare too superhuman status depends on mastery of death. Julius Caesar claims to be "constant as the Northern Star, / Of whose true-fix'd and resting quality / There is no fellow in the firmament" (3.1.60–62). Yet in swimming the roiling Tiber, Caesar nearly drowned, causing Cassius to play the mythic hero Aeneas and rescue the father figure Anchises, "the tired Caesar." Hence Cassius's contempt: "And this man /Is now become a god" (*JC* 1.2.115–16). It could be argued that Antony routs the conspirators by resurrecting Caesar in his eulogy, turning the pitiful corpse into a mythic hero in the public imagination, acting out the slain man's will by proclaiming his will. The plays are critical of divine ambitions and idolatry. In the tragedies, sacredness "goes with the recognition of the human impossibility of being divine, realized in a dread attempt, which brings destruction."[29]

Christian iconography usually visualized heaven as a process of per-

Vittore Carpaccio, *The Ten Thousand Martyrs of Mt. Ararat*. Venice, Accademia. Courtesy of ALINARI / Art Resource, New York, New York.

sonal validation. The elect bask in palpably valuable gold, their individual faces framed by golden haloes. In paradise an imperial God crowns the Virgin before an audience of saints, in an idealized temporal rite. All the might in heaven and earth focuses on one humble woman, raising her from mortal insignificance to cosmic life. The Jesus tortured in crucifixion imagery becomes the risen Lord, divinity with an individual human face.

In Shakespeare as in the world outside the theater, rulers and patriarchs are predictably the most eligible for promotion to divinity, and in later chapters I examine the grounds and consequences of that pattern. The late plays, however, conspicuously elevate regal women. Evoking the Virgin's exaltation, *The Winter's Tale*'s Queen Hermione returns from an apparent grave and, with echoes of the New Testament's promise of eternal life, delivers a kingdom deadened by grief (5.3.102–3). Like the Queen of Heaven, Hermione is a model of long-suffering virtue, not to mention the mother of a redemptive child. She becomes both an agent of deliverance and the object of universal reverence, giving the trite epithet "most sacred lady" (1.2.76) uncanny validation. Although Hermione is individualized, as I noted in Chapter 2, parallels between the two figures suggest that the Jacobean audience took special satisfaction in seeing an abused wife and mother reverenced with a nostalgic piety suggestive of the old religion. As C. L. Barber puts it, "the problematical role of women in Shakespeare . . . reflects the fact that Protestantism did away with the cult of the Virgin Mary. It meant the loss of ritual resource for dealing with the internal residues in all of us of the once all-powerful and all-inclusive mother" (Barber 1980, p. 196).

By contrast, it is Henry V's violence that makes him a star more glorious than Caesar and the object of his followers' prayers (*1H6* 1.1.52–56). In the following chapter I show how Henry's awful righteousness, no less than Hermione's patient love, becomes the ground of behavior for an entire society. Through hero worship individuals may participate in a conviction of apotheosis. Those who survive Henry V, for instance, act as if his supernatural will empowers them to throw off conventional restraints on violence and hate. Caliban inflates himself by making gods of Trinculo and Stephano. To Sicilia the statue-queen Hermione almost literally becomes a life-giving idol.

Finally, I use the term apotheosis because it captures the scope of the imaginative striving in Shakespeare and the world around us. In

the Capulets' orchard—"the place death, considering who thou art"—
Romeo envisions himself reborn, "new baptiz'd; / Henceforth, I never
will be Romeo" (2.2.64, 50–51). Juliet would make his "gracious self /
. . . god of my idolatry" (113–14). Like Antony and Cleopatra, they
would seek out new heaven and new earth. The rhythm of play-death
and apotheosis expresses a desire to remake the world that may be as
natural as breathing and yet a project of messianic scope.

It goes without saying that fantasies of transcendence are often latent in criticism as well as in Shakespeare. In their imagery critics carry
on culture's undeclared war against the grim invader, as in this melodramatic agon: if the bond of love holds in *Romeo and Juliet*, "Death is
robbed of the greater glory; the ending is a triumph, a transcending
the limits of mortality by holding fast, in a union of suffering, to what
is best in the mortal condition."[30] In his *Letters* (1926) W. A. Raleigh
claimed immortalizing powers for criticism itself, vowing that "the
main business of criticism . . . is not to legislate, not to classify, but
to raise the dead. Graves, at its command, have wak'd their sleepers,
op'd, and let them forth." In her famous study of imagery Professor
Spurgeon finds anxious realism in every image of death but the one
that she declares to be Shakespeare's personal attitude (Sonnet 146),
and that one she makes triumphal: "Here we see . . . the greedy feaster
on the flesh of men . . . annihilated . . . by the spirit of Man grown
strong."[31]

Chapter 4

Heroism and Hero Worship

Socially conceived, Shakespeare's imagery of play-death and resurrection expresses fantasies about self-effacement and autonomy. Shift the focus to the supremely autonomous figure of the hero, male or female, and the dynamics of play-death appear again, but in a new light. In the hero autonomy becomes tantamount to superhuman purpose, and hero-worshippers tacitly play dead in order to share vicariously in it. Alternatively a hero may force others to sacrifice themselves to his or her appetite for aggrandizement. Although most of my examples come from the early histories, my concern in this chapter is not primarily with traditional heroic roles such as the *milites*, but with systems of belief and the social behavior they energize.[1]

A logical place to begin is where Shakespeare apparently began, with the mourners eulogizing Henry V at the opening of *1 Henry VI*—perhaps his first play. In a sense all the motive energy of the histories originates in the problem presented by Henry's corpse: how to overcome dread and recover the power lost with the hero's fall. The survivors do not merely grieve over Henry V, they invoke play-death and apotheosis. Bedford prays to Henry's "ghost" (1.1.52) and "A far more glorious star . . . than Julius Caesar" (55–56). Losses in France "Will make [Henry] burst his lead and rise from death" (64). Gloucester then quips that "If Henry were recall'd to life again, / These news would cause him once more to yield the ghost" (66–67). The speakers acknowledge death yet excite hopes of heroic immortality.

Gloucester opens the scene by identifying Henry with the warrior-Christ of the Apocalypse. He tries to keep alive the conviction of indestructible righteousness which the king aroused in his followers:

His brandish'd sword did blind men with his beams;
His arms spread wider than a dragon's wings;

His sparkling eyes, replete with wrathful fire,
More dazzled and drove back his enemies
Than midday sun fierce bent against their faces.

Abruptly the duke becomes self-conscious about this rhapsody and catches himself: "What should I say? his deeds exceed all speech: / He ne'er lift up his hand but conquered" (1.1.10–16).

Exeter then deflates the naive wish for the hero's resurrection. "Henry is dead," he insists, "and never shall revive. Upon a wooden coffin we attend" (18–19). Yet the deflation actually deepens the wish for omnipotence since he urges ritual violence: "We mourn in black, why mourn we not in blood?" (17). Henry's loss, he complains, degrades the hero-worshippers themselves: "death's dishonorable victory / We with our stately presence glorify, / Like captives bound to a triumphant car." Conquered, enslaved, the mourners are helplessly "bound" by a new obsession with death. To break loose, Exeter recommends killing those French "Conjurors and sorcerers, that, afraid of [Henry V], / By magic verses have contriv'd his end" (26–27). He reduces death to a military humiliation that the survivors can undo by destroying the French and, through them, death itself.

At this point the bishop of Winchester lauds Henry as

. . . a king blest of the King of Kings.
Unto the French the dreadful Judgment Day
So dreadful will not be as was his sight.
The battles of the Lord of hosts he fought;
The Church's prayers made him prosperous."
[28–32]

This speech also associates the fallen hero with the Christ of the last days. However self-serving, the bishop's vision draws upon themes that originated in early medieval theology, where "Christ was regarded as the lord and hero *par excellence*, unremitting in his demand of obedience, who overcame Satan's power and his claims over the loyal Christian retainer. He had triumphed over death and one day would preside . . . over the eternal and blissful banquet of his chosen and faithful followers."[2]

The alternative to Henry's holy triumph is slavery to the lord of darkness.[3] By linking personified death to the satanic French and crying for apocalyptic revenge, the mourners compulsively elaborate a

degraded theology. As scapegoats, fiendish magicians killing a messianic king, the French embody the mourners' unconscious motives.
The English associate Henry's demise with usurpation. Bedford
blames "bad revolting stars" (4) and worries about "civil broils" (53).
Exeter speaks of "our glory's overthrow" as "plotted" (24). And for
decades after this scene English nobles will be wishing for a new
demigod while untiringly plotting against their leaders. Worshiping
Henry V, urging extermination of the French, the survivors seek to
control their own homicidal urges for power.

As the scene develops Henry's followers first reconsecrate the feeling of power he inspired in them by exciting convictions of cosmic
righteousness. Then, in part by projecting all their ambivalence onto a
scapegoat, they seek to substantiate their illusions through sacred revenge. In Otto Rank's words, "the death fear of the ego is lessened by
the killing, the sacrifice, of the other; through the death of the other,
one buys oneself free from the penalty of dying" (Becker 1973, p. 99).

Throughout the histories death provokes obsessive dread that is
superficially relieved by aggression, which in turn produces revenge
and, in an endless spiral, more anxiety and sadistic triumphalism.[4] The
participants in this process impose cosmic categories on one another
(God, devil, glory, Judgment Day) so that once released from paralyzing dread, they can act with "superhuman" freedom and resolve. To be
sure, there is a note of cynicism in speeches about divinity that justify
looting and lust, yet the cynicism controls terrifying conflicts never far
beneath the surface. A warrior may be bluff and witty about death
without in the least disavowing the cosmic fantasies that sustain him.

Rarely do the warrior-heroes begin to see through their own enchanted language, however sterile. In *3 Henry VI*, for example, Warwick faces his end with sudden resignation:

> . . . of all my lands
> Is nothing left me but my body's length.
> Why, what is pomp, rule, and reign, but earth and dust?
> And live we how we can, yet die we must.
>
> [5.2.25–28]

In the larger chronicle of slaughter this speech begins to evoke the
sense of futility that the mourners around Henry V deny: that divested
of aggrandizing symbols, the self is nothing. Yet Warwick's own perspective is limited, "an old moral expressed in language as stale as
itself" (Spencer, p. 148).[5] His comrades immediately comfort him by

reasserting his heroic supremacy for Montague, who "to the latest gasp cried out for Warwick" and died beseeching not the Redeemer but the kingmaker (34, 41). Like Henry V's brothers, Montague would merge with a "sweet brother" as commanding as death itself—"who liv'd king, but I could dig his grave?" (21).

As Montague's devotion suggests, heroism is a system of enabling beliefs. Followers release their own strength through a leader. Yet their interdependency also creates instability. Like any other lovers, the hero-worshippers may tire of effacing themselves: they may become envious or fickle or ambitious. And no hero can forever live up to the ideal. In this perspective the struggle over heroic authority in the early histories is a long, tragic effort to sustain and dramatize violence capable of fusing inner conflicts into furious purpose.

II

Shakespeare's histories, then, begin with a crisis in heroic relationships. To revere a leader who is more fearful than Judgment Day (*1H6* 1.1.29) is to identify with inexhaustible vitality. Ernest Becker understands such worship as transference:

> Realistically the universe contains overwhelming power. . . . The child takes natural awe and terror and focusses them on individual beings. . . . The transference object, being endowed with the transcendent powers of the universe, now has in himself the power to control, order, and combat them. As ultimately power means power over life and death, the child can now safely emerge in relation to the transference object. . . . All he has to do is conform to it . . . conciliate it if it becomes terrible; use it serenely for automatic daily activities.
>
> [Becker 1973, pp. 145–46]

Transference merges the hero-worshipper with an idealized other, and this symbiosis effectively produces an "us" superior to any lone individual. (If necessity is personified, then even fatalism may become a self-sacrificing submission to a superior will, precisely as in hero worship.)

Nowhere are transference and symbiosis more striking than in the feudal rituals of lordship in the early Middle Ages. They are ancestral forms that starkly clarify social bonds in Shakespeare's world. Originally, for instance, a vassal was a young male slave or *vassus*:

These young men (*juniores*) submitted to the authority of an older man, or *senior* (from which seigneur), in a curious ceremony, the "commendation," in which the younger man placed his clasped hands between the hands of the master, who enfolded them in his own. The vassus thus entered into a new realm of protection and mutual services. Through the touching of hands the warrior chief caused to pass from his own body into the body of the vassal something like a sacred fluid, the *hail*. Made taboo, as it were, the vassal thereupon fell under the charismatic power, pagan in origin, of the lord. . . . This ceremony went beyond the mere notion of paternal protection and filial service. This new kind of relationship, of inferior to superior, derived its force from pagan notions of interpersonal relations. Behind every individual who wielded power the pagans saw the cosmos itself, which they represented anthropomorphically.[6]

Transference in this ritual is remarkably potent but not, Becker would argue, unique. The inheritors of Henry V ascribe to their lord a personal force comparable to the protofeudal *hail*. And it is worth pointing out that while Charlemagne consolidated his government by means of these male ties, with his death—as with Henry's in the scene above—heroic bonds degenerated into civil war.

Society itself is a network of transference relationships: a specific historical arrangement of heroic roles. The official network in the Renaissance was an interlocking sequence of upward identification following the chain of being from dead matter to the throne of the everlasting father. Ideology regulated transference so that deference had a quasireligious quality, as in the mystification of noble blood. Yet unauthorized transference also flourished. Lovers could validate each other with or without parental approval, as Juliet makes Romeo "the god of my idolatry" (*RJ* 2.2.114). No sooner does the ruthless Edward seize the throne in *3 Henry VI* than he is seized by the idea of a woman "whose perfections challenge sovereignty" (*3H6* 3.2.86). As mother of the future, a woman may rival the greatest lord as a guarantor of immortality.[7]

As a symbolic action, transference may engage any object at any distance. The miserly Shylock worships "his" ducats, while the Christian merchants—unconvincingly—preach devotion to friends and contempt for mere gold. The transference object "always looms larger than life because it represents all of life and hence all of one's fate" (Becker 1973, p. 146). Having won Portia, Bassanio experiences transference in the same way a crowd would respond to a "beloved prince." He feels a "confusion in my powers" like a crowd whose mingled voices turn "to a wild of nothing, save of joy / Express'd and not express'd" (*MV* 3.2.177–83). In this image the release of feeling makes Bassanio an entire society and yet also "a wild of nothing." Ineffably fulfilled, he is also potentially destroyed.

To appreciate the plasticity of transference it helps to remember that theater itself can be an arena of hero worship, as Thomas Heywood noticed: "What English blood seeing the person of any bold English presented and doth not hug his fame and hunny at his valor, pursuing him in his enterprise with his best wishes and as being wrapt in contemplation, offers him in his heart all prosperous performance, as if the performer were the man personated? so bewitching a thing is lively and well-spirited action, that it hath power to new mould the hearts of the spectators."[8] As the "wrapt" spectators lose themselves in "contemplation," the actors become the glorious figures they "personate." The fantastic heroes in turn "mould" anew the "bewitched" spectators. Like Bassanio's love, the spectators' wishes for "all prosperous performance" recreate them: make them more and less than they really are. And since this process appears endlessly renewable, it whispers of immortality.

Regarded this way, the will to worship is as potent as a hero's charisma. The nobles invoking Henry V are not merely wishing him back to life but externalizing their own still-vital feelings about him. The survivors try to reobjectify the king's presence in themselves, as if by his "inspiration" he has breathed life into them like God. When their rhetoric of prayers and conjurations accomplish nothing, they try to rekindle inspiration from revenge.

Revenge is a negative form of transference; it concentrates complex emotions into a primary hatred so that hatred can be a means of "taming terror" (Becker 1973, p. 145). In the Quarto *2H6* York stands up to Clifford's rage by vowing, "now my heart hath sworne immortall hate / To thee" (5.2.21–22), as if hate may be everlasting. In addition, retribution rationalizes death. "You may slay me, but retribution guarantees that you too will die." More profoundly, vengeance supports fantasies of triumphal apotheosis, as when Richard III plays the scourge of God. The bayed York displaces his will into a supernatural future, where, he claims, "My ashes, as the phoenix, may bring forth / A bird that will revenge upon you all" (*3H6* 1.4.35–36).

Since revenge magnifies the self, the need for it may precede any injury. Like the feud in Romeo's Verona, the war in France plunges on, every aggression called retaliation, its first cause forgotten. The English and the French enchant each other with supremely meaningful rage. By acting in the name of an absent leader, the revengers displace their responsibility for atrocities, so that events seem to unfold with cosmic fatality.

Revenge may reinforce the bonds of hero worship, promising transcendence not only of death but also of insoluble conflicts in social structure. Winging off to heaven "Coupled in bonds of perpetuity," the slain Talbot and his son "shall scape mortality" (*1H6* 4.7.20–22).[9] But their sacrifice also dissolves the usual generational ambivalence by turning the pair into brotherly lovers and projecting all patriarchal hostility onto "antic Death," whose "insulting tyranny" their love defeats.

The same release of ambivalence into vengeance and supernatural vitality appears in *Henry V* when Exeter reports mangled York's kissing Suffolk's wounds as they "fly abreast" to heaven (4.6.11–19). Loving another's wounds, the warrior atones for his own homicidal rage against the enemy and pities his own mortality—the "cause" that battle would revenge in the first place. Such love is part of a broader social drama as well. In this instance the witnessing Exeter and Henry V behave like ambivalent parents for whom the "pretty and sweet" sacrifice is performed (28). York offers his death to his sovereign Henry (22) and expires kissing his "brother" Suffolk's lips. Thinking about it, Exeter claims, "all my mother came into my eyes" (31), and Henry sympathizes with this maternal response. Yet in his next breath the king acts out the rage of a vindictive father-hero by commanding that the French prisoners be slain. On one level the father is revenging his lost sons. In the symbolic logic of the scene, however, the sacrificial love of good sons deflects parental rage onto scapegoats and, reciprocally, that hidden rage energizes the good sons' conviction of immortality.[10]

In the *Henry VI* plays Shakespeare tests various figures such as Talbot, Joan of Arc, Duke Humphrey, Warwick, and Henry VI against his own deepening awareness of the real limits of conventional heroic forms. It becomes clear that people cannot thrive without some form of transference: when a feeble or even saintly king like Henry VI is unable to act out the fictions of warrior immortality, he arouses anxiety and aggression among his followers, and so jeopardizes the community he represents. He admits—in both senses—death. Equally clear is

the potential for evil delusion in transference, as Richard III obligingly demonstrates when he wins over—apparently against her own
will—Lady Anne, whose husband and father-in-law he has slain. The
eventual victory of Richmond is meant to be a healthy solution to the
problem of heroism, yet Richmond remains mostly off stage, as un-
tested and ghostly as the lost Henry V.

There are two interrelated problems here: one is the inherent ambivalence of all transference; the other, the tragic inadequacy of specific historical forms of heroism. To consider the second of these problems, which is the larger aim of this book, requires a closer examination of the first.

III

As witnessed by the calamities chronicled in the histories, transference is the essential problem of heroism. Again and again hero and
hero-worshippers betray each other. They may prove fatally unen-
chanted like the supposed coward Falstaff and the timid Henry VI, or
treacherously ambitious like Suffolk and York. Rival heroes such as
Talbot and the Pucelle would murder one another to substantiate their
authority. Richard III, by contrast, cynically uses transference as an
instrument of policy, undermining all who would depend on him.

The ambivalence of transference comes in part from its totality. "In
some complex ways," says Becker, "the child has to fight against the
power of the parents." Although the child controls his or her fate
through a crucial surrogate, that surrogate becomes his new fate: "He
binds himself to one person to automatically control terror . . . and to
defeat death by that person's strength. But then he experiences 'transference terror': the terror of losing the object, of displeasing it, of not
being able to live without it. The terror of his own finitude and impotence still haunts him, but now in the precise form of the transference
object" (Becker 1973, p. 146).

This paradox makes itself keenly felt in love. The lover reads his or
her life and death in the beloved's face.[11] Othello equates Desdemona
with the cosmic order—"when I love thee not, / Chaos is come again"
(3.3.91–92)—and ambivalently links love to damnation: "Perdition
catch my soul / But I do love thee! (90–91). In Juliet's eye Romeo sees
the menace of rejection as well as tenderness, since "There lies more
peril in thine eye, / Than twenty . . . swords" (2.2.71–72).

When the swords are literal, the peril of the eye becomes lethal.

Henry V's "sparkling eyes . . . dazzled and drove back his enemies" (*1H6* 1.1.12–13). Henry VI reads Suffolk's murderous will in eyes which, like the basilisk, "kill the innocent gazer with [his] sight" (*2H6* 3.2.53). "Look not upon me," he begs, "for thine eyes are wounding" (51). Richard III also exudes hypnotic fatality (*R3* 4.1.54–55). In each of these examples eyes radiate superhuman force. The more terrifying the object, the stronger the transference, and the greater the potential for terror and release from terror. Hence the attempt to dispel transference by decapitating its apparent personal source, and the practice of exposing a beheaded enemy's visage on London Bridge. In *3 Henry VI* the captive York rails at Clifford that his own "frown hath made [Clifford] faint and fly ere this!" (1.4.48). Logically, Clifford makes himself terrible by killing the source of the terrible "frown," and the decapitated head is "set on York gates" (179) to celebrate its impotence. Eventually Clifford's visage is tamed by the same technique.

One way of understanding the intrinsic ambivalence of hero worship is to consider the hero and his clients together as a single supra-individual creature. This image underlies Talbot's joke when the Countess of Auvergne imagines she has captured him in *1 Henry VI*. "I am but the shadow of myself," he teases her. "[M]y substance is not here" (2.3.50–51). His soldiers provide the punchline, for they "are his substance, sinews, arms, and strength, / With which he yoketh [her] rebellious necks" (63–64). Temporarily Talbot, like Henry V, unites his quarreling countrymen.[12] In his modest formula his followers are the substance and he merely their shadow: he plays dead to be magnified in them. Yet at the same time he implicitly envisions his followers as prosthetic extensions of his own will.

On the one hand, the hero lives through hero-worshippers and owes them everything; their combined strength is synergistic. On the other hand, such followers are merely his instruments, as slaves are, and the more—and more absolutely—he controls, the more there is of him: the more he exists.[13] In one model hero and followers thrive through mutual love and the followers' emulation. In the other model the hero dreads his followers' dependency and their independence as well, and therefore he turns tyrannical, seeking to incorporate them into his projective "body." In one model the hero sacrifices himself for the group, as Talbot claims to do. In the other, epitomized by the Richard III born "to bite the world," he symbolically devours others in order to aggrandize himself through their strength.

The distinction is of course artificial insofar as the plays tend to keep asunder what historical reality intermingled. However benevolent they may have been, king and nobleman lived off their subjects, creating resentment and conceptual discord that had to be contained. While Shakespeare trenchantly dramatizes the viciousness of privilege, he also reconciles spectators to it when heroism splits into the pure forms of Richmond and Crookback, one of which scapegoats and routs the other. This is akin to the strategy in the prologue to *Henry V*, where the spectators are called "monarchs" and invited to "behold the swelling scene" in which Harry routs England's enemies: "For 'tis your thoughts that now must deck our kings, / Carry them here or there, jumping o'er times" (*H5* pro. 4, 28–29). The prologue splits the audience in two: into imaginative "monarchs" who, like the kingmaking Warwick, are as gods to kings, ordaining established authority; and into those wretches, in the playhouse and out, who would withhold life from the king by refusing to "deck" or "carry" him. One group silently displaces the other. Coaching the spectator-monarch, the prologue objectifies transference in a form flattering to marginal hero-worshippers. "The ideal king must be in large part the invention of the audience, the product of a will to conquer which is revealed to be identical to a will to submit."[4]

Nowhere is this ambivalence more radical than in *Hamlet*, whose opening scenes recreate the dilemma that animates *1 Henry VI*. Like the survivors of Henry V, Hamlet anxiously mourns a lost hero. This time, however, the fearful wish for resurrection comes true:

Let me not burst in ignorance, but tell
Why thy canoniz'd bones, hearsed in death,
Have burst their cerements, why the sepulchre,
Wherein we saw thee quietly interr'd,
Hath op'd his ponderous and marble jaws
To cast thee up again.

[1.4.46–51]

While Hamlet recalls an idealized father, the Ghost he conjures to speak is obsessed with vengeance and envisions no future for Hamlet or Denmark beyond that. On the contrary, this father would live through the son like a vampire. From "the table of my memory" Hamlet vows to "wipe away all trivial fond records," all traces of his identity, so that "thy commandment all alone shall live / Within the book and volume of my brain" (1.5.98–103). Such self-effacement would be a panicky regression to infancy, where the soul "is yet a white paper unscribbled with observations of the world, wherewith at length it becomes a blurred notebook. [The child] is purely happy because he knows no evil. . . . He kisses and loves all, and when the smart of the rod is past, smiles on his beater."[15] In Hamlet as in this dehumanized infant, violent domination would produce only "smiles on his beater."

Hamlet imagines being nullified and filled with the ghostly father's fierce, supernatural purpose. They would become one, as in the imagery that equates the son who would "burst in ignorance" (1.4.46) with the father whose "canoniz'd bones" have "burst their cerements" (47–48). And from time to time, as in his speech about "the witching time of night, / When churchyards yawn and hell itself [breathes] out / Contagion to this world" (3.2.388–90), itself a fantasy of play-death and displaced rage, Hamlet could be speaking with the Ghost's voice.

This tomb-bursting play-death signals a collapse of repression in Hamlet: an inability to keep the internalized, ruthless father "out of mind."[16] In Hamlet's experience heroic transference has acquired a hallucinatory life of its own. It takes the prince's own play-death and deliverance at sea to release him from this spell.

In *Hamlet* as in *1 Henry VI* a survivor conjures a lost hero in an effort to preempt despair and ambivalence.[17] Unresolved dependency leads to compensatory fury against a rival—Claudius, France—who supposedly destroyed the hero by "witchcraft." As in Hamlet's brooding over the praying Claudius, cosmic extermination of the adversary promises to restore heroic integrity. In both plays the survivors come to struggle fratricidally against each other—as Hamlet and Laertes do—and themselves perish. The new hero who finally breaks the cycle of rivalry and revenge—Richmond, Fortinbras—enters as if from the outside.

The comic analogue of this pattern is the materialization of a hero or god such as *Cymbeline's* Jupiter, who confirms the integrity of transference after it has been broken and reestablished. *As You Like It's* Hymen validates marriages that reintegrate families and dispose the lovers to cherish one another. In *A Midsummer Night's Dream* the fairies' love juice exposes the irrational nature of transference, whereupon the feuding lovers reorient themselves in marriages authorized by the duke and, in the phenomenological distance, the fairy king.

IV

Shakespearean drama, again, begins with a crisis. A hero's sudden death evokes fears about the loss of creative will, and incites rage directed outward, against foreign scapegoats, and fratricidally (or suicidally) inward, against countrymen. By the time Crookback fights his way to the center of the stage, the righteous frenzy has become maddening. Would-be heroes have grown decadent or collapsed into futility. Henry VI loses credit the more saintly he becomes. His selflessness strikes Queen Margaret as an irresponsible play-death: "What is it, but to make thy sepulchre, / And creep into it before thy time come?" (*3H6* 1.1.236–37). Crookback inherits a world in which the code of heroic immortality has deteriorated.

Richard dramatizes the insight with which the histories began: that dread may disrupt transference and produce a vengeful, wolfish appetite for survival. While critics often ponder the origins of the remarkable Richard, I would emphasize how directly he plays out the consequences of that initial traumatic loss: how he re-presents the conniving, viciously idealistic and anxiously inadequate voices around Henry V's bier.

From the outset he calls attention to his helplessly mortal body, whose grotesqueness measures his unfitness for the symbolic immortality of love and glory. He sees his crooked back as "an envious mountain . . . / Where sits deformity to mock my body" (*3H6* 3.2.157–58). "Deformity" literally tyrannizes him. The image presents the personified cruelty of the perverted heroic ideal. Such a psychic force can seem more substantial than the man it inhabits, who is "disproportioned" in every part, "Like to a chaos or an unlick'd bear-whelp" (160–61): scarcely formed into being. Richard's own monstrous body becomes an object of negative transference for him. As it obsesses him, it gives him all-absorbing purpose.

Like the mourners for Henry V, who soon turn against one another, Crookback meets the temptation to usurp the crown in order "to o'erbear such / As are of better person than myself" (*3H6* 3.2.166–67). He too would compensate for his inadequacy by exterminating scapegoats, dispatching Hastings, for example, in a tantrum against "witchcraft" that has supposedly "blasted" his body (*R3* 3.4.67–72). In effect, Richard directly manipulates the psychic forces that in the mourners are repressed and devious. They rhapsodize about Henry

V's annihilating righteousness; Crookback deliberately stages his own piety "aloft, between two Bishops" (*R3* 3.7.s.d.). Where they are covertly hostile to women, Richard is blatantly antagonistic:

> The *Henry VI* plays begin by mourning the loss of a world of male bonds and locating degeneracy in the power of women to seduce magically and then dominate: the triumph of Margaret over both Suffolk and the young king is both emblem and cause of this degeneracy in England, as Joan's triumph over Charles is both emblem and cause in France. The agent of corruption is specifically identified with a female force when the struggle of these histories is relived tragically in the person of Richard III, who believes that a "she"—simultaneously identified with love, nature, and mother—has deformed him in his mother's womb. [*3H6* 3.2.155][18]

Enticing his victims to greedy hero worship or overwhelming them through terror, Richard subsumes others. Hence the images of cannibalistic self-aggrandizement that follow his bloody career. "Teeth thou hadst in thy head when thou wast born," cries Henry VI, "To signify thou cam'st to bite the world" (*3H6* 5.6.53–54). Richard is a "wolf" (7); a "dog" (77; *R3* 1.3.288–90); and of course a rogue boar. Old Queen Margaret calls him and his brothers "bloody cannibals" (*3H6* 5.5.61), and Richard a "carnal cur" who "Preys on the issue of his mother's body" (*R3* 5.4.56–57).[19]

Nevertheless, Crookback's cavalier hatred of his own ugly body expresses how profoundly heroic idealism has shaped him in spite of his apparent cynicism. He is not free to be indifferent to his culture's models of perfection; on the contrary, he is idealistic in a negative way, substituting wishful omnipotence for the basic self-love by which imagination ordinarily anchors personality in the world:

> I'll make my heaven to dream upon the crown,
> And whiles I live, t' account this world but hell,
> Until my misshap'd trunk that bears this head
> Be round impaled with a glorious crown.
>
> [*3H6* 3.2.168–71]

Richard's "dream" is idolatry. The crown would transform his "misshap'd" self. He would be "round impaled" as if in the enclosed paradise of medieval iconography.

Despite his scorn, that is, Richard relies on the dynamics of transcendent heroism, in his negative way as dependent as any other person on its authority for life. In context, for instance, his monologue is a compensatory reaction to his brother Edward's infatuation with Lady Grey. Conjuring up purpose for himself, he appears envious not merely of love's pleasures but of its profound authority. He is aroused by Edward's ecstatic vision of command over, and surrender to, a being whose "perfections challenge sovereignty" (3.2.86). And so Richard's boasts to "drown more sailors" and "slay more gazers" project relationships with mythic heroes of spellbinding potency: the mermaid, the basilisk, Ulysses, Nestor, Sinon, and Proteus. Hence his fantasies of unlimited persuasiveness as an actor who can "murther whiles I smile" (182). Acting not only invites illusions of perfection but also dissociates the actor's imagination from his merely human—for Richard meaning deformed and mortal—feelings. In time, with godlike fluency, he will parody his culture's idealized roles one after another: warrior, king, lover, sage. Armed with a Bible, flanked by bishops, and meekly declining the crown, he will mimic even the saintly, feeble Henry VI (*R3* 3.7.95ff). For him mimicry is a mode of incorporating others akin to oral appetite.

The underlying ambivalence of heroic apotheosis emerges in Richard's groping promise to act the deliverer. Trying to tempt Queen Elizabeth to let him marry her daughter, he acknowledges killing her sons, the princes, "But in your daughter's womb I bury them; / Where in that nest of spicery they will breed / Selves of themselves, to your recomforture" (4.4.423–25). Fantasizing about the phoenix, Richard plays upon the dynamics of play-death. He depicts himself as the agent of renewal whose good offices will enable his victims to "breed / Selves of themselves," apparently without end.

My basic premise is that Richard's rage to devour others originates in terror of death and feeds an illusion of omnipotence.[20] By the end of his career, when the all-important crown has brought him no lasting security, he wakes in the night at Bosworth Field to find his psyche full of the victims he has swallowed up. The ghosts he beholds are lives he has engorged yet cannot digest. As their encouraging appearance to Richmond suggests, they can be construed as internalized models of heroism: providing guidance and comfort to the righteous and terrorizing others. Momentarily Richard disintegrates in panic. "What do I fear? Myself? There's none else by" (5.3.182). Yet dread seizes him, "Lest I revenge." But now revenge explicitly means self-destruction: "What, myself upon myself?" (186).

Shakespeare's Richard is "born to bite the world," imagery that has a profound historical context in Paul's promise of immortality, that "the trumpet shall sound, and the dead shall be raised incorruptible, and we shall be changed." Then "shall be brought to passe the saying that is written, Death is swallowed up in victorie" (1 Cor. 15.52–53). Paul depicts resurrection as conquest: summoned by the trumpet of a fearless lord, himself once liberated from the tomb, the faithful will all rise up "incorruptible," no longer bedeviled by mortal deformity, and defeat the dread adversary. Immortality will be a triumph of oral incorporation, an aggressive "swallowing up" of the enemy, and bring the apocalyptic satiation of mortal appetite or desire. Identifying utterly with the cosmic hero, the follower will live forever in Christ.

Richard III presents a pathological version of the fantasy that heroic killing and incorporation can feed life without end. Richard finally swallows up the crown itself but with no relief from anxiety. If anything, his fears intensify. Critics often argue that Crookback's inspiration mysteriously wanes as his fortunes peak. A better explanation might be that Shakespeare dramatizes a progressive failure of symbolization to control an underlying rage for survival. For Richard the crown is a symbolic substitute for the power of death over others, and as it loses its efficacy, he becomes more brutally literal, provoking former allies and escaped victims to retaliation so he can slaughter them.

Logically the play culminates with a homicidal Richard enacting "more wonders than a man" at Bosworth Field (5.4.2). There he stabs at an adversary who springs indestructibly back to life in a parody of the schemer's homicidal career: "I think there be six Richmonds in the field; / Five have I slain today" (11–12). In this imagery Richmond is akin to the Henry V imagined bursting from his tomb at the beginning of the histories, whereas Richard becomes ghostly. He cries out for a horse to magnify his own failing strength and make flesh equal to his will. And at last, "Seeking for Richmond in the throat of death" (5), Richard is himself consumed by the death he would have swallowed up in victory.

V

Let me distinguish two kinds of heroic apotheosis. The first, the affirmative, emphasizes the creativity of the ego-ideal and ranges along a continuum from benevolent narcissism such as Bottom's to variations on the role of deliverer. It yields active and passive scenarios of rescue from death. Prospero claims to have waked the dead through his magic (*Tem.* 5.1.48–50), whereas Queen Hermione restores life indirectly. Passive heroism tends to be associated with martyrdom, as in Calpurnia's dream that a statue of Caesar "Did run pure blood" and "many lusty Romans" bathed their hands in it (*JC* 2.2.76–90). The dream combines fear of the hero-worshippers' parasitic cannibalism with a vision of the hero's godlike gift of immortality to his people. As Decius explicates it: "from you great Rome shall suck / Reviving blood" (87–88).

Negative apotheosis, on the other hand, ranges along a continuum from narcissistic withdrawal to apocalyptic rage. At the extreme the hero strives to destroy all mortal imperfection. In the beginning at least Hamlet, for example, internalizes the righteousness of a parental Hyperion that would turn him not only against Claudius but also against his own "sallied flesh" and the "weary, stale, flat, and unprofitable" world (1.2.129, 133). In the active form of negation Richard III acts to devour the vitality of others, and Coriolanus becomes "The son, the husband, and the father tearing / His country's bowels out" (5.3.102–3). In different ways both figures act out Coriolanus's urge to be perfectly autonomous "as if a man were author of himself / And knew no other kin" (36–37).[21] In practice these categories often intermingle. The Henry V blessed of the King of Kings is capable of sadistic fury. The magnanimous Prospero uses magic to subsume everyone else in the play. It is the politics of transference, the circumstantial negotiations of heroism, that give the plays depth. Yet however complex, heroic fantasy is inescapable, at work even in moments of resistance, as in Williams's conversation with the king in *Henry V*, and Hamlet's efforts to escape from paralyzing transference into existential "readiness."

Gender is among the most problematical determinants of heroic fantasy in Shakespeare. In the rhetoric of apotheosis men become devils and demigods, women witches or goddesses. Although figures such as Sycorax and Hermione perpetuate these stereotypes in the late plays, Shakespeare does try to move beyond them by dramatizing underlying infantile ambivalence toward woman-as-mother and undoing the misogyny of his earlier plays. In the first tetralogy a shepherd's lowly daughter suddenly becomes the savior and queen of France, only to be demonized and annihilated. *The Winter's Tale* gives this scenario a sly, wish-fulfilling outcome when Sicilia honors the supposed daughter of a Bohemian shepherd as a savior and queen. Like the Pucelle, Perdita inspires visions of "a world ransom'd, or one destroyed" (5.2.15).

Nevertheless, the change from demon to goddess keeps woman transfixed by masculine transference, and there is an ongoing debate about the degree to which women in Shakespeare are male fantasies in female dress.[22] One consideration in that debate should be the dramatist's attempt to keep heroic fantasies in critical focus through irony. While irony deflates pretensions to glory, it may also contribute to the illusion of depth and autonomy in a character. "Let me give light," says the teasing Portia, "but let me not be light" (*MV* 5.1.129). With its superabundant meanings, this gnomic play makes Portia to some extent unaccountable. Such resonant female heroes are constructed to exceed conventional categories.

The truest heroism, Shakespeare insinuates, exists in ironic excess of, or contradistinction to, heroic conventions. But ironies themselves have to be read as historical-cultural productions. In mystical love poetry, for example, or in the strategic riddling of Queen Elizabeth, irony protected the illusion of autonomy as it does onstage.[23] Yet readings of irony are notoriously inexact, especially with a historical subject as elusive as gender. When we respond to Hermione and Portia, say, we are not simply responding to a direct representation of personality but to character as a criticism of conventions: a negation of "common" social prescriptions.[24] The catch is that this dialectic of prescriptive transference and resistance to transference affects nearly everyone in Shakespeare. There are as many cogent yet incompatible interpretations of Henry V and Hamlet as there are of heroic women in the plays. Implied is a social system in which heroic transference operated so pervasively and urgently that individuals compulsively transformed others into ego-ideals or scapegoats. In such a society people controlled insecurity by fictionalizing each other's "characters," magnifying qualities that justified submissive admiration or righteous contempt. The more nakedly mortal the individual—and the more he or she exposed mortality in others—the more radically valorized the personality, and the more overt the social imagination's drive toward apotheosis.

Later chapters explore specific cultural expressions of heroic behavior such as patriarchy (Chapter 8) and prophetic history (Chapter 9).

Chapter 10 reconsiders the emergence of the hero in light of conflicts over individuation. In the meantime, however, I want to look at some ancient forms that influenced ideas of play-death and heroism in Shakespeare, in particular the long shadow of the archetypal hero.

Chapter 5

The Hero and the Tomb

A "commercial writer" like Shakespeare, says Leslie Fiedler, "can rediscover antique fable only in the cliché," yet "fortunately, every stereotype is a sleeping archetype, a myth which seems moribund or dead
until resurrected by the Kiss of the Prince, the touch of a great popular artist."[1] This flippant assessment, which links Shakespeare's use of
myth to his preoccupation with revival, reminds us how commonplace
mythic forms may be, even as it remystifies myth by touting the artist's
magical touch.

Since empirical proofs are out of the question, the subject of archetypes invites academic impressionism and compensatory theorizing.
Whether universal archetypes even exist is debatable. Putting discre-
tion before valor, the present chapter tiptoes past such controversies.
Instead it considers archetype as a source of heroic authority. My concern is with recurring patterns of heroic imagination whose antiquity
and representation of fundamental human concerns have made them
useful paradigms. After weighing analogies between play-death, the
quest of the archetypal hero, and ritual sacrifice, I examine Shakespeare's tactic of subverting naive archetypes in order to evoke more
sublime meanings. Attention then turns to Christian paradigms, and
finally to the tomb viewed as a conceptual device for controlling the
boundary between life and death, an inquiry Chapter 6 continues by
treating heroism as movement in a psychic landscape determined by
death-defying boundaries.

World history is replete with myths of the hero that celebrate an
awakening or deliverance from death. In Joseph Campbell's synthesis
the formula of the hero's so-called rites of passage calls for

> a separation from the world, a penetration to some source of power,
> and a life-enhancing return. The Greeks referred fire, the first support

of all human culture, to the world-transcending deeds of their Prometheus, and the Romans the founding of their world-supporting city to Aeneas, following his . . . visit to the eerie underworld of the dead. Everywhere . . . the really creative acts are represented as those deriving from some sort of dying to the world; and what happens in the interval of the hero's nonentity, so that he comes back reborn, made great and filled with creative power, mankind is also unanimous in declaring.[2]

The thousand-faced hero functioned as a modeling device by which groups shaped values and behavior. Stories of heroes conceptualize and stake out a range of human aspirations and limits. Which is to say that the hero served as an enabling fantasy, a technology for securing innovation and improving control over life.

In his survey of initiation rites in premodern cultures Mircea Eliade finds the passage into adulthood virtually always structured as a rebirth into a heroic role. "By dying ritually, the initiate shares in the supernatural condition of the founder of the mystery. Through this valuation, death and initiation become interchangeable. . . . Initiatory death becomes the *sine qua non* for all spiritual regeneration and, finally, for the survival of the soul and even for its immortality. And . . . this religious valuation of ritual death finally led to conquest of the fear of real death, and to the belief in the possibility of a purely spiritual survival for the human being."[3] When the majority of initiatory patterns lost their ritual reality, "they became what, for example, we find them to be in the Arthurian romances—literary motifs" (Eliade 1975, p. 126). The same fate of course befell the heroes.

So adaptable and multiform is the basic pattern that, like aboriginal genetic material, the thousand-faced hero persists in incongruous guises. Critics have claimed, for example, that "our exultation in the death of Hamlet is related in direct line of descent to the religious exultation felt by the primitive group that made sacrifice of the divine king or sacred animal, the representative of the tribal life, and, by the communion of its shed blood, felt that life . . . renewed."[4]

From primordial times people have taken significant individuals to be deliverers or redeemers. In archaic Greek folk belief "the hero was a dead man who walked about corporeally," a ghost who was "thought to appear in very concrete form," and to whom "people applied . . . for help in all their needs"[5]—just as the Duke of Bedford prays to the ghost of Henry V to "Combat with adverse planets in the heavens" (*1H6* 1.1.53). In *The Winter's Tale* Leontes owes his restoration to a ghostly wife: "I saw her / (As I thought) dead; and have (in vain) said many / A prayer upon her grave" (5.3.139–41).

In theory the ancient Greek heroes were not demigods but a separate class of beings. Figures who influence human affairs from beyond the grave, however, readily acquire attributes of divinity, and as the archaic hero evolved with later religious developments, so did his eschatological status. The oracle of Delphi "prescribed that a hero cult should be devoted to a dead man if it appeared that a supernatural power was attached to his relics, and the pope canonizes a saint for similar reasons. The cult of heroes corresponded to a popular need which was so strong that it continued to exist in Christian garb" (Nilsson, p. 20). Saints George and Thomas à Becket, among others, were capable of the sort of superman miracles attributed to Saint Augustine Novello (Figure 1). Erasmus (1516) derived kingship from ancient heroism: "In the very early times, the kings were selected through the choice of the people because of their outstanding qualities, which were called 'heroic' as being all but divine and superhuman."[6] Ralegh believed that the practice of idol worship began with the Assyrian king Belus (sometimes associated with the Tower of Babel), who was "the first of all men . . . ever honored by their subjects with the title of Deitie."[7]

While the hero converts death into energy for life, usually there is an economy of sacrifice implied, in which giving—or giving up—life brings more life in return. René Girard contends that all myth and religion derive from the murder of a victim whose death "curtails reciprocal violence and imposes structure on the community." If the scapegoat's murder appears to free the group from the plague of violence or some other horror, he acquires the superhuman aura of the hero. If he "can extend his benefits beyond death to those who have killed him, he must either be resuscitated or was not truly dead. . . . In order not to renounce the victim's causality, he is brought back to life and immortalized."[8] Like the gods, he combines beneficent and maleficent qualities, becoming savior and monster, source of peace and rage. Emphasize the hero's relinquishment and tragic paradigms emerge. Stress his access to generativity and comedy or romance appears.

John Holloway holds that "the intrinsic design of Shakespearean tragedy is human sacrifice."[9] As in play-death, the protagonist's career dramatizes life and death "in prolonged and intimate interpenetration" (p. 144). He becomes a hunted animal as well as a demigod, his ordeal akin to rites in which bloodshed reinvigorates the forces of life as "the vital energy of the victim is redistributed among those he leaves behind" (p. 141). Whatever its cosmic function—to discharge violence or insure fertility—sacrifice reorders the transference conflicts within communities. The hero-victim focuses all the antagonism and dread in social experience, so that the release of conflicted emotion in others becomes a source of power for them.

Comedy, too, often employs imagery of hunt and harvest, as the "green world" symbolizes the victory of summer over winter. In "Summer's Last Will and Testament," which C. L. Barber saw as a prototype of festive comedy,[10] expiring Summer charges Autumn and Winter to immortalize Queen Elizabeth with a bounteous harvest in the "charmed circle" of perpetual summer. Young lovers effectively sacrifice the *senex* they outwit. In *Twelfth Night* the "drowned" Sebastian and Viola become the paradoxical personage—the "natural perspective"—who frees Illyria from the spell of mourning. Freed from the lead casket as from a coffin, Portia becomes a "Daniel" who revives the law to give Antonio "life and living" (5.1.286). In various ways these play-deaths draw on archetypes for their potency. But a qualification is in order inasmuch as archetypes are cultural productions and—in the Renaissance routinely—fabrications of authority.

II

In England a host of ancient and national heroes shared the imaginative heavens with the Christian Savior. Beholding Queen Elizabeth, her subjects professed to see this or that pagan goddess, the Fairie Queen, and other tutelary spirits. Since symbolic forms may lose their potency, privileged Englishmen were continually scavenging for new myths. The great maintained themselves on the edge of apotheosis by dispatching artists and propagandists to raid the past for authority the way Drake and others raided the New World for the reified immortality of gold.

Shakespeare often mocks the conjuration of heroic authority out of a mystified past. "Great Hercules" may prove to be an imp and his sally against death a pedantic boast that his "club kill'd Cerberus, that three-headed *canus*; / And when he was a babe, a child, a shrimp, /

Thus did he strangle serpents in his *manus*" (*LLL* 5.2.588–91)."" In this instance the players burlesque the Renaissance obsession with precedent and authority, reducing archetype to stereotype. Yet Hamlet despises Claudius for being "no more like my father / Than I to Hercules" (1.2.152–53), demoralized by his own failure to measure up to the paradigm.

Even when the dramatist does honor archetypal forms, irony qualifies them. Borrowing cash to "venture" for Portia as any impecunious Elizabethan aristocrat might, Bassanio is a lowly fortune hunter yet also a mythic Jason among self-regarding Argonauts. The play undercuts and protects his pretensions, requiring him to prove himself by risking all for meager lead, the antiarchetype. As the mad outcast Poor Tom, Edgar likewise earns the authority to put his blinded father through a providential parody of Satan's temptation of Christ to suicide (Luke 4.9–12): "It was some fiend; therefore, thou happy father, / Think that the clearest gods, who make them honors / Of men's impossibilities, have preserved thee" (*KL* 4.6.72–74). Cassius compares himself to Aeneas with a mixture of strategic cynicism and urgency not easily sorted out (*JC* 1.2.112–15).

The late romances project their revelations through dream and riddle in an attempt to put them beyond contrivance. As Antigonus guiltily abandons the infant Perdita, Hermione arises in his mind:

I have heard (but not believ'd) the spirits o' th' dead
May walk again. If such a thing be, thy mother
Appear'd to me last night; for ne'er was dream
So like waking.

[*WT* 3.3.16–18]

The oracular mother excuses Antigonus's cruel deed (27–30) yet also ordains his punishment—or self-punishment: "For this ungentle business, / Put on thee by my lord, thou ne'er shalt see / Thy wife Paulina more" (34–36). Because self and nature, logic and archetype, seem to meet in the unconscious, the old man's dream can appear both self-serving and profound. No less equivocal, *Pericles* makes poignantly absurd the "resurrection" in which Queen Thaisa evokes the goddess Diana who in turn may evoke the Virgin Mother as well as "the internal residues in all of us of the once all-powerful and all-inclusive mother" (Barber 1980, p. 196). Imagination may appear incoherent or irrational yet embrace archetypal logic. The decisive question in the plays is the extent to which that logic is felt to originate beyond the contriving conventional self.

Pericles dramatizes psychic development as a discovery (or recovery) of progressively deeper archetypes. Trying to assume manhood through marriage, reaching for a "fair Hesperides, / With golden fruit, but dangerous to be touch'd" (1.1.27–28), the callow Pericles plays Hercules. In English society as in the play-world, courtship was in part a propaganda contest to resolve critical issues of wealth and status, and the prince inflates himself so he can face a greedy, incestuous father figure who slaughters would-be inheritors. Where the early "Jason" Bassanio meets the challenge of a safely deceased patriarch while his fellow Argonauts free Jessica from a miserly alien, Pericles is routed. To escape retaliation by the ogreish Antiochus, he flees in panic from his own throne and is promptly shipwrecked, whereupon he clutches at a new identity by donning his late father's rusty armor. But this salvaged identity comes to nothing. Although Pericles marries, he soon loses his new family at sea and, traumatized, falls mute, playing dead until his long-lost daughter restores him.

As contrived ("rusty") models fail him, Pericles unwittingly plays out a sacrificial pattern that opens the play-world to a new sort of awareness. At last he is able to recreate the evil parent figures Dionyzia and Antiochus as the goddess Diana and the benign father-in-law Simonides ("Heavens make a star of him!" [5.3.79]). The play begins with a loss of idealized parents that makes psychic development a scramble to fabricate an identity out of cultural junk such as "Hercules" and the rusty armor. Only the rediscovery of wife and daughter—a deliverance from the unconscious—allows the recreation of parental archetypes and a belated validation of the self. In metadramatic terms, by moving from the formulaic, derivative style of the opening to the resonant dramaturgy of the last three acts, *Pericles* itself opens toward the unconscious. To be sure, there is an element of silliness and self-mystification in this quest for archetypes that epilogues usually deflate. As *The Winter's Tale* slyly confesses, "we are mock'd with art" (5.2.68). Yet each play renews the quest.

Dream and intuition enable Pericles and Marina to recover others as Lord Cerimon does the drowned Queen Thaisa. Cerimon, however, evokes not the mighty Hercules but Christ, whose miracles affect the design of more plays than one.

III

Seen through the lens of tragedy, Christ is the scapegoat whose confrontation with death purchases eternal life for humankind. From a comic perspective he is the humble preacher who revives Lazarus and others as he himself will ascend to heaven and resolve history. As sacrificial tragedy may strengthen social bonds (Holloway, p. 145), so "many Shakespearean comedies resemble the Mass described by O. B. Hardison: 'The mythic event celebrated is rebirth, not death, although it is a rebirth that requires death as its prelude. The experience of the participants is transition from guilt to innocence, from separation to communion.' "[12] The subject of Christian archetypes in Shakespeare is too large to be encompassed here. Instead I pursue a cluster of images centered on the tomb, comparing accounts of Christ's miracles with fantasies of deliverance in the plays.

To begin with, the Gospels recount that Herod, who had murdered John the Baptist, feared that Christ was "John risen from the dead" (Luke 9.7). Behind Herod's anxiety is the old idea that "murder will out," as in Macbeth's fear that he sees the slain Banquo before him. But it might also remind us of the archaic Greek folk belief that the hero was "a dead man who walked about corporeally" (Nilsson, p. 18). In popular belief Christ perpetuated important characteristics of the Greek heroes, including the resurrected Heracles/Hercules.[13] As devotion celebrated the Savior's emergence from the tomb, so the archaic hero was thought to range abroad freely from the grave that housed him. Christian relics became charged with significance as the archaic hero's remains had been. Cimon, for example, brought home the bones of Theseus from Scyros. (In the Middle Ages, I would argue, it was partly vestigial cult behavior and not simply the wish to be buried at home that prompted followers to cut up and boil nobles who had died abroad in order to extract the bones for shipment home. Henry V returned by this route, as did various other English notables who had fallen in France [Huizinga, pp. 142–44].)

Like his heroic antecedents, Jesus, "the firstborn from the dead" (Col. 1.18), opened the tomb to life. Confronting the mourners for Lazarus, "Jesus said, Take ye away the stone. Martha, the sister of him that was dead, saith unto him, Lord, by this time he stinketh; for he hath been dead four days." Commanded to live, Lazarus "came forth bound hand and foot with graveclothes: and his face was bound about with a napkin. Jesus saith unto them, Loose him, and let him go" (John 11.39–44).

In such narratives the tomb epitomizes the confinement and alienation of conventional life—life deadened by the effort to contain dread. In "loosing" Lazarus, Christ releases the mourners, not only from their immediate horror and grief, but also from anxiety, guilt, and the latent rage for life that leads to scapegoating.

> [G]rief, shame, and guilt are not very far removed from feelings of anger and rage. The process of grief always includes some qualities of anger. Since none of us likes to admit anger at a deceased person, these emotions are often disguised or repressed and prolong the period of grief or show up in other ways. . . . The ancient Hebrews regarded the body of a dead person as something unclean and not to be touched. The early American Indians talked about the evil spirits and shot arrows in the air to drive the spirits away. Many other cultures have rituals to take care of the "bad" dead person, and they all originate in this feeling of anger which still exists in all of us.[14]

Christ's command reunites the group. It strips off the binding graveclothes just as it banishes the demons infecting "the man with an unclean spirit" who "had his dwelling among the tombs" in Mark 5.1–17. The possessed man is "a prisoner of his own madness . . . a living corpse," shunned, persecuted. Like Martha appalled by the stinking Lazarus, the community would repudiate the "unclean" madman and, through him, the contagion of death. Jesus would exorcise not simply one man's demons but the displaced rage of an entire community (Girard 1986, pp. 168).

Each of Shakespeare's late romances culminates in just such a release. Like Christ's miraculous voice, Prospero's command has waked the dead from their graves (*Tem.* 5.1.48). Through his tempest he would awaken his old persecutors from destructive obsessions with their own powers of survival. No less redemptive are Thaisa and Marina, Imogen/Fidele, Hermione/Paulina and Perdita. One and all, they represent a will to release life from madness and mourning.

Nevertheless, deliverances in Shakespeare are usually indirect—in part to avoid charges of blasphemy. New Testament echoes notwithstanding, *The Winter's Tale* diffuses the source of its miracles. Behind the regenerative Hermione lie Paulina, "Julio Romano," the oracle, "great creating nature," and more removed mysteries. The play's redemptive figures are emphatically selfless. They are mediators or actors through whom a pervasive, baffling Providence works, not agents of a personalized Father-God.

By contrast, direct intervention in deliverance invariably proves suspect. No sooner do the nobles conjure Henry V to rise from his coffin than their homicidal rhetoric and his silence subvert their vision of a savior for England. The cry for deliverance stands exposed as vicious manipulation. But then, the plays often challenge aggressive piety, as when Friar Lawrence schemes to reconcile all Verona by raising Juliet from the tomb, a scenario that parodies Christ's resurrection of the daughter of the ruler of the synagogue:

> And he cometh to the house of the ruler of the synagoge and seeth the tumult, and them that wept and wailed greatly.
>
> And when he was come in, he saith unto them, Why make ye this ado, and weep? the damsel is not dead but sleepeth.
>
> And they laughed him to scorn. But when he had put them all out, he taketh the father and the mother of the damsel, and them that were with him, and entereth in where the damsel was lying.
>
> And he took the damsel by the hand, and said unto her . . . Damsel, I say unto thee, arise.
>
> And straightaway the damsel arose, and walked; for she was of the age of twelve years. And they were astonished with a great astonishment.
>
> [Mark 5.38–42]

Friar Lawrence contrives to minister to grief-stricken prominent citizens and enjoy their gratitude later. He would allot himself the redeemer's role but his hubris proves fatal. Given his morally equivocal pharmacy (2.3.7–22), in fact, the friar begins to resemble the wonder-working magus, whose lineage goes back through Faustus to the biblical Simon Magus cast down for his arrogance.

Shakespeare's mages, Prospero and Cerimon, personally perform resurrections, yet critics have felt obliged to apologize for them as "white magicians" because their arts raise the spectre of Satanic presumption as well as the dead. "Graves at my command," says Prospero, "Have wak'd their sleepers, op'd and let 'em forth / By my so potent art" (5.1.48–50). In *Pericles* a pious onlooker praises Cerimon because, like Christ (Luke 7.16–17), he inspires glory to God as well as himself: "The heavens, / Through you, increase our wonder, and sets up / Your fame forever" (3.2.95–97). Still, Cerimon works by human "virtue and cunning" (27), with a characteristic Renaissance fantasy of Christlike humility and aristocratic opulence:

Your honor has through Ephesus pour'd forth
Your charity, and hundreds call themselves
Your creatures, who by you have been restored,
And not your knowledge, your personal pain, but even
Your purse, still open, hath built Lord Cerimon
Such strong renown. . . .

[43–47]

Discovering the "corse" of the drowned Thaisa "balm'd and entreasur'd / With full bags of spices," Cerimon marvels, as if expecting the stinking Lazarus, "how fresh she looks!" (3.2.63–66). Whereupon he sets about reviving her:

Death may usurp on nature many hours,
And yet the fire of life kindle again
The o'erpressed spirits. I heard of an Egyptian
That had nine hours lien dead,
Who was by good appliance recovered.

[82–85]

Conceivably the dramatist's conception of Cerimon is a tribute to the good appliance of his son-in-law, Dr. John Hall, whose casebook records his own "miraculous recovery from a debilitating fever: 'thou hast saved me . . . ' he addresses his maker, 'restoring me as it were from the very jaws of death to former health.'"[15] Whatever his connection to the Ephesian lord, Dr. Hall's report suggests a mental world in which the grave and Christ's miracles were very close.[16]

Release from entombment fascinated Shakespeare. Within the gold casket in the *The Merchant of Venice* the Prince of Morocco finds a skull. Like "whited sepulchres, which indeed appear beautiful outward, but within are full of dead men's bones, and of all uncleanness" (Matt. 23.27), "Guilded tombs do worms infold" (*MV* 2.7.69). Choosing the lead casket, by contrast, Bassanio damns false religion (3.2.77–80) and chooses to "give and hazard all he hath" (2.9.21) as if heeding the injunction, "Whoever shall seek to save his life shall lose it; and whoever shall lose his life shall preserve it" (Luke 17.33). Portia's hair is "like a golden fleece," and "many Jasons come in quest of her"

(1.1.169–72). Yet Bassanio's heroic "hazard" is an act of faith that re-leases Portia from the casket as from a sarcophagus. Instead of a "car-rion Death" (2.7.63), he brings into the world a living picture of per-fection akin to Julio Romano's seemingly immortal statue—"What demigod hath come so near creation?" (*MV* 3.2.115–16)—and frees an advocate who can deliver others. The action resonates with archetypal significance that intensifies and mystifies, rather than clarifies, it.[17]

That entombment was a preoccupation of Shakespeare's culture we can see from Anthony Munday's Lord Mayor's Show of October 29, 1611, a pageant entitled *Chruso-thriambos: The Triumphe of Golde*. Leof-stane (who represents London's first mayor, Henry Fitz-Alwyn) re-veals that Time has raised him from the grave for this occasion: "See in how short a while a quiet Soule, / Hid from this world five hundred years and more, / May be forgetfull of great Times controule, / . . . My selfe . . . could tell this worthy Lorde, / Time had reviv'd me, to attend this day."[18] Like the mourners at the opening of *1 Henry VI*, the pag-eant characters are gathered around a tomb, and their theme is the restoration of a former hero. Time then resurrects a fourteenth-cen-tury mayor, Nicholas Faringdon, reviewing his accomplishments and summoning him: "Arise, arise I say, good *Faringdon*, / For in this tri-umph thou must needs make one." Says the stage direction: "*Time striketh on the Tombe with his Silver wand, and then Faringdon ariseth*" (Bergeron, p. 128).

In this pageant no less than in Shakespeare we are witnessing a complex interplay of imaginative materials. Time operates with autho-rial power over the past, like *Pericles*' resurrected Chorus: "To sing a song that old was sung, / From ashes ancient Gower is come" (1.1.1–2). Time behaves like Jesus in Nain, who also touches the dead man's bier and says "Arise," even as he uses the style and props of a magus such as Prospero. He is also an archaic folk figure and, like his counterpart in *The Winter's Tale* (4.1), "Father" Time. In his "controule" over the tomb he acts out a fantasy of patriarchal omnipotence in which the father awes the multitudes of London by using his "silver wand" to regenerate life from the womb/tomb. (Compare the tragic violence of the rebellious patriarchal son Romeo, for whom the phallic wand becomes a crude pry-bar when he has to force open the "womb of death"—the Capulet tomb—in his effort to "resurrect" Juliet [5.3.45].) In the pageant Father Time specifically regenerates heroism as mascu-line governance in the person of a London mayor, acting out the same godlike power that Warwick enjoyed when making and unmaking kings in *3 Henry VI*.

In *The Winter's Tale*, Time expresses the ambivalence latent in the hero. Although he bestows new life, he warns that "it is in my pow'r / To o'erthrow law," "O'erwhelm custom," and "make stale / The glistering of this present" (4.1.7–14). This father is also *tempus edax*, the destroyer, and he sounds for a moment like the lawless Richard III, whose nihilism likewise takes the glister out of experience.[19] As Christ the lamb is also the grave-opening destroyer of the last days, and as the wooer Henry V is also awful as Doomsday (*1H6* 1.1.29–30), so "Father" Time may devour as well as nurture his children. All creatures must submit to him as children to a sometimes incomprehensibly sinister patriarch. As in the revelation of Jupiter in *Cymbeline*, irony distances us from an archetype that would as readily appall as delight us.

When Christ or Father Time turns the tomb into a womb, he expands the boundaries of life, reopening a space death has closed. Analogously the intervention opens the minds of the spectators. In the resurrection at Nain "there came a fear on all: and they glorified God, saying, That a great prophet is risen among us; and, That God hath visited his people" (Luke 7.16).

IV

As a rule imagination attributes a radical otherness to death, and consistently places it "there" and not "here" in conventional reality. When repression is effective, people can behave as if everyday life is absolutely real, and death remote. When someone does "go to heaven," the survivors experience death as a shocking break in the continuity of experience. They are apt to blurt helplessly, "I just can't believe it." This is the forbidding imaginative boundary that the archetypal hero negotiates, the conceptual basis of play-death and apotheosis. One way of approaching that boundary is to consider how people have used the tomb to give it form.

In the last years of Elizabeth's reign funeral pageants and monuments achieved extravagant proportions. The funeral acted out the idea of triumphal cynosure: the honored dead led a procession of mourners blazoned with heraldic badges of worth, ranked to proclaim the eminence of the deceased and the everlasting social order, to a tomb whose architecture might duplicate the triumphal arch that crowned a victorious military campaign. Such shows radically fused religious and secular forms, the roles of clergy and the College of Heralds, all the while self-consciously celebrating an awe-inspiring financial sacrifice. The resulting spectacle evoked not only Christian but archetypal transcendence, since it was "as if Duke Hector, or Ajax, or Sir Launcelot was buried."[20]

Some Renaissance tombs directly invoked the idea of play-death. "Die to the world," exhorts the tomb of John Colet, the Dean of St. Paul's (1519), "that you might live for God." But the promise of survival was more than a doctrinal statement. The humblest grave can be a house that lasts till doomsday (*Ham.* 5.1.58–59). Hewn from stone and enshrined within a stone cathedral, a monument advertised permanence. With its artful symbols and symmetry it perfected life even as it contained death. Most importantly, such a monument objectified the psychological shell, the idealized self-image, that individuals develop. If it was crowned by a sculpted portrait, it gave its inhabitant a surrogate self rather like a mummy, not literally alive yet not annihilated either. Insofar as Hermione is supposed to be a funerary statue, her tomb may be said to come to life as she does. For the king of Navarre his personal fame can "live regist'red" on a tomb, buying "honor which shall bate [Time's] scythe's keen edge," making heroes "heirs of all eternity" (*LLL* 1.1.1–7). In effect, the tomb summarized Renaissance ambivalence inasmuch as it represented a massive denial of death even as it confirmed the Christian view of the body as a prison or tomb that confines the soul (Spencer, pp. 5, 99–103).

Until the middle of the fourteenth century tombs typically showed the deceased in the costume and symbols of his earthly glory, serenely awaiting the general resurrection. "But under the terrible scourge of the bubonic plague . . . [and the] Hundred Years War . . . Europeans began to add tomb carvings of fleshless skeletons, or cadavers in the process of decay."[21] In two-bier tombs the "superior" figure is the robust, idealized worldling, while the "inferior" is the same figure rendered as a hideously shrunken cadaver, displaced to reveal the "other" reality of decay. As in the theater, however, where from moment to moment a character may seem more real than the actor impersonating him, the two figures on the tomb are interchangeable and the robust "superior" figure may seem as substantial as the corpse. The design of such a tomb risks disenchantment in order to reinforce the beholder's faith. By admitting the physical reality of death more than earlier tombs had, the design may have tried to strengthen psychic defenses that had been too naively based on denial to withstand awareness of mortality.[22]

Such a monument spatially separates decay from the idealized reality in which we usually live. Contemplating the corpse, imagination "goes" into death and returns to conventional reality where death is in effect unthinkable. In these terms denial is a boundary or screen through which imagination momentarily passes. The tomb's design presumes that the movement "into" the reality of death may be readily reversed, with an intensified sense of the heroic values embodied in the superior figure and the church. The "trials" of the forbidden sphere may seem to open the constricted mind and renew its immortality symbolism. Inability to make the return, as in Hamlet's case, is apt to strike others as melancholic madness.

From my perspective this oscillation may also be seen as a kind of playing dead. The onlooker's imagination enters and returns from the sphere of death, testing, expanding its own life-space by trying out the possibility of its own demise. Then, identifying with the "monumentalized" dead man and with Christ, the beholder may participate in a form of apotheosis.

Shakespeare employs a version of this imaginative situation when he makes Juliet envision entombed corpses in shocking detail, a violation that intensifies her commitment to immortalizing love, and presumably excites the audience's wish to believe in the lovers' final triumph (*RJ* 4.1.81–85, 4.3.39–54). When Hamlet calls the Ghost "dead corse" (1.4.52), "the description suggests that (despite its 'complete steel') this Ghost is cadaverlike, resembling one of those *transi* tomb effigies in which the signs of decay have already appeared" (Neill, p. 179). Hamlet's passage into taboo territory takes him into the graveyard and into physical contact with the skull of the father figure Yorick, where instead of apotheosis he experiences disgust at the actual smells, conceiving the archetypal world-conqueror Alexander as dust to stop a bunghole. Only later does Hamlet come to a tenuous vision of "providence in the fall of a sparrow" (5.2.220).

Like Yorick's skull and the *transi*, the anamorphic skulls in Renaissance painting serve not merely to disabuse naive imagination but to test defenses against death and potentially to arouse an awareness of transcendent mystery.[23] Kneeling at an oblique angle to Holbein's *The Ambassadors*, the viewer suddenly recognizes the meaningless distortion before his eyes as a death's head, even as the conventional scene dissolves. The viewer loses the familiar world in the discovery of death, realizing that the skull has been there all along but unperceived, on a different plane of reality. Yet the painting also allows the beholder to withdraw again into conventional reality, where death is no more than an inconvenient blur on the official face of life. In fact, the perspectives in *The Ambassadors* are such that the viewer actually cannot leave the painting with the death's head the dominant image. At the same time it is teasingly difficult to shake off the sensation of having experienced the threshhold of an expanded reality. Anamorphic distortions construe death as a topographical displacement of consciousness. To make out the death's head in the Holbein painting, the viewer must adopt an oblique, figuratively self-effacing stance. The imagination may return to its original perspective with increased integration or increased disquiet.

The anamorphic image is of course only one of many ambiguities that imagination may use to control the boundary of life. Like the tomb, mummification, as I noted in Chapter 3, also simultaneously mystifies and clarifies that boundary. A mummy is an ambiguous personage, no longer animate yet not rotting either. Embalming suspends the deceased on the edge of life, creating a kind of paradox or riddle that enlarges the possibilities of the mortal world even as it counteracts fears of an absolute end to existence. While their physical remains reposed in a sarcophagus in fact, pharoahs braved the underworld like other archetypal heroes. Hence Marlowe's logic in having his boundary-transgressing Tamburlaine order his wife's body embalmed so he can carry it with him as he struggles to subdue death through conquest.

Like the modern world—where the practice of embalming also suspends distinctions between life and death, most incongruously in the display of Lenin in atheistic Moscow—Renaissance English culture had equivalents of the mummy. Funeral effigies are facsimiles of life and were a familiar feature of Shakespeare's world, as in

> the custom of carrying atop the coffin a manikin-like representation or effigy of the deceased so designed as to be a faithful rendition of the person. In the case of kings, this can vividly illustrate the symbolism of the king's two bodies, the effigy being the sign of kingship that survives while the mortal remains are in the coffin. Such an effigy was

constructed for Elizabeth's funeral. . . . In 1606 when King Christian of Denmark came for a visit, one of the things he went to see in Westminster Abbey were the effigies of some sovereigns and spouses which had been newly "repayred, robed and furnished at the King's Majestie his charge."

[Bergeron, p. 132]

The effigy of Prince Henry, who died in 1611, was to be "jointed so that it would be capable of 'sundrie accions first for the Carriage in the Chariot and then for the standinge and for settinge uppe the same in the Abbye'" (Bergeron, p. 132).

Like "Julio Romano's" statue in *The Winter's Tale*, such facsimiles of life perpetuate transference relationships and defer loss. For the on-lookers in Paulina's chapel the distinction between life and death momentarily blurs even before the statue moves. They are willingly entranced. Likewise, Olivia's obsession with her lost brother in *Twelfth Night* blurs the reality of death for her. She tries to create an idol of the mind akin to the funeral effigy. Hence the joke about mummification in her use of "eye-offending brine . . . to season / A brother's dead love, which she would keep fresh / And lasting in her sad remembrance" (1.1.29–31). In both cases the ambiguous reality of "living" memory blurs the fatal limits of life. I will be arguing that mourning and escape from mourning pervade the conventional world in Shakespeare far more deeply than meets the eye. But first let me show how the boundary I have been describing relates to the wider topography of mind and landscape in the plays.

Chapter 6

The Topography of Death and Heroism

"Going" to sleep or "falling" in love, we construe mental life in spatial terms. By extension, an imaginative world onstage in the theater is implicitly a mental space. *A Midsummer Night's Dream*, for instance, associates consciousness with a city whose laws and walls define conventional reality. Outside Athens lies a magical wood that mirrors the city yet remains associated with the unconscious. Over and over in Shakespeare, as in myths of the archetypal hero, consciousness is similarly bounded. Often the plays discover that the authority enshrined in a city or court has become moribund or perverse. Their plots are a death-defined venture outward and back, into an enchanted wood, the sea, or "great creating nature," a movement that revitalizes the city. The city dwellers—and theater audience—come to sense the crushing immensity of the world but also transcendent meanings ("something of great constancy") that support their lives. In this section I want to examine the margins of experience where such symbolic resurrections may take place.

The ancients buried their dead outside the city—out "there" and not "here" in conventional reality. Early medieval Christians brought the tomb into the church, yet souls continued to depart to an underworld or the heavenly city. Later imaginations including Dante devised intricately circumstantial maps of the afterlife. While it symbolized the infinite and ineffable, eschatological topography was highly particular.[1] Although superintended by angels and monsters, the old religion's heaven and hell mirrored society and the family: the "court" of heaven was an ideal patriarchy as in "Abraham's bosom," whereas hell was a regime of terror. The earthly city had a heavenly counterpart. Life and death were destinations in a closed system.

The Reformation repudiated all such maps, and eliminated the Church's guides to eternity, from chantries to intercessory saints. Calvin and Luther both insisted that what lies beyond death is ineffable, although they used traditional imagery to make the point.[2] By 1552 the reformers' campaign against the papist doctrine of purgatory had effaced even the gates of hell from the second Book of Common Prayer. Officially at least, the afterlife was becoming "the undiscovered country" that Hamlet queasily contemplates (3.1.78).[3]

When the older topography persists in Shakespeare's imagery, it is apt to be explicitly subjective. Othello foresees the moment when not God but Desdemona's look "will hurl my soul from heaven" (5.2.274). In Mistress Quickly's opinion the late Falstaff is "not in hell; he's in Arthur's [Abraham's] bosom" (*H5* 2.3.9–10). Expose the conventional basis of thought as Shakespeare does, and such images stand revealed as fictions. The city is apt to be an Athens surrounded by "fairies" who burlesque the unseeing city folk, acting out the claims of denied imagination. The supernatural status of "something of great constancy" is problematical. The beyond has become ineffable and the readiness is all.

II

One way to approach this psychic topography is to look at the analogue presented by the walled city of the Middle Ages that the Elizabethans inherited. There city walls marked an impregnable, strictly monitored boundary between executive reason and righteousness on the inside, and muscular, illiterate unconsciousness without. Picture angels in a goldleaf sky over a minster and palace which epitomized authority and dominated the countryside from inside the fortified circle. Beyond the walls, at the margin of control, agriculture and the hunt harvested energy for life. The land bestowed riches and obedience on the minster and palace in exchange for transcendent authority for life.

The minster and palace reproduced the larger configuration of city and wilderness inasmuch as their architecture concentrated imagination on the heroic authority inside. The minster's stained glass windows reconstituted the external world in the static images of authorized myth, and its great doors, like city gates, barred the profane. As in social hierarchy so in architecture, restrictive structures were designed to concentrate imagination and authority upward, toward altar and throne. Within the minster funeral monuments epitomized the fortified city inasmuch as their stone walls idealized the heroic lives inside and banished chaos. The tomb exemplifies the way repression structures death into lawful forms, justifying life.

Yet the city has always had a double nature, creative and violent, as founded (according to Puttenham's *The Art of English Poesie*) by the poet Amphion, or (according to Augustine's *City of God*) by the first killer, Cain.[4] In some measure fortified authority could not help but be alienated from a landscape that could produce wolves and destabilizing heroes like the Pucelle as well as pastoral piety and vital food. As the avenue of invasion, the alien horizon implied vulnerability and menace. All life-giving commerce therefore had to enter the city through defensively monitored gates. In the painting by David Vinckboons mentioned in the last chapter (n. 19) death is at a city gate shooting arrows into a crowd that tries to defend the entrance with humble pikes. The skeletal marauder evokes the brigand, warrior, and huntsman. The city is humankind's refuge, and the "outlaw" world a fertile yet annihilating wilderness.[5]

In most Renaissance English towns people still lived in an area enclosed "by whatever remained of an ancient wall, or some sort of boundary such as a river bank and a ditch, and entry was through two or more gates which were locked at night and passage through which was to some extent supervised, even in daylight. Such gates, with their massive housing, would often, as it were symbolically, contain the town's lock-up or prison" (Youings, p. 68). Yet the towns were outgrowing their medieval defenses, and Shakespeare dramatizes the rewards and dangers of expansion. A disenfranchised daughter and son find refuge in the Forest of Arden and return to a liberated domain. In *Lear* a maddened king is driven onto a stormy heath where he begins to recognize the falseness of the old social order. In his withdrawal to "the very hem o' th' sea" (*TA* 5.4.66), self-entombed, Timon finds a treasure that forces open the walls of Athens to a purifying Alcibiades. These plays share a conviction that fortified authority is suffocating, and that vitality is a heroic interrogation of the horizon. Yet by insisting that to remain outside is to suffer insanity and degradation, they also warn that renewal is preferable to any wish for renegade autonomy.

The situation of the playhouses in this psychic scheme is critical,

David Vinckboons, *Men and Animals Struggling against Death and Father Time* (after a painting known through an engraving by Boetius Boiswert): Copy after Flemish, 1576–1632. Oil on panel: 28.2 × 44.0 cm. (11⅛ × 17⅜ in.). Courtesy of the Museum of Fine Arts, Boston, Massachusetts.

since they were built in The Liberties, the equivocal territory outside the city's official jurisdiction. John Stockwood took for granted the claims of the old medieval topography of authority when he grumbled about the players' "houses of purpose built . . . and that without the Liberties, as who woulde say, 'There, let them say what they will say, we wil play.'" The London theaters located the function of play on the margin of culture, where conventional and alien energies could inter-act and recreate each other.[6] The players were literally in a unique position to appreciate the city's double nature.

III

The city's doubleness is a function of the hero's ambivalence. "Great cities are founded by those who have murdered their brothers, proba-bly *because* they have murdered their brothers; aspiration is compensa-tion, shadowed forever by guilt. But, the human challenge to time and nature that great cities also represent . . . also nurtures a sense of kinship with the divine" (Paster, p. 11). The mark of Cain is on Shake-speare's Rome and also his on his Verona, where rival houses compete like warring cities. A forbidding wall encircles Capulet's house, and at the ball Tybalt keeps watch over the arriving guests to spy out enemies (1.5). As love challenges established authority in Verona, imagination is concentrated upward to Juliet's bright window rather than to a spire or cloud-capped towers. While the landscape outside Verona's gates is the source of the friar's death-mocking herbs and Romeo's lovesick ecstasy, Romeo finds a forbidden paradise in the orchard beside Ju-liet's bedroom, as if Capulet has annexed the uncanny fairy woods to his house. By the play's end the house has become the Capulet tomb, and the city has begun to reintegrate itself around golden funerary statues that (wishfully) promise to supplant church and palace.

When the city becomes transfixed by the struggle to control death, it comes to resemble the tomb. For the funeral monument is a model of social values as well as "the secret house of death" (*AC* 4.15.81). By rigidly idealizing life, hiding decay inside, the monument images the repression by which society would subdue death. Like the Capulets' vault and "Ninny's" tomb, where Pyramus and Thisbe meet, it freezes the vitality it would immortalize. To promote eternal fame through "brazen tombs," the king of Navarre would extirpate love (*LLL* 1.1.2). The "groaning shadows" in his family's sepulcher demand that Titus

Andronicus slaughter Tamora's captured son Alarbus (*Tit.* 1.1.125–26). The tomb of the Andronici becomes associated with the devouring pit that destroys Bassanius and others, and finally with Rome itself. Similarly, the "something rotten" in Denmark turns out to be, among other horrors, the unquiet "corse" of its murdered king. Grieving at her husband's banishment in *Cymbeline*, Imogen feels entombed within the court: "There cannot be a pinch in death / More sharp than this" (1.2.130–31). By contrast, when the tomblike social world is leveled, death may then open toward cosmic meaning, as when Kent concludes: "I have a journey, sir, shortly to go: / My master calls me, I must not say no" (*KL* 5.3.322–23).

In this perspective conventional life is inherently—often insidiously —colored by mourning. Behind the imagery is the idea, at least as old as Plato's *Cratylus*, that the body is the tomb or prison of the soul, while the world outside, including the "green world" of comedy, is sacred territory (Garber, p. 124). The hero promises to open up the tomb/city and overcome despair. This is the plot of *Twelfth Night*, *A Midsummer Night's Dream*, and *The Winter's Tale*, among other plays. It is also the plot of Henry V's reign, at least as his followers would like to imagine it. By contrast, when dread subverts heroism, as in the tragedies, tyrants would lock up or repress the body and the city (the body politic) in a mad effort to preempt death.

Where the benign hero would open quotidian reality to the risky horizon, freeing life to develop and die, false heroism creates vainglorious illusions, fortifying the self against change, seeking to dominate or consume everything outside the self. While Perdita arouses wonder, as at a world ransomed or destroyed, in *Coriolanus* "Volumnia, as Rome, [becomes] the unnatural dam eating up her children in order to survive, starving with feeding" (Paster, p. 88). In *Pericles*, the prince would be Hercules freeing a maiden from a father who marks his palace walls with the heads of slain suitors, literally using death to fortify his greed for life.

What lies beyond the city? For Renaissance Englishmen an anxious response might point to a Protestant island encircled by Catholic nations plotting its annihilation. Hence the rationale for heroic sallies into the Netherlands and Ireland, as well as the grim watch kept on the Welsh and the Scots. Yet the horizon was more than a phalanx of enemies.

On the edge of memory and geography shimmered the ancient

world. Recovered from oblivion, Alexander the Great and Cleopatra lived in imagination like "Julio Romano's" statue, ephemeral as fictions and yet historically substantial, demigods yet dust to stop a bunghole. Such figures originated on the edge of Terra Incognita, their prestige magnified by so many centuries of miraculous survival. They provided the Renaissance with new models or "laws" of heroic authority.

As in the Middle Ages, Christian culture also looked outward toward Jerusalem, the sacred site of death and revelation. In Donne's "Hyme to God my God, in my sickness," the blood of Christ is shed in the place of Adam's creation and burial, so that death becomes the source of universal regeneration:

> We thinke that Paradise and Calvarie,
>   Christs Crosse, and Adam's tree, stood in one place;
> Looke Lord, and finde both Adams met in me;
>   As the first Adams sweat surrounds my face,
> May the last Adams blood my soule embrace.

Shakespeare's penitent regicide Henry IV vows to lead a crusade "As far as to the sepulchre of Christ" (*1H4* 1.1.19). Henry V dreams of a son who will slay the infidel Turk with sanctified violence (*H5* 5.2.209). However cynically, the two kings draw upon an archetypal fantasy of locating the place where life and death meet, and then wresting control of it from demonized enemies, appropriating its wondrous efficacy.

In the Old World's interpretations of the New the same dynamics are discernible. The Americas signified a possibility of renewal at once economic, political, and religious. Within a decade of Shakespeare's death English Puritans in the wilderness of "New" England set about founding a new Jerusalem, spurred on by anxiety about corruption and impending doom in England.[7] But from the first hazardous crossings, Europeans ventured into a sphere of diminished restraints and enlarged ambitions. Again and again they were greeted as gods, and they exploited this gratuitous apotheosis in a fury of self-aggrandizement. As in Prospero's domination of Caliban, even hostile subservience could be taken to legitimize the master's authority if labeled barbaric or demonic.

Trade between the Old and New Worlds developed as a mode of heroic economy: Europeans forcibly extracted treasure, land, labor, and obedience from savage hero-worshippers, and converted these raw materials into heroic power. In return for this symbolic immortality the Old World imagined that it gave back transcendent authority for life in the forms of missionary Christianity and European law.[8] Englishmen such as Drake and Ralegh who personally traded in that heroic economy aroused fierce jealousy and suspicion back at court, partly because the symbolism of apotheosis was so compelling, and partly because they represented a temptation to taste renegade freedom.

Like Prospero's island or the seacoast of Bohemia, the New World was a sphere of renewal, explicitly so in legends of the fountain of youth. In Lucas Cranach's painting *Der Jungbrunnen* (1546) decrepit bathers are wading into an Arcadian pool and emerging on the other side pink with decorous erotic vigor. The fountain divides the landscape into a conventional milieu on the left and, on the right, a golden age of courtly delights. As in the European encounter with the New World, the fountain marks a passage from an aging, socially inhibited world to a paradise of youthful appetite where life is idealized as well as rejuvenated. The bathers implicitly shed the dust of experience and the doom of original sin, undoing the expulsion from the Garden.

Some of Shakespeare's plots are psychic excursions into a regenerative landscape of this sort. Fleeing sterile Athens, young lovers lose themselves in a fairy wood and awaken, bedazzled, to find the city transformed. A newly sympathetic Theseus displaces the aged, embittered Egeus, and marriages promise fertility. As in Cranach's painting, a pastoral setting affords a magical liquid (fairy love juice) that renews society. Like the edenic Forest of Arden and the fanciful seacoast of Bohemia, where lions and bears prowl, the fairy wood combines mortal terrors with the pastoral dream of nature's undying vitality.

Like the archetypal rite of passage, these plays act out an expansion and integration of imagination. In each, a community literally widens the range of things it can bear to think about, adapting more fully to the world. In the process characters leave behind their "old" conventional identities and, passing through states akin to madness or exaltation, arrive at a new sense of themselves and each other. Like a ritual rebirth, such an adventure appears to recreate personality—although the process is equivocal inasmuch as the new life may merely reinforce the status quo.

Lucas Cranach, *Bathing Scene.*
Courtesy of Marburg / Art Resource, New York, New York.

IV

The city's patriarchal order also overlays this topography. Shakespeare's husbands often seek to lock up wives and daughters as symbols of value, only to have the women escape. A Portia, Rosalind, or Perdita may then assume heroic roles with archetypal associations: Daniel, the marriage-maker Hymen, and the life-giving Persephone. The greater the investment in women, the more appalling the prospect of loss, and the greater the likelihood of masculine ambivalence. Mystified, overestimated, woman, like any other hero, potentially becomes a dangerous alien. To apprehensive males a Desdemona or Rosalind may be a ministering angel or a witch. In the early *1 Henry VI* the English try to engross alien France by exterminating the demonized French and their fiendish angel, the Pucelle. Yet after her execution the Pucelle's dangerous energy infiltrates England in the enticing, ruthless Margaret. Since the condemned Joan claims to be carrying the child of Margaret's father, Reignier, king of Naples,[9] Margaret can be regarded as Joan resurrected in an incestuous alter ego and thus a precursor of the depraved daughter of Antiochus in *Pericles*. In the late romances, however, the women who inhabit visionary terrain prove at last to be deliverers. In a later chapter I argue in detail that sexual desire and childbirth make palpable women's life-giving powers, and that patriarchy can be understood as a strategy for gathering that power toward apotheosis. For the present I want only to consider one mode of gender relations—one that returns us to the topography of mourning and play-death.

During Perdita's supposed demise in *The Winter's Tale* she calls upon Proserpina (4.4.116–18), who is the prototype of Perdita herself inasmuch as "Hermione has been 'killed' by her husband's perverse notion of her sexuality and bound below the earth for a winter's season, while her daughter, also 'killed,' reaches the bloom of maidenhood. Like Persephone, then, Hermione has returned a young virgin in her daughter Perdita" (MacCary, p. 40).[10] Furthermore, in the earliest source of the myth "Hades is a father-figure to Persephone—Zeus and Hades are brothers, and . . . he comes to her as both sexual threat and forbidden but (or therefore) desired lover" (MacCary, p. 38). Consequently, the final release of Persephone from bondage to Hades resembles the situation of young women in many other plays of Shakespeare's. "The archetypus archetypi of this material must be the pattern of death and rebirth ritualized in the mystery cults and . . . mythologized as the rape of Persephone by Hades (who is death personified), and dramatized throughout the history of Greek comedy, tragedy, and satyr-play" (MacCary, p.37). The essential paradox presented by comedies of the Persephone pattern is that "men desire young women for their fertility and then, by means of marriage, walls, or underground chambers, attempt to control that mysterious force" (MacCary, pp. 40–41).[11]

The topography of the Persephone myth places the superhuman abductor, the fatal father himself, in a dark stronghold that mirrors the conventional city or court, and is as well a type of the tomb. Between the two domains is the fertile sphere of Ceres—"Great Creating Nature." When a suitor ventures to rescue the captive maiden, he may play Jason (as Bassanio does), Theseus braving the Minotaur (Suffolk in *1H6* 5.3.187–89), or Hercules (*Per.* 1.1.27–29). A figure of Persephone who returns on her own from the underworld brings renewal as the archetypal hero does, yet her potency is usually diffused in a magical aura, as Perdita's is, or obliquely curbed. In *Love's Labor's Lost* the princess of France releases the king of Navarre from the perverse immortality of ascetic study, only to be herself closed in by her father's sudden demise. For one turn of the seasons she must "shut / My woeful self up in a mourning house" (5.2.807–8). After stipulating that her lover must test his desire against "frosts and fasts, hard lodging and thin weeds" that may "Nip . . . the gaudy blossoms of your love" (801–2)—as in the wintry absence of Persephone—the princess disappears into the psychic distance where renewal may take place. Only after a year's "reckoning" (798) may she and her lover win life for themselves.

In *Love's Labor's Lost* the hermitage and "mourning house" extend the association of the self with the walled city and the "little academe" with the tomb. As Olivia forsakes life to preserve her brother's love and her own sense of security in *Twelfth Night*, so the princess and Navarre entomb themselves to preempt death. Since the symbolic logic of the plot insinuates that daughters kill fathers by abandoning them to marry, the lovers' self-entombment expiates guilt aroused by the transfer of love from father to suitor (or by the suitor's theft of love). But in addition, their behavior creates a ritualistic solution to the obsession with fruitless immortality that inspires the entire play. For ideally deprivation will not only test but also increase the lovers' desire, arousing them to go outside into the natural world of fertility and decay. Their sacrificial play-death may produce a comic apotheosis structurally related to the tragic sacrifice of lovers like Romeo and Juliet, who also come to believe that they must pass through death to be united.

V

Conventional reality, I have been saying, is inherently shadowed by mourning. Sooner or later everyone is a survivor, and every bereavement is also an escape from one's own death. Again and again Shakespeare makes mourning the starting point for his plots. Like Olivia in *Twelfth Night*, *Measure for Measure*'s Mariana has lost a heroic brother, isolating herself in a moated grange. Egeon spends most of *Comedy of Errors* imprisoned "for the sake of them [he] sorrowest for" (1.1.121). In *The Merchant of Venice* her late father's will closes Portia in a casket as Shylock shuts Jessica in his house (3.2.40–41). Shut up in forms of the mourning house, the tomb, or the fortified city—and in the mental state such images imply—survivors in Shakespeare dwell on lost authority, suspended between life and death.

To break out of this circle requires exceptional intervention. Bidding Portia, "Promise me life" (3.2.34), the "Jason" Bassanio finally rescues her from the casket. Having won her, he vows that "when this ring / Parts from this finger, then parts life from hence; / O then be bold to say Bassanio's dead!" (185). Whereupon he gives his life to, and regains it from, Portia. Like Portia, who is at first "a-weary of this great world" (1.2.1–2), Hamlet laments the "weary, stale, flat, and unprofitable" world (1.2.133), imagining himself bounded in a casketlike nutshell (2.2.254–56). Withdrawn into "the pales and forts of reason" (1.4.28), grieving for a lost father, Hamlet could think himself a cosmic hero, a "king of infinite space," were it not for "bad dreams." Making Laertes' warnings about love into a "watchman to my heart," Ophelia unwittingly turns her heart into a threatened city akin to Elsinore itself (*Ham.* 1.3.33, 46). When her lover murders her father, mourning destroys her.

Without a prospect of deliverance, grief may lead to a mad effort to fortify the self. Brooding on "the hollow crown / That rounds the mortal temples of a king," Richard II pictures himself as a fortress, "As if this flesh which walls about our life / Were brass impregnable" (*R2* 3.2.160–61, 167–68). Yet death mocks the monarch's pretensions and "at the last . . . with a little pin" he "Bores through his castle walls, and farewell king!" (169–70). The castle-self becomes a tomb. Richard bewails the uselessness of cultural and psychic armor against death. In his anticipatory grief, drastically passive, Richard plays dead as if to preempt death. Symbolically entombed, he laments his end. Within the hollow crown as in a nutshell, he counts himself a king of infinite space, conjuring armies of angels while haughtily denying his bad dreams. Weeping for himself, he monumentalizes his futility in a theatrical effort to give himself significance.

Whenever Shakespeare's characters are compulsively austere, it is reasonable to look for signs of mourning. In *Measure for Measure*, Angelo's regime of blighted purity suggests mourning, as does the duke's insidious endorsement of rigor, not to mention his satisfaction in preparing Claudio and others for doom. Vienna's rulers insist that mourning behavior is wholesome discipline. Having himself "ever lov'd the life removed" (*MM* 1.3.8), Duke Vincentio associates mourning with realism, renunciation, and fidelity to values. If "fond fathers" fail to contain youth, he fears, then "liberty plucks justice by the nose; / The baby beats the nurse" (23, 29–30). Children will destroy the father's heroic vitality if his will becomes "more mock'd than fear'd" and "[his] decrees, / Dead to infliction, to themselves are dead" (27–28). The duke's anxiety is a reminder that law is an essential defense against dread. A child grows up in a network of commands that not only screens out the overwhelming mysteries of the universe, but also contributes to the child's sense of worth, the conviction of rightness that makes personality possible.

Duke Vincentio would compel Vienna to mourn for a kind of absolute lawfulness that once guaranteed life and now admits the possibility of death. But force cannot revive Eden or the city of God in the walled city—in this instance Vienna. No ruler can banish the sorrow of the fallen world. As enacted by Angelo, in fact, the duke's reverence toward the law reveals a potential for cruel obsession. Angelo has "bestow'd [Mariana] on her own lamentation" (3.1.228) in the "moated" grange. Like Hades in the Persephone story, he would capture Isabel for his own dark uses. His decrees would turn the mourning house into a prison and, with the executioner's help, a tomb.

If the hero's quest is to overcome basic grief, he fails when grief subverts and possesses him. As he succumbs, the insidious relationship between tyranny and mourning becomes momentous. The hero himself becomes death's agent. In *Love's Labor's Lost* mourning is aggression. The king's edict acts out his fantasy of immortalizing study, which is a disguised form of self-entombment undertaken to cope with the "disgrace of death" (1.1.3). Advertising his masked ball to Paris, Old Capulet uses imagery that disguises his own heartache, resentment, and dread. Praising young women as "earth-treading stars," he promises:

> Such comfort as do lusty young men feel
> When well-apparell'd April on the heel
> Of limping winter treads, even such delight
> Among fresh fennel buds, shall you this night
> Inherit at my house.
>
> [*RJ* 1.2.26–30]

Doomed and downtrodden winter—old man winter—resembles Hades, who will be forced to release Juliet from his mourning house. His buried grief presumably supports the rage that fuels the feud between the Capulets and Montagues.

More acutely, at the height of his butchery Macbeth's dirge for life, the "poor player" (5.5.19–28) reveals "a mind diseas'd" by "a rooted sorrow" (5.3.40–41). His rage can be understood as a wild effort to counteract a wasting grief akin to Richard II's. Mocked by the prediction that Banquo will produce an undying race of kings, Macbeth has tried to empty the world of rivals for life. In fortified Dunsinane he finds himself staked like a bear (5.7.1), the marginal wood closing in to kill his ravenous appetite for life (5.5.43–45). Finally his delusion of immortality succumbs before a hero who appears to come from beyond nature: "I bear a charmed life which must not yield / To one of woman born" (5.8.12).[12]

Unchecked, mourning directs aggression against the self or others. It becomes a disease, a self-perpetuating obsession that transforms the hero into a destroyer. Christians were working to control that obsession when they devised a Satan who has lost heaven and now exists to nullify others: a sadistic despot at the center of a tomblike, imprisoning city whose gate Christ will have to force open at the end of the world; and a scapegoat who can be happily repudiated.

In countless guises mourning may subvert the hero. No sooner does the princess of France free Navarre from symbolic entombment than she imprisons herself in sorrow. Just when she might reach for the fruits of autonomy she disables herself. Something comparable happens in *As You Like It*. Throwing off his "sadness" (1.1.5), the orphan Orlando rebels against his oppressive brother and finds a surrogate father in the Forest of Arden. But then, "Under an old oak, whose boughs were moss'd with age / And high bald with dry antiquity" (4.3.104–5)—imagery that evokes the lost father—Orlando spies his sleeping brother Oliver, who "doth seem as dead" (128). Fighting off a lioness, he raises Oliver from this doom as a new man. In the rescue Orlando gives up his own just rebellion and reconciles himself to patrimonial authority: behavior characteristic of mourning. For Hamlet in the ruthless Danish court such self-disablement becomes immobilizing, even suicidal.

In this perspective the quest to recreate or replace lost heroic authority is inescapably ambivalent. Hence Shakespeare's rhetoric of madness and wonder. *Twelfth Night* opens with an entire society immobilized. The deaths of father-heroes and intermediary brothers have blocked marriage and—given the duke's lovesickness—paralyzed Illyria's governance. Yet the way to recovery is through play-death. Olivia entombs herself, the duke wishes that his "appetite may sicken, and so die" (1.1.3), and Viola daydreams of perishing for love (2.4.112–20). The quest motif in the play is the outward voyage of the twins and their initiatory shipwreck, in which the tomblike vessel is forced open to experience. Sebastian survives a watery grave believing his sister "drown'd . . . with salt water, though I seem to drown her remembrance again with more" (*TN* 2.1.30–32).

Engulfed in sorrow the self can perish—witness the mad Ophelia— or be transformed. "Snatch'd one-half out of the jaws of death" like her brother (3.4.360), Viola uses a surrogate father, the captain, to change into Cesario, a form of "Caesar," or leader. Yet both mourning and sea change presuppose loss of identity, the one through self-denial, the other through role-playing. The twins come to evoke the archetypal hero because play expands their identities, confounding conventional distinctions between male and female, noble and commoner, and life and death. They become one paradoxical personage, Viola-Sebastian, a "natural perspective" that opens minds fixed on loss. When the hero's expansion of identity is merely vainglorious, his quest is mania. The overweening Malvolio, for example, is locked up in "hideous darkness" (4.2.30) as a madman. By comparison, though madness discomfits Viola and Sebastian more than once, they meet incoherence with selfless poise. Playing, they behave as if there is an inexpressible sense in the chaos that would drown them.

To play is to be heuristic and improvisatory in spirit. It means, terrifyingly, to unbar the gates of the city-self.[13] The hero needs "to open his soul beyond terror to such a degree that he will be ripe to understand how the sickening and insane tragedies of this vast and ruthless cosmos are completely validated in the majesty of Being" (Campbell, p. 147). What the hero encounters is not meaningless but supercharged with meanings. The plethora of significance the plays call wonder is the life-giving analogue of the engulfing grief figured as shipwreck and drowning. In the utter stillness of near-death, dread and sorrow may be transmuted into awe. Symbolically Leontes dies as Hermione and Perdita do. At Perdita's recovery, he and Camillo "look'd as they had heard of a world ransom'd, or one destroy'd. A notable passion of wonder appear'd in them" (*WT* 5.2.14–16). What is in fact ransomed or destroyed is the conventional mind, which like the ghostly archaic hero, simultaneously in and out of the world, suddenly leaves behind customary boundaries.

Play, again, represents not just pastoral escapism or instinctual release, and not simply an effort to test and withstand death, but also an effort to recreate authority for life in the margins of experience. The comedies offer a glimpse of Hymen and Jupiter and the king of the fairies, even though their epilogues slyly disclaim any supervisory guarantees. Despite supplications, Henry V neither bursts from his coffin nor sends a blessing. Scotland's salvation Macduff is superhuman only by virtue of a mischievous prophesy. Like mythic heroes braving the underworld, Romeo and Juliet enter the tomb of her forefathers in hopes of pacifying Verona, only to be transformed into statues. Numinous experience, insofar as it exists at all in Shakespearean drama, is always arguable.[14]

Ultimately heroic striving does not resolve ambivalence so much as try to suspend it in wonder or a "natural perspective." Like the plays' topography, the symbolism of twinning expresses the hope of expanding the self to accept conflict. No action can be altogether pure. Noble sacrifice may imply an element of self-aggrandizement that must be subsumed, just as rescue implies a dynamic of dominance and submission. The close of this chapter looks more closely at such contradictions in yet another topographical paradigm in Shakespeare: the Garden of Eden.

VI

As a story of aspiration and disobedience, Genesis reflects the psychological dynamics of play-death and heroism. Given Adam as a figure of Christ, and Christ's resurrection as Adam's redemption, the story of the fall itself becomes a type of play-death and apotheosis. Expelled from paradise, humankind returns to dust and yet arises at last to the union with God. This is the archetype associated with Cordelia: "Thou hast one daughter / Who redeems Nature from the general curse / Which twain have brought her to" (*KL* 4.6.205–7).[15]

Shakespeare's imagination of Eden usually construes it concretely, as an earthly paradise. In the "brave new world" of *The Tempest* (5.1.183), Ferdinand finds an Eve in Miranda and rapturously exclaims: "Let me live here ever; / So rare a wonder'd father and a wise / Makes this place Paradise" (4.1.122–24). Ferdinand's paradise is a function of transference: like Adam absorbed in praise of God, the child lives in the father who "makes" paradise. As one critic aptly puts it, "The supreme validation of the father's creating power is the central wish-fulfillment of *The Tempest*."[16] While the father's "creating power" could be despotic, as a paradise it transfixes the imagination of a son traumatized by a fatal shipwreck. For the grieving Ferdinand, in fact, Prospero's magic isle is a wishful version of the mourning house I described earlier, in which the child can honor both the "drowned" father Alonzo and the surrogate father whose "every third thought shall be my grave" (5.1.312), while gladly perpetuating paternal will in a predetermined marriage and symbolic regeneration.[17] The rapture of paradise suspends all conflicts, and Ferdinand appears happily oblivious to the deferment of his own autonomy.

Paradise in this sense is a world already completed, without beginnings or endings, fear or desire. Its fulfillment is static. So conceived, paradise paradoxically resembles the psychic topography I have associated with the walled city—or the tomb that epitomizes the walled city—within which reality is transfixed. The trees of knowledge and of life correspond to the central minster and palace that authorize the city's life (compare Prospero's cell). Like Eden's gates before the fall, the city's walls circumscribe consciousness so that the life inside appears harmonious and immutable. The intrusion of death into such highly conventionalized reality is catastrophic.

In Ferdinand's mind paradise is conventional reality made trancelike by transference to a father-hero. As long as he can remain spellbound in the aura of Prospero's magic, he is a godlike Adam, unaware of limits. On the threshold of marriage, in the full conviction of sexual immortality, he can take his own vitality for granted and happily submit to the servitude of log-carrying. At the same time his ecstasy is a form of the compensatory mourning I have been describing. He has recreated his drowned father in the fantastic Prospero as Olivia would sequester herself in her father's house to preserve brother and father. In short, Ferdinand can love because the play imagines wishfully perfect mourning for him.

Like Prospero, Henry V "the world's best garden achieved" (*H5* epi. 7). The archbishop of Canterbury equates the hero's own body with Eden, linking the king and the God of Genesis:

> The breath no sooner left his father's body,
> 'But that his wildness, mortified in him,
> Seem'd to die too; yea, at that very moment,
> Consideration like an angel came
> And whipt th' offending Adam out of him,
> Leaving his body as a paradise
> T' envelop and contain celestial spirits.
>
> [*H5* 1.1.25–31]

The archbishop's imagery insinuates that Hal has come to perfection through a play-death and apotheosis in which his willfulness has perished and revived as "celestial spirits." Moreover, this paradise is another form of the mourning house wherein a departed father holds a child spellbound on the edge of maturity. If Hal is God's child Adam, and the scourging angel "consideration" is the father Henry IV in—or in addition to—Hal's grieving conscience, then the archbishop implies that purgatorial mourning creates paradise.

By implication, Hal's wildness was, like Adam's, an ambition to "be as gods" and to rival the father. For Hal as for Ferdinand, paradise resolves Oedipal conflict. Hence the symbolic logic of the conspiracy Henry V exposes. The play allows the lordly Henry V to seem nearly omniscient compared to the routed traitors. Like God himself, he deems "this revolt of [theirs] . . . / Another fall of man" (2.2.141–42) and pronounces death on the wretches. In this way Hal becomes the father who casts out the usurping son he would otherwise have been himself.

The Henry V who wages war on France confounds the archbishop's symbolism. Springing to life out of the stasis of Eden, he undergoes a twofold apotheosis, as the pagan war god Mars (Pro. 6) and the warrior-Christ of the Last Judgment (*1H6* 1.1.28–30). The change of images disguises the king's resumption of "th' offending Adam's" wildness. For in his ambitious rage he would "bend [France] to our awe, / Or break it all to pieces" (*H5* 1.2.224–25). After the slaughter he can tell Kate, "I love France so well that I will . . . have it all mine" (5.2.173–74). As in Genesis, vicarious life in the blissful spell of the Garden is finally not enough. Adam and Eve chose to aspire and so, with a vengeance, does Henry. The irresistible desire, he confesses, is to be immortal, "as gods." He would conquer not only France but history, so that posterity would praise him with its "full mouth" like a mourning child obsessed with the ideal, lost father. Were he to fail, by contrast, he would end up in a "tongueless" grave, "Not worshipp'd" (1.2.230–33).

In this example Eden holds insoluble contradictions in suspension. Desire is implicitly aggression against the world and the father who stands for the world. Obedience, however, would mean living in the father, in a play-death of self-oblivion. In the archbishop's fantasy the son's mourning allows him to merge with the father and therefore enjoy both expansive aggression and static righteousness. Even in its structure the fantasy expresses the expansive appetite it would dispel inasmuch as Hal/Adam—exactly as the serpent promised—comes to incorporate all the available roles. And the instant this Edenic rhapsody is tested against historical reality in the plays, the hero's privileged status begins to disintegrate, and a nightmarish cycle of mourning and triumphalism begins.

Othello plays out this dream of paradise with tragic perversity. Cassio's praise prepares us for a pagan apotheosis:

> Great Jove, Othello guard,
> And swell his sail with thine own pow'rful breath,
> That he may bless this bay with his tall ship,
> Make love's quick pants in Desdemona's arms,
> Give renew'd fire to our extinct spirits,
> And bring all Cyprus comfort!
>
> [2.1.77–82]

Cassio plays dead ("extincted spirits") to a life-giving Prometheus. Yet ironically he figures the Moor as the rivalrous hero whom Jove eventually punished, and in killing Desdemona, Othello will pervert the role of benefactor. "With Jove's assistance, Othello is propelled toward paradise," but as a competitor of the gods, not a reconciled Adam (Coursen, p. 191).

Unconsciously and ominously Othello himself sees Cyprus as a paradise:

> . . . O my soul's joy!
> If after every tempest comes such calms,
> May the winds blow till they have waken'd death!
> And let the labouring bark climb hills of seas
> Olympus-high, and duck again as low
> As hell's from heaven! If it were now to die,
> 'Twere now to be most happy; for I fear,
> My soul hath her content so absolute
> That not another comfort like to this
> Succeeds in unknown fate.
>
> [2.1.184–93]

Having survived the chaotic sea, Othello "compares the storm to death and the calm beyond to paradise, and, in one sense, he is right. He has reached his greatest moment and can only fall 'as low / As hell's from heaven'" (Coursen, p. 188). No less than Cassio, the hero himself longs for rebirth. But this is an ecstatic reprieve more than an access to vital joy. He dreams of absolute stasis akin to the suspended animation of mourning, and he will try to force that perfection on Desdemona, turning her into a tomb of "monumental alabaster" (5.2.5) and murderously abandoning the quest for life: "I know not where is that Promethean heat / That can thy light relume" (12–13).

Othello's ambition for paradise and his implied competition with the gods points this inquiry back toward Genesis. For as soon as the serpent's temptation brings dynamic instability to Eden's perfect stasis, heroic aspiration begins to obsess Adam and Eve. They would be "as gods," rivaling the majestic Father as Lucifer does in the mystery cycles. With the apotheoses of Adam and Eve the cosmos would revert to the polytheistic competition of paganism. From this standpoint original sin is both a denial of transference—of life in the Father—and a threat of role reversal. While living in a state of praise, absorbed in

God, Adam and Eve were blissfully oblivious of themselves, whereas the desire to be as gods is a desire for existential authority: to know good from evil is to be able to make personal righteousness the basis of autonomy. This is a fantasy of being self-created that counteracts the knowledge of human dependency and finitude. Eating the forbidden fruit is a Promethean act, an attempt to acquire heroic authority for existence.

The first play-death, in retrospect, was that original state of transference in which humankind lived in God, and from which Adam and Eve awakened with a desire to be gods. The narrative draws upon the idea of play-death in its effort to contemplate the source of ontological authority. Having transgressed, Adam and Eve react to the Father's accusations by deliberately seeking refuge in play-death again, this time by hiding in the Garden, as if no longer there. Their effort to disappear is an attempt to lose themselves again, as in the original state of transference. But now desire and guilt have defined them into personal existence. The punishment that follows is humankind's discovery that death is not simply reversible like the fertile sleep that created Eve, but final, and that life must always begin anew in painful birth.[18] Cain's murder of his brother reenacts the original temptation to rivalry, and he suffers an analogous curse. (In *Richard II*, having murdered a king to make a king, Exton is cursed like Cain [5.6.43]). Eventually the figure of Abraham reconciles heroic expansiveness with the Lord's demand for worship. He mediates between God and his people, and Renaissance Christians spoke of the afterlife as a return to, or slumber in, the bosom of Abraham, so that the patriarch became associated with the mastery of death found in archetypal heroism. In theology Christ ultimately becomes the "second Adam," so that Adam's doom becomes a form of play-death fulfilled in the resurrection of the Lord.

In Genesis the serpent's promise leads not to equality with God, but to aggression against God, alienation from the Garden, dread of death, and the competition for heroic authority later acted out in Cain's murder of Abel. The Elizabethan state accordingly used Adam's disobedience as a crucial text in its untiring campaign against political dissent. The monarch guarantees life; rebellion unleashes death.

Logologically, says Kenneth Burke in his explication of Genesis, "guilt is intrinsic to the idea of a Covenant."[19] Mortification is intrinsic to the ideas of dominion and order inasmuch as "the scrupulous subject must seek to 'slay' within himself whatever impulses run counter to the authoritative demands of sovereignty" (p. 206). As a result,

Even if you begin by thinking of death as a merely natural phenomenon, once you come to approach it in terms of conscience-laden *mortification* you get a new slant on it. For death then becomes seen, in
terms of the socio-political order, as a kind of *capital punishment*. . . .
[Death] in the natural order becomes conceived as the fulfillment or
completion of mortification in the socio-political order, but with the
difference that, as with capital punishment in the sentencing of trans-
gressions against sovereignty, it is not in itself deemed wholly 'redemptive,' since it needs further modifications, along the lines of placement
in an undying Heavenly Kingdom after death.

[p. 207]

In this formulation the guilt is inherently a form of play-death, and it
is fulfilled by apotheosis in "an undying Heavenly Kingdom." From
the violated covenant Burke goes on to derive the principle of sacrifice
and, beyond that, "the idea of outright redemption by victimage"
(p. 216). These terms suggest that the archetypal hero's rites of passage
may be understood as an exploration of the problem of intrinsic guilt
and expiation, alienation and atonement.

Insofar as Shakespeare's edenic imagery implies play-death as mourning—as traumatic enclosure in houses, cities, tombs, a crown, and
paradise itself—it points to the problem of violated covenant, and to a
conception of identity that is obsessed by the violent paradoxes of
order. Viewed from within this metaphoric system, Henry V plays out
contradictions supposed to be primordial and absolute. Consider once
more the archbishop's description. His father's death leaves Henry V
"mortified": a tacit death in which the son's "wildness" also dies, is
split off and "whipt out" of him, symbolically becoming the "offending" traitors soon to be executed and the defiant French whom the
now-"celestial spirit," the godlike Henry, will first seek to crush and
then to reincorporate through "loving domination" of the alien
woman Kate. For in courting Kate, Henry besieges French cities
"turn'd into a maid; for they are all girdled with maiden walls that war
hath never ent'red" (5.2.321–23). As a sacrifice to peace, Kate placates
his threat of rape. Their union will in turn produce a son intended to
displace the violent paradox of dominion by going still farther afield to
assault the Turk, not only scapegoating yet another alien Adam but
also, metaphorically, pulling down yet another formidable father "by
the beard" (5.2.209). By such a succession of pseudo-demises and re-
births, heroism enables mortification to become self-aggrandizement

while anxiously preserving the fantasy of ontological righteousness so crucial to Elizabethan Christian ideology.

To stress this metaphoric substructure in *Henry V* is of course to narrow its concerns for the sake of analysis. The extent to which Shakespeare endorses Henry's ideological authority is an open question. The insoluble paradox of dominion itself helps to explain the doubleness critics have repeatedly rediscovered in the play.[20] As a hero, "the King finally has difficulty, on the eve of Agincourt, in sustaining the responsibility which seems to belong with the ideological power which he has engrossed to himself: thus the fantasy of establishing ideological unity in the sole figure of the monarch arrives at an impasse which it can handle only with difficulty."[21]

More transparently perverse than the archbishop of Canterbury's use of paradise is Crookback's equation of the crown with paradise in *3 Henry VI*: "How sweet a thing it is to wear a crown, / Within whose circuit is Elysium / And all that poets feign of bliss and joy" (1.2.29–31). Where for Richard II the crown is at last a bitterly absurd tomb, for the future Richard III the "circuit" of paradise defines a fantastic, omnipotent self. Though he calls upon the pagan Elysium, he is meditating on usurpation and murder, and his ambition cannot help but recall Genesis. Like the envious Cain, he would purchase chimerical bliss through the deaths of others, including King Henry VI and his own brother Clarence.

There are other versions of paradise in Shakespeare that allude to heroic origins, violation, and recuperation. In the Forest of Arden, Duke Senior daydreams that he has recovered Eden: "Here we feel not the penalty of Adam" (*AYLI* 2.1.5). Most "invectively," however, Jaques mourns the slaughter of Arden's other "citizens," the deer (58, 55). Jaques

> . . . pierceth through
> The body of the country, city, court,
> Yea, and this our life, swearing that we
> Are mere usurpers, tyrants, and what's worse,
> To fright the animals and to kill them up
> In their assign'd and native dwelling-place.
>
> [58–63]

Jaques' insight, that humankind lives by killing and eating other creatures, "pierceth through" the boundaries of civilization—country, city, court—as if to kill the lords playing at paradise the way they themselves kill deer. His demystification of humankind's need to murder for nurture strikes through topographical defenses exactly as Richard II imagines death boring in fatally upon the king (*R2* 3.2.161–68). Shortly thereafter old Adam gasps "I die for food!" (*AYLI* 2.6.1–2), and in response Orlando, like an outlaw, at sword point, demands food from the duke's "outlaw" band, in a parody of the Lord's prohibition in Eden: "He dies that touches any of this fruit" (2.7.97). The play contrives a comic resolution in which there is food and love enough for all, yet it is "pierced through" by the anxiety that just beyond paradise lies carnage.

The following chapter, on *Venus and Adonis*, examines a hero who lives for the hunt and regains an ambiguous paradise. It would be possible to regard Adonis as an incarnation of the archetypal hero. After all, he operates outside the defensive circle of culture, in an uncanny wood where love and death reveal themselves. Pursuing death, sacrificing himself, Adonis attains an equivocal immortality—a version of paradise—in the eyes of Venus. Which is to say, Adonis acts out the mythic origin of the mourning that grips humankind.

Part Two of this book examines fantasies of heroism in individual works, placing them in the historically specific world outside the Globe Theater. Where the goddess and hunter dramatize the situation of the courtier-hero in the last years of Elizabeth's reign, Romeo and Juliet's Verona acts out conflicts that defined patriarchy. The third chapter, on the histories, demonstrates how prophecy became a strategy for recreating the self by projecting it into a supernaturally sanctioned future.

Part Two

What is our life? a play of passion,
Our mirth the musicke of division,
Our mothers wombes the tyring houses be,
Where we are drest for this short Comedy,
Heaven the Iudicious sharpe spectator is,
That sits and markes still who doth act amisse,
Our graves that hide us from the searching Sun,
Are like drawne curtaynes when the play is done.
Thus march we playing to our last rest,
Onely we dye in earnest, that's no jest.

—Ralegh, "The Life of Man"

Chapter 7

Love, Death, and the Hunt in Venus and Adonis

Since death itself is ultimately inconceivable to us, the metaphors used to substantiate it reveal as much about the constructive imagination as about death itself. The metaphors that kill Adonis and thereby govern the meaning of *Venus and Adonis* seem to me especially significant, for they define a historical moment in which the Elizabethan fantasy of aristocratic heroism began, under stress, to reveal the social and psychic conflicts that inspired and perpetuated it. Like the histories treated in the previous chapter, *Venus and Adonis* expresses a larger cultural drive to ground authority in cosmic heroism. The poem, however, makes heroism erotic and female as well as violently masculine, and tries to capture the treacherous vitality released when these different values come together.

The poem celebrates the death of the hunter Adonis as the mythic origin of love's sorrow in the world. This is an elegaic epyllion. Yet death in the poem takes sublimely metaphorical forms. One critic, for example, invokes "paradise regained in the union of love and death," and goes on to assimilate Venus and Adonis to Antony and Cleopatra in a crescendo of affirmation: "In the last analysis . . . Chaos is an illusion; the Boar and Caesar are not fortune, but fortune's knaves. And Venus and Adonis, fallen and risen as Cleopatra and Antony, live in triumph in the kingdom of the second chance."[1] Despite its mystification, this is useful insight: that Adonis's demise and reunion with Venus at Paphos are tacitly a play-death and apotheosis. The final tableau of Adonis transformed into a flower at the breast of the goddess makes the apotheosis especially suggestive, evoking a nursing mother or even a pietà.

Much of the critical consternation over *Venus and Adonis* stems from the perplexing nature of this transformation. For most readers it suggests some sort of deliverance. One concludes that Venus "crops the stalk" of the flower that springs from Adonis's blood, and so "Adonis was twice butchered, once in blindness by the boar, and the second time in equal blindness . . . by Venus." The poem's theme thus becomes "the destruction of something exquisite by what is outrageously vile. Man and the cosmic process are at irreconcilable war; the ends of man are denied by the world he lives in."² Yet even this uncompromisingly tragic view offers consolation, blaming nature or the cosmos for death and casting humankind in a lofty Promethean role. Like an Elizabethan reader, the critic assumes the hunter Adonis to be innocently superior to his "vile" prey and the world.

In my view Venus and Adonis play out crucial fantasies of immortality that were in radical conflict in Shakespeare's England, and nowhere more acutely than in the mythically charged milieu of his patron, the young earl of Southampton. Through heroic violence the hunter would overcome the boar, the evil embodiment of death itself, while the goddess promises immortality through love. Although love and the hunt undermine one another in action, the poet projects an ambiguous play-death and apotheosis that allow him to celebrate these culturally sanctioned fantasies even as he exposes them to demystification.

For all its wit and eroticism, the poem's principal source of dramatic tension is the threat of death. Obsessed with the hunt, Adonis disciplines himself to be the master killer, seeking out situations in which he must kill or be killed, dominate or die. His final adversary, the boar, becomes death itself. At the same time love, too, is a hunt, and Venus, among other things, a predatory eagle. Both roles magnify the self, making human motives superhuman.

If subliminal images are counted—such as the opening vision of the sun taking "his last leave of the weeping morn" (l. 2), which anticipates Adonis's fatal leave-taking (ll. 817–40)—the text's preoccupation with mortality and grief becomes even more striking. Consider moments where loss of autonomy is figuratively death, as in the many descriptions of love-play as war and of lust as a murderous tyrant, and the pressure of dread begins to appear formidable. Convention and wit may domesticate these tropes, yet their anxiety subtly persists.

The hunter is the archetypal hero, the life-giving provider, slayer of monsters. The beautiful Adonis dramatizes the power of spirit over the mortal animal body. Yet he is potentially a dangerous figure as well. To use Elias Canetti's term, he is a survivor, and "the moment of *survival* is the moment of power. Horror at the sight of death turns into satisfaction that it is someone else who is dead. In survival, each man is the enemy of every other, and all grief is insignificant measured against this elemental triumph."[3] In this context the hunter metaphorically evokes the warrior and the ruler.

Imposing death on the animal world, the hunter, like the Renaissance king, may seem to exercise godlike control over life and death. In this way the hunt plays out a desire for apotheosis which, since it is founded on a fantastic wish, must be repeatedly revitalized, usually by killing either a greater quantity or quality of victims. Aristocratic hunters in the Renaissance reveled in copious slaughter, and ennobled selected animals such as the hart to increase the significance of the kill. By analogy, matching himself against the boar, Adonis makes it the spellbinding source of all meaning and value for him. The boar becomes death itself. The poem pits the hero against the principle of annihilation much as a masque might oppose the queen to the god Proteus, the principle of mutability and the Elizabethans' nemesis.[4]

The hunt, in short, makes possible a conviction of immortality in which a reader may subliminally share. Yet needless to say, that mastery over death is finally an illusion: only as long as the spell is intact can the hunter feel godlike. Hence the obsessiveness of Adonis. His mastery is jeopardized not only by actual death but also by demystification. Hence the goddess's attempt to win Adonis away from the hunt is as menacing as the boar, and arouses his hostility toward her. Venus reminds the hunter of death even as she advertises love's joys. "What is thy body but a swallowing grave[?]" she demands, comparing his independence to suicide: "So in thyself thyself art made away" (ll. 757, 763). Her extravagant "prophesy" of his doom (l. 671) focuses the danger she poses.

At first Adonis protests that love is "a life in death" (l. 413). He wishes to remain safely immature, denying his own aggression as a hunter: "Who plucks the bud before one leaf put forth?" (l. 416). Later he displaces the overwhelming threat of death onto lust, which has usurped love's name and "fed / Upon fresh beauty," destroying it "As caterpillars do the tender leaves" (ll. 793–98). Heroic confrontation promises better results against a boar than against insidious caterpillars. The metaphors converge in the threat to devour in which the hunter is no less implicated than his quarry.

"Loving" heroic violence (l. 4), the hunter obeys an urge that darkly links him to the boar he would put to death. For the boar is "bent to kill" (l. 617). Like the most elemental type of the survivor, the boar lives by annihilating others: "His snout digs sepulchers where'er he goes; / Being moved, he strikes whate'er is in his way, / And whom he strikes his crooked tushes slay" (ll. 622–24). In this respect the animal objectifies the sadistic root of the hunter's fantasy of immortality. As such, he dramatizes a compulsion akin to lust that the heroic youth must somehow transcend in himself, the compulsion Shakespeare associated in the homicidal Richard III with "the wretched, bloody, and usurping boar" (*R3* 5.2.7).

Trying to captivate Adonis, Venus inadvertently exposes the equivocal core of heroic immortality: although the hero may love and so give life to others, the pressure of dread may produce a lust for survival. Venus can empathize with a victim such as "poor Wat" the rabbit, showing a capacity for mercy that would require the hunter to kill in a spirit of sacrifice or not at all. Her passion for Adonis would supplant the fantasy of the hunt by substituting love for heroic aggression.

Ideally love would create a symbiotic intimacy based on mutual worship. Heroism would be the symbolic action of generating value, not the physical act of destruction. In *Venus and Adonis* love would compel the hero to sublimate his superhuman violence in worship: he is to be "more lovely than a man," a living "wonder" (ll. 9, 13). Yet love can no more guarantee immortality than the hunt can. Venus herself proves a tragicomic servant of desire, fleshy and importunate. Impulsively wrestling Adonis off his horse (l. 42), she defeats him as a warrior would a foe, inadvertently demonstrating his mortal limits. Moreover, because love magnifies the beloved as well as the lover, possession of something so precious automatically entails a dread of loss. "If I love thee," Venus laments, "I thy death should fear" (l. 660).

Paradoxically, the love that would conquer death may intensify dread. Worse, dread can make love as violent as the hunt itself: "For where Love reigns, disturbing Jealousy [anxiety] / . . . suggesteth mutiny, / And in a peaceful hour doth cry 'Kill, kill!'" (ll. 649–52). Which is to say, the dilemma is not merely the inadequacies of Venus, not just her lust or the other faults seized upon by moralists, but rather humankind's tragic incoherence as the godlike animal, the god who must die. Maddened by the inevitability of loss, desire may turn to lust, "murd'rous, bloody, full of blame," as in Sonnet 129.

As the poem reveals the dark underside of heroic aspiration, then, it also recognizes the destructive potential of love. Although she is the masterful tamer of Mars, the goddess projects the humblest of human needs. Like the status of Queen Elizabeth in a patriarchal society, divinity in the poem combines heavenly rhetoric with conditional power. Like any ordinary mortal, Venus is helpless to control death and compulsively magnifies her hero. Through transference, she over-estimates Adonis, identifying herself with his supremacy.[5] She would feed on the "steam" of his breath (l. 63), as if to incorporate his soul. In such hero worship the lover vicariously shares in the beloved's perfection as a child would merge with a parent.

To lose oneself in the imagined majesty of the other is to risk enslaving oneself or becoming parasitical, so that eventually anxiety may turn hero and hero-worshipper fatally against one another. Ostensibly so free, the goddess is as driven as the mortal Adonis is, frantic to center her life on an object of unshakable value. Without something to live for, some purpose that could counter the senseless immensity of the universe, immortality itself would be a horror. And any conception of the gods that shrinks from that ultimate perspective is bound to seem childish. Only in these terms, I think, can we understand the ferocity Shakespeare discovers in love.

When Adonis resists her, Venus "murders" his words and tacitly his volition "with a kiss" (l. 54). She kisses him like a "devouring" eagle (l. 57). With violence constrained by pretty antitheses she equates love with death: "But now I lived, and life was death's annoy; / But now I died, and death was lively joy. / O, thou didst kill me, kill me once again!" (ll. 497–99). Dying the play-death of love, she would live in her lover. Adonis in turn protests against the parasitical nature of this behavior: "You do it for increase" (l. 791). It "soon bereaves" or destroys the beloved "As caterpillars do the tender leaves" (ll. 797–98). Mastered in the hunt, nature reasserts the imperatives of change and death through love. Even as they replenish the world with children ("increase"), lovers are dying. The imagery reflects the conventional belief that the act of lovemaking—"dying"—uses up irreplaceable vitality and reduces one's lifespan. (As Donne laments in "The First Anniversary," "We kill our selves, to propagate our kinde.") Implied is a world haunted by dearth, a subsistence economy for sexual energy as well as food. Like patriarchy, the hunter's chastity is a restriction of gender relations grounded in anxiety about health.

Venus's "devouring" appetite for Adonis (l. 57), with its latent cannibalistic threat, reveals love, no less than other human relationships, to be tragically conditioned by a hunger for power that is, finally, life itself. She feeds on him "as on a prey" (l. 63). Since the appetite for perfection and transcendence can be boundless, in the end desire may consume the vitality of the self or the beloved. The revelation that Adonis plans to hunt the boar directly precipitates her most ecstatic longing, the excitement of violence euphemized in chivalric imagery in which she is herself a participant: "Now is she in the very lists of love, / Her champion mounted for the hot encounter" (ll. 595–96). And this is the same will to annihilation that can make the hunter a monster.

In her rapture love is a hunt founded on infantile greed and wishful omnipotence.[6] Her experience is radically polarized. Though she is a goddess, she is disposed to play the mother as well as the infant. At once she is supplicant and conqueror, passively "faint" yet brutally dominant. These intolerable contradictions culminate in a "blindfold fury" of lust, "planting oblivion, beating reason back" (ll. 554–57). As the ultimate concentration of the self, the hysterical blackout that releases her from tension is the furthest reach of transference and akin to death. And Adonis's experience, too, is polarized between dominance and submission. The proud hunter is also tacitly the infantile flower of the conclusion.

What governs these extremes is the fantasy of play-death and resurrection. Rapturous oblivion is transparently a form of play-death in hopes of revival in the beloved. In their kiss "Incorporate . . . they seem; face grows to face" (l. 540). "Say that the sense of feeling were bereft me," Venus fantasizes, "And that I could not see, nor hear, nor touch"—as in death—"O, what banquet wert thou to the taste, / Being nurse and feeder of the other [senses]" (ll. 439–46). Out of this state of nullity she would be reborn as a lavishly nurtured infant. In her final withdrawal to Paphos with the flower embodying Adonis at her breast, the fantasy is reversed. The hungry infant becomes the cosmic mother, agent of eternal love.

For Adonis the sequence is reversed. Though in the end the goddess plucks him from death as a flower, earlier the fantasy of play-death entails lordly gratification. His one moment of release from inhibition, for example, comes when Venus appears to faint, falling suddenly passive "as [if] she were slain" (l. 473). "The silly boy, believing she is dead," gives up his urge to "reprehend her" (ll. 467–70). Instead he "seeks to mend the hurt that his unkindness marred" (l. 478), and he kisses her. The moment bristles with sadomasochistic feeling. Adonis can renounce his "sharp" anger, savoring instead a pleasurable tenderness which, heroically, may save her life since "love by looks reviveth" (l. 464). At the same time her prostration allows him a moment of exhilarating dominance unmistakably colored by sadism. He "claps" her cheek red, "wrings her nose," and "strikes her on the cheeks" (ll. 468–77). Associating this assault with orgasm, the roused Venus is made to pant: "But now I died, and death was lively joy" (l. 498).

The hunter's sexual feeling arises from his triumph over her. He can "kill" her and yet undo any guilt since "his breath breatheth life in her again" (l. 474). Venus's mock demise not only frees him from his obvious fear of her as a woman, but also liberates him from his own dread of death by means of the role reversal in which he becomes the godlike giver of life. In this moment of teasing necrophilia sexual fulfillment means apotheosis as the modest hero causes the sun to shine through her eye "and all the earth relieveth" (ll. 482–83).

This resurrection from mock death plays out the wish "to be as gods" that brought Adam and Eve to grief.[7] Venus introduces a forbidden knowledge that reveals man's godlike imagination yet also confirms its fatal disjunction from the imprisoning body. She makes Adonis self-conscious, redefining him as the paradigm of beauty, "more lovely than a man" (l. 9), that must perish. Yet at the call of instinctual desire, the dissociated body, like Adonis's stallion, may bolt (ll. 259–354). The problem is not merely disobedience, but the tragic incompatibility of imagination and flesh. "Banning his boist'rous and unruly beast" (l. 326), Adonis in effect curses his instinctual self. Left anxious and vulnerable, he attacks love as he would the boar: "My love to love is love but to disgrace it; / For I have heard it is a life in death" (ll. 412–13). In making him self-conscious about ideal beauty and death, Venus brings about alienation akin to original sin.

As I read *Venus and Adonis*, it shows how fantasies of immortality through heroism and love subvert one another. Challenged to renounce the triumphalism of the hunt, Adonis repudiates Venus. Yet love unconsciously penetrates his defenses. Returning to the chase, fleeing from the goddess's empathy and idealism, he is no longer able to be the masterful killer, and the boar now destroys him. In psychoanalytic terms, the possibility of love creates an insuperable conflict in the hunter. He can no longer project all aggression onto his prey and then, by killing it, play lord of creation. Instead he is abruptly confronted by his own sadistic drives, now dissociated in the boar, and that alienated rage overwhelms him.

As a result there is an element of self-destruction in Adonis's end. Rage and love fuse in the nuzzling kiss of "the loving swine" (ll. 1114–16), and this sexualized death allows otherwise irreconcilable forces to collapse into each other, but in a violent regression that only stabilizes when the hunter becomes a supremely harmless flower and is safely enraptured, infant to mother, at Venus's breast. Through his death Adonis expiates his anger at the Venus who "Like a milch doe" would succor him with "swelling dugs" in his suddenly mortal suffering (ll. 875–76). His atonement prepares for the wishful apotheosis at Paphos, beyond death and terror. Desire for the life-giving validation of a mother's love, furiously denied by the active hero, at last surfaces in an eschatalogical embrace.

But if the goddess undermines the hunter, the opposite is also true. If we recognize that mythic aggrandizement compensates for the deepest fears, Venus's contradictions become more coherent. For in her behavior with Adonis she begins to use love for power. Her idealism comes to seem compensatory, and her lust a desperate effort to project, and lose herself in, an object of cosmic majesty.

For Venus no less than Adonis the retreat to Paphos is irreducibly equivocal. For Venus the flower is ambiguously both Adonis and his son, her baby. To dote eternally on the flower is to be transfixed as if in surrender to a lover, and yet be the self-possessed mother as well. She can lose herself in spellbinding worship yet maintain a conviction of autonomy also. This would seem to be the perfect fantasy resolution were it not that she "crops the stalk" of the flower to possess it (l. 1175). "[But] know," she apostrophizes, "it is as good / To wither in my breast as in his blood" (ll. 1181–82). Even her final generosity has something despotic and life-denying about it. "Venus is unwilling to allow the flower to grow and wither naturally," and this attempt to control death produces "deluded idealizing."[8] In its hallucinatory urgency ("Here was thy father's bed, here in my breast" [l. 1183]) her last role, like Cleopatra's, evokes the pathos of a mad scene in the theater.

Yet this final tableau holds other ironies in balance as well. Although sacrificed, Adonis undergoes a form of play-death, and his metamorphosis is a compensatory resurrection. Though he will "wither," the poem does not insist on his extinction. On the contrary, the hero will exert an everlasting spell over the goddess. For Adonis, this final self-effacement is circuitously a strategy of lordly assertion. "In his total passivity, he dominates Venus, but she also dominates him."⁹ In Paphos, Adonis will keep Love "immured" in total and invisible stasis (l. 1194). Metaphorically, this death is sublimation: it euphemizes all that Adonis represents to create in art a strategic closure impossible in life.

II

Historically, Venus objectifies a challenge to a heroic fiction crucial to Shakespeare's audience. As a fantasy of immortality, the boar hunt expresses the righteous aggression through which the Renaissance warrior-courtier sought exaltation. For ultimately the courtier ethos depended on the deaths of others, whether hunted animals, enemies felled in combat, or heathens exterminated in conquest. To be sure, culture evolved symbolic substitutes for triumphal killing, including battle pageants and the atavistic jousts revived by Tudor aristocrats, not to mention the hunt itself. But culture also authorized the sacrifice of others, as religion did, for example, in the virtually endless campaigns to exterminate doctrinal foes at home and abroad. In Elizabethan Christianity, especially Calvinism, the saved were themselves types of the survivor whose ascendancy was measured, in iconography and sermon alike, by the swarming hosts of the damned excluded from eternal life.

Reared in a fantasy of heroism that combined the superhuman gentleness of Christ with the triumphal violence associated with the warrior and hunter, the Elizabethan courtier-hero embraced an identity founded on apocalyptic stress. In his relations with authority and his obligation to pursue danger such a personality had to reconcile impossible self-aggrandizement with intolerable humility: the more so at a time when in spite of its warrior ethos the English aristocracy was becoming an elite administrative corps.

Rooted in triumphal violence, courtly heroism was inherently self-expansive. For "at the root of the cult of honor, as of the lust for power, lay . . . the hugely inflated ego of the young courtier himself."¹⁰ When forcibly controlled, as under Queen Elizabeth, young men such as Ralegh and Essex continually required new, safely sublimated forms of glory or risked the demystification of the beliefs that sustained them. Yet the impersonation of gods in masques, the resurrection of knighthood in Accession Day tilts, and cutthroat competition for ceremonial posts at court could never wholly compensate for the inhibition of aggressive energy. As an imaginative struggle over the ground of identity itself, by young men who felt themselves to be the "very gods of this earth," the resulting strife had a religious intensity (Esler, p. 164).

The queen's task was not only to master that masculine energy but to make it enhance her own power. As Louis Montrose has shown, the queen and her people fashioned her into a mythic creature, a goddess who combined the roles of maiden, wife, and mother. The virgin queen actively encouraged lovemaking, using erotic energy to enhance her power.[11] For courtiers the quest for patronage "came to be understood as an act of wooing the queen. This was the form such political negotiations assumed from the early years of her reign."[12] As the supremely potent personality in the land, Elizabeth's love was readily analogous to the absolute will of the Venus who boasts that she has reduced the invincible Mars to her "prisoner" and her "slave" (ll. 110, 101). Bidding Adonis "brag not of thy might, / For mast'ring her that foiled the god of fight!" (ll. 113–14), Venus directly competes with him for potency, and tacitly asserts her own superiority.

By 1593, the date of the poem, the queen's flirtations had become dangerously self-parodic, not merely because she continued to bare her breasts in the fashion of a maid at an age when her blackening teeth and other intimations of death created disquiet, but also because her flirtations had plainly become contests of wills. The ideology of virginity made wooing behavior a mode of exaltation—ideally a symbiotic, reciprocal exaltation of ruler and subject. In action, however, the cult of Gloriana entailed struggle. As Venus herself warns, "where Love reigns, disturbing Jealousy / Doth call himself Affection's sentinel, / . . . / And in a peaceful hour doth cry 'Kill, kill!'" (ll. 649–52). Imprisoned in 1593 for his secret marriage, as Southampton eventually would be, Ralegh explicitly identified the queen with Venus, among other deities.[13] In the end Elizabeth struggled with nearly every one of her favorites, to the death of Essex and the near ruin of the poet's patron Southampton.

While this is not the place to summarize the many connections between the poem and Southampton, Shakespeare's Venus dramatizes the threat to a young courtier's autonomy that the jealous Queen Elizabeth inevitably represented: a threat that would be acted out in her repeated frustration of Southampton's military aspirations and her wrath over his secret marriage to one of her Maids of Honour. In 1593, says G. P. V. Akrigg, "Southampton's good looks had so obviously won the interest of Queen Elizabeth that he stood a good chance of taking over Essex's place as royal favourite."[14] Although Venus insists "Thou canst not see one wrinkle in my brow" (l. 139)—and given Elizabeth's famously thick makeup, it is fair to wonder if her favorites could see the wrinkles they knew to be in *her* brow—the queen of love bears down on Adonis with an imperious will that must have stirred complex pangs of recognition in those with experience at court.

Similarly, Adonis's play-death and apotheosis would have had resonance at court. At the close of his *Ocean to Cynthia*, for example, Ralegh seizes on self-sacrifice as the only means to action with the queen: "She is gonn, Shee is lost! She is found, she is ever faire! / Sorrow drawes weakly, wher love drawes not too. / . . . / Do then by Diinge, what life cannot doo" (ll. 493–96). To the courtier the queen's manipulation of her favor (she is "gonn . . . lost . . . found!" reflects the rhythm of play-death and leads to the courtier's own wish to play dead ("Do then by Diinge") as a way of sublimating his otherwise condemned will to action.

Clearly it would have been lèse majesté for Shakespeare to depict the queen as a predatory oppressor or to mock the martial pretensions of the aristocracy. Understandably the poem is equivocal about this troubling material. Neither Adonis nor the poem itself can imagine a heroic alternative to regression. If life becomes an obsessive hunt, Venus warns, victims will cringe in terror like "poor Wat" the hare: in a metaphor that could apply to the predatory competition at court, "Each envious brier his weary legs do scratch" (l. 705). Were Adonis to slay the boar, he would become supremely powerful and, if anything, even more indifferent to love. He would exist outside any ideology of service to a monarch, especially a female monarch.

In the symbolic logic of the poem, momentary distraction by maternally invested eros exposes the young man to the retaliatory rage, itself sexually domineering, of the murderously masculine boar. This is akin to the struggle over the orphaned boy in *A Midsummer Night's Dream*, since Titania wishes to feminize the boy with flowers, while Oberon would make the boy a "Knight of his train, to trace the forests wild," where the boar prowls (2.1.15). While Oberon's magically empowered patriarchy contrives to resolve the changeling boy's future, in *Venus and Adonis* the only irresistible masculine force turns out to be the demonic boar. As Venus symbolically embodies the force of an all-powerful mother, the boar objectifies the aggressive patriarch empowered to execute those—especially sons—who threaten his dominance. The boar's masculinity is reified in his sexual and lethal tusks which, combining functions in the slaying of Adonis, parody the erotic aggression of Venus. These opposed figures caricature a child's awe of its parents, specifically the awe of an Elizabethan child who had to fashion an identity out of, and be fashioned by, the culture's incompatible forms of gender and ideology.

Hence the strategic martyrdom of Adonis, which opens to Venus the sort of superhuman maternity of Eliza's famous vow to her subjects that "[you shall] never have a more natural mother than I mean to be unto you all."[15] Doting on Adonis at her breast, "Like a milch doe, whose swelling dugs do ache" (l. 875), Venus will forever prove his worth even though, strictly speaking, he no longer exists at all. Maternalized at Paphos, compensated for her loss by this parodic generativity, the goddess can venerate the warrior who has "melted like a vapor from her sight" (l. 1166). Like Hamlet's suicidal impulse "to melt, / Thaw, and resolve . . . into a dew" (1.2.129–30), Adonis's transformation comes at a moment when no heroism seems possible.

Adonis and Venus end up suspended between life and annihilation, in the mythic space of metaphor. In historical terms, the poem brings us into the dreamlike sphere of cultural fantasy. We can speculate about the spirit in which this ambivalent accommodation at Paphos is offered, but we are unlikely to ascertain exactly how cynical or sublime it is intended to be.[16]

Unlike *Hero and Leander's* "actively self-dramatizing narrative persona" (Keach, p. 115), say, the poet in *Venus and Adonis* is self-effacing. He employs a sophisticated comic technique that minimizes the personal impact of love and death. He sacrifices the solemn passion that tacitly makes the artist a heroic mediator between his mortal audience and the cosmos. Instead his wit keeps his readers and patron imaginatively poised between engagement and detachment. In part such poise is aesthetically and politically determined. At once it mocks and slyly consoles for humankind's narcissistic illusions. Yet as the equivocation of the withdrawal to Paphos suggests, the poet's own feelings may have needed some protection.

In the end, however, the poet himself also plays the hunter, capturing his mythic quarry in art even as he acts to understand, and influence, the privileged world of his patron. However much the poem may flatter, it also offers the reader some new control over the ordinarily inaccessible mystique of heroic authority. Despite his inescapable subjectivity, the artist as hunter uses the weapon of imagination, and captures and kills through demystification, making the energy of his prey available to others.

In addition, the poet impersonates the goddess too. For the prophesy Venus speaks is also the voice of the poem. This might be a quibble were it not that ultimately the prophesy would disenchant us, its readers, as Venus has Adonis. "Sorrow on love hereafter shall attend," she vows, beginning a litany of sorrows from war to madness. Her incantation discovers the world to come—Shakespeare's world, plague-ridden London—turned upside down and at the mercy of gross contingency. "The boar that kills Adonis," one critic maintains, "may be a direct symbol of the plague, for the wound is in the flank or groin, where the dreaded plague spots, the 'bubos,' appeared—under the armpits and at the crotch."[17] Which is to say that the poem mythically reenacts the discovery not only of love but of chaos and death as well.

Ernest Becker and others have argued that all cultural production ultimately serves to deny death. But the historical background of *Venus and Adonis* specifically suggests a need for denial. For in 1593 plague had closed the theaters and for the time being finished Shakespeare's career as a dramatist. Whether or not he was actually living in Southampton house in London or at Titchfield, manifestly dependent on his new patron, the dramatist was himself undergoing a sort of play-death, aspiring to a renewal of his fortunes.

Meanwhile in the streets of London pestilence made life catastrophically tenuous. Let me recall Simon Kellway's pamphlet of March 21, 1593, *A Defensative against the Plague*, which discovers dreadful portents in what would ordinarily be a harmless childhood game: "Certaine signes foreshow the plague, as when . . . young children flock together in companies, and feigning one of their members to be dead, solemnize the burying in mournful sort." In this mental climate there must have been a special urgency to Venus's praise of Adonis—a conceit that Shakespeare used more than once in this period: "stargazers, having writ on death [that is, predicted an epidemic], / May say the plague is banished by thy breath" (ll. 509–10). Even as the beloved's breath might save the lover from plague, so the breath of the young earl must have promised Shakespeare himself new life inasmuch as the affection of Southampton—literally a good word—could transform the commercial entertainer into a voice of England's ruling elite, and a creator of its empowering mythology.[18]

But I think there is a deeper relation as well. Playing dead and ritually "solemnizing" it helped the children Kellway observed to come to terms with their anxiety. I would like to suggest that Shakespeare's eulogy for mortal Adonis is a culture-specific adult version of the ritual play by which those Elizabethan children allayed dread. For all the patent differences, these two forms of play invoke sacramental behavior to master the spectres of contingency and annihilation. The poet plays the masculine role of priest to bury the arrested hero Adonis in the bosom of the maternal queen.

Shakespeare's personal situation demanded that he live by deference. And certainly his readers and patron expected him to intensify their heroic claims on life. And so the poet worked by self-effacement in order to assert control over dangerous and obstinate materials: materials fully capable, given the pride of privilege, of destroying a poet caught stalking them. For the poem threatens to disenchant heroic culture and the compensatory cult of Gloriana, revealing, as the rampaging, parodically loving boar does, vulnerability and a need for renewal.

Chapter 8

Love, Death, and Patriarchy
in Romeo and Juliet

Recent criticism has tended to depict patriarchy primarily as an authoritarian institution for the regulation of society.[1] Where Elizabethan theorists praised the system for its order, we now have difficulty seeing beyond its flagrant injustices and limitations, especially its misogyny. Yet repression is not the whole picture. What made patriarchy tolerable, even valuable, to so many Elizabethans? No one in Shakespeare's Verona, for example, openly rebels against its patriarchs. Like Romeo, Juliet blames fate that she "must love a loathed enemy" (1.5.141); she desperately tries to placate her father with "chopt-logic" (3.5.149). For all their touchiness about being thought slaves, even the servants identify with—are willing to fight for—their houses. Why would individuals consistently subordinate their own desires to the will of a patriarch?[2]

The answer I read from the play is that like religion, patriarchy systematized heroic fantasies of immortality. Anxiety about death pervades *Romeo and Juliet*. The word "death" itself shows up more often here than in any other work in the canon. In the lyrical balcony scene (2.2.53–78) no less than the ominous Prologue, love is "death-mark'd." Even before Romeo's first glimpse of Juliet, as he laments Rosaline's vow of chastity, he plays at being dead: "in that vow / Do I live dead that live to tell it now" (1.1.223–24). Even then he worries that "untimely death" will overtake him (1.4.111). This "Black and portentous" dread, I shall be arguing, dramatizes the breakdown in Verona of patriarchy's ability to control people's anxiety about death, and unconsciously anticipates the dangerous consequences of that breakdown.

Patriarchy evolved from ancient systems of social order based on heroic dominance.[3] In Roman law a male child of any age "remained under the authority of his father and did not become a Roman in the full sense of the word, a paterfamilias, until the father's death. More than that, the youth's father was his natural judge and could privately sentence him to death" (Veyne, p. 27). The early Roman paterfamilias not only ruled over the family, but was priest of the family ancestor cult. In various ways this access to superhuman power persisted into the Renaissance.

Like Christianity, whose priestly fathers commonly exercised worldly as well as spiritual influence, patriarchy associated the father with the king and God: he created and validated his child's personality. As Duke Theseus formulates it to a daughter as disobedient in love as Juliet:

> To you your father should be as a god;
> One that compos'd your beauties; yea, and one
> To whom you are but as a form in wax,
> By him imprinted, and within his power,
> To leave the figure, or disfigure it.
>
> [*MND* 1.1.47–51]

Ultimately the patriarch guaranteed the psychic life of all who depended upon him. The father may be invested with maternal nurturance: "Where should the frighted child hide his head, but in the bosom of his loving father?"[4] Tasso reveals the underlying premise when he reports that he confided in his patron "not as we trust in man, but as we trust in God. It appeared to me that, so long as I was under his protection, fortune and death had no power over me" (Bradbrook 1980, p.73).

In early modern England, "in spite of all the subordination, the exploitation and the obliteration of those who were young, or feminine, or in service, everyone belonged in . . . a family group," a circle of affection, but also a likely scene of hatred (Laslett, p. 5). Patriarchal dominance was supposed to stabilize the family. By subsuming the personalities of those dependent on him, a father or master reconciled or if need be overrode their conflicts. His strength energized the entire family and his purpose gave it meaning. In this perspective patriarchy was a means of consolidating diverse wills into one extraordinary will and generating a communal feeling—in effect, a spell—of immortality.

The potency of that spell derived from dread as well as devotion. A patriarch could annihilate as well as make men. The prince acts to rein in his "Rebellious subjects" by threatening their lives (1.1.97). Old Capulet curses the uncooperative Juliet: "hang, beg, starve, die in the streets" (3.5.192). Servants joke anxiously about the gallows. More than mere discipline is at stake here, since one who can command death may seem to transcend it. Symbolically the patriarch appropriated the role of death himself, subjecting it to human rules. By being perfectly obedient one could hope to placate if not control death. Even unconscious anxiety about a rejection akin to death must have reinforced identification with the father.

In a system such as ancient Rome's, where "famulus" or family also meant "slave" or "servant," only self-effacement brought a share of the father's power and security. In theory, either one identified with one's master and vicariously shared his glory by lording it over inferiors, or one was dominated. Hating to be thought slaves (1.1.13) but also fearful of the executioner (5), the Capulet servants associate aggression on the master's behalf with escape from the nullity of servitude. Yet their inferiority is the creation of masters and produces volatile ambivalence in them. They summarize their situation with an ambiguity too dangerous to be consciously faced: "The quarrel is between our masters, and us their men" (19–20)—that is, not merely between houses but between masters and servants as well.

In seeking to dominate, the servants act out the submerged values of their masters. Since patriarchy is founded upon the promise of security to dependents such as women, Sampson imagines humiliating his enemy by violating his women. Likewise, he appropriates the patriarch's role as judge when he fantasizes, "I will be civil with the maids—I will cut off their heads" or maidenheads (21–23), equating rape with execution. By contrast, Romeo acts out patriarchy's benevolent generativity when he first approaches Juliet, assigning her an identity (the sun) and commanding her to arise and claim her rightful place in the order of things (2.2.3–9). These examples reflect a paradox that becomes increasingly significant the deeper we look into the play's imaginative world: that even those who seemingly oppose patriarchy internalize patriarchal values.

The marriage Old Capulet would make for his daughter helps to explain the submissiveness of dependents. By meekly wedding the paternally sanctioned Paris, making him a patriarch in his own right, Juliet would fulfill her father's will and transform herself. Lady Capulet fetishizes Paris as a book of spellbinding value that "in many's eyes doth share the glory" (91). Marrying him, Juliet too would be glorified, sharing in "all that he doth possess, / By having him, making [herself] no less" (1.3.93–94). With its connotations of worship, "glory" exactly expresses the religious assumptions underlying the patriarchal system. Compelling admiration from others, Juliet's marriage would exalt her and by extension her parents. For a dependent deference can be a means to vicarious triumph.

In Verona, however, patriarchy is under stress. The prince envisions himself protecting the city's "ancient citizens" from the turmoil of "rebellious subjects" (1.1.82, 97). A servant's spiteful taunts can provoke a full-scale brawl in the streets. At the same time romance has begun to rival patriarchy as an alternative mode of devotion and deliverance. As a result, the fathers' demand at least for deference, at most for total self-sacrifice, sets off a violent chain of events. Social patterns and preoccupations inherent in the patriarchal system create conflicts that make rebellion inevitable.

II

To begin with, in patriarchy the conviction of immortality must be maintained by mystification, since in the end every master's strength is finite and people do helplessly die. Any threat to that spell jeopardizes the community's sense of security. The principal threat, however, is the direct replacement of fathers by more vigorous sons. An aging father may become apprehensively tyrannical, or the child disenchanted and rebellious.[5] Withdrawing its strength from the father, weakening their shared identity, the child cannot help but evoke dread. To her father, Juliet is "My soul, and not my child" (4.5.62), and with her loss "life, living, all is Death's" (59).

Since the system polarizes roles into extremes of dominance and submissive identification, the moment when those roles at last reverse may be terrifying. Hence the potential violence of paternal retaliation. Acting the righteous judge, a father can pronounce doom on an unruly child and thereby—however painfully—make the loss of the child (and the child's loss of self) confirm his own vitality.

One solution to the problem of succession makes the father an unmoved mover, as it were, a conscience figure or judge who controls a seemingly static house or kingdom by directing his powers of life and death inward in the form of blessings and executions. By contrast, the annihilation of enemies acts out the heroic mastery of death, and that power may be delegated to sons and followers. In this way the potency of the father remains safely incontestable.

Since Verona has no outside enemy, however, heroic violence has turned inward. When Old Capulet calls for his sword, he is about to assault Old Montague, who is tacitly his "brother" in relation to the patriarch who governs them, the prince. In this context the otherwise peculiarly gratuitous feud is a device that allows males to seek forbidden self-aggrandizement by scapegoating rivals, and each house kills in the name of righteousness. The feud helps to preserve the illusion of immortality essential to patriarchy's survival by providing a safety valve for aggressive feelings against masters, yet it only postpones the inevitable crisis of succession.

Hence the need to glorify the submission of the child while making the father godlike. The model for that submission is Christianity, in which the central action is the atonement of the Son with the omnipotent Father. Christ resists Satan's temptation to personal dominion over the earth and by sacrificing himself earns eternal life for humankind. While God remains the unmoved mover, his son struggles in the world and earns through his faithful death a resurrection that transforms him from lamb to fatherly shepherd, and from victimized mock-King of the Jews to the militant warrior who will harrow hell and rout Antichrist in the last days. In this arrangement the shepherd/warrior can share in the identity of the Father without threatening his preeminence as everlasting judge.

In a fallen world, however, as Renaissance sectarianism made plain, the urge to rebellion remained strong. Reformers repudiated the patriarchal pope (*il papa*) and feuded among themselves, seeking to dethrone each other's "false" god and win the eternal life afforded by the true Father. The English, typically, depicted their own rebellion as the rescue of true faith from Antichrist. The patriarchal analogue to religious schism is Verona's feud. Like rival dispensations, each house kills in the name of righteousness. Cursing Benvolio, Tybalt cries, "I hate hell, all Montagues, and thee" (1.1.71). In psychoanalytic terms, fanaticism such as Tybalt's suggests a reaction formation, a means of suppressing one's own taboo impulses by killing off the devilish enemy of authority one might otherwise become.

In Verona as in Christianity the patriarchal role is split between incontestable control and heroic expansiveness, yet any reconciliation is repeatedly subverted. The prince functions as conscience and judge, commanding obedience "on pain of death" (1.1.103). But Prince Escalus seems weak and his unruly "sons" deviously aggressive. While the "sons" profess obedience, they maneuver for power. Instead of suffering abuse as Christ did, they seize on indignities to promote a spiral of violence. Their rivalry ambivalently allows "sons" to challenge and curry favor with their lord. Old Capulet, for example, insists on Juliet's marriage to the prince's kinsman Paris, which presumably would give him an edge over his rival Montague. His marriage scheme expresses the mentality of the feud and also signifies an effort to identify with the supreme source of strength in Verona. And not surprisingly: for in a larger context these "sons" are themselves fathers covertly challenged from below.

Within his own house a lord such as Old Capulet is himself a weakened conscience, his role as warrior being appropriated by actual or surrogate sons such as Tybalt, and below them unruly servants. Tybalt, after all, boldly usurps the role of warrior lord. Wishing to assault Romeo at the ball, he tests his surrogate father's authority to the limits, provoking Old Capulet to roar: "Am I the master here, or you?" (1.5.78).

As a potential son-in-law, Romeo himself is tacitly a rival son with Tybalt, competing to inherit Old Capulet's power. Like Old Capulet and Old Montague, Tybalt and Romeo displace their resentment of superior authority onto one another. Furthermore, Romeo scales the patriarch's orchard wall to steal his daughter's heart and thereby his posterity, yet he denies all hostility in himself and others. "There lies more peril in thine eye / Than twenty [Capulet] swords" (2.2.71–72). Eventually, as Verona's sons destroy one another, Romeo will join Mercutio, Tybalt, and Paris in the graveyard.

As the source of new life and immortal posterity, marriage is one means of mediating the anxious replacement of the parent by the child, especially when subject to stringent parental control.[6] As Old Capulet insists, "[all] my care hath been / To have [Juliet] matched" (3.5.177–78). Marriage compensates the father for his losses by putting his consent—his will—at the center of the formalities. In theory he creates the union. Hence the tragic nature of the parental dread that spurs Juliet's defiance. Lamenting Tybalt's death, prevented by the prince's edict from taking comfort in the usual fantasies of triumphal revenge, Old Capulet keenly feels his own mortality—"Well, we were born to die"

(3.4.4). Promptly he makes a "desperate tender / Of my child's love" to Paris (12–13). For a moment he loses faith in his own ordained mastery and tries to secure the future by force. Bullying his daughter to wed Paris, fatally alienating her, the old man brings on the horror he seeks to dispel. Vowing to "drag" her to wed Paris "on a hurdle" like a doomed criminal, he behaves as if she has actually acted to destroy him. In his mind marriage and the feud cannot be separated.

But then the feud is part of a larger system of behavior that involves everyone in Verona. While the prince champions peace, for example, the feud actually serves to protect his limited power from expansive ambitions from below. By blaming the fathers, he can exercise his threat to execute troublemakers and thus "maintain his posture as a decisive ruler."[7] Until the night of the ball at least, the fathers have similarly profited from the distressing competition that has distracted feisty impatient for power. Old Capulet has had reason to worry about "lusty young men" taking "comfort" when "well-apparell'd April on the heel / Of limping winter treads" (1.2.26–28). While he plays the vigorous master inviting Paris to his feast, in his imagery he is old man winter, impotent and jealous and doomed.

The feud presupposes, then, that one "son" may kill another to identify with the father's strength as warrior-hero. With the emphatic symmetry of "Two households, both alike in dignity" (Pro. 1), Capulet and Montague are virtual alter egos, as are Tybalt and Romeo, and in the opening brawl the opposed servants. Externalized, the doubling plays out fratricidal rivalry. Fully internalized in a vulnerable character, patriarchal conflicts may produce self-murder. And that, I maintain, is what finally destroys Romeo and Juliet.

III

For all their lyrical tenderness, Romeo and Juliet create their love out of the tragically conflicting materials of their own culture. In Romeo's shifting passion, for instance, the Chorus implies a struggle to inherit a father's position: "Now old desire doth in his deathbed lie, / And young affection gapes to be his heir" (2.Pro. 1–2). The lovers attempt to evade the world of the feud, yet in making love they unwittingly act out patriarchal and Christian forms. Construing love as worship, substituting the beloved for father and God, they seek apotheosis in each other.

In an imaginative world where children grow up transfixed in the aura of a protective lord or else face nullity, it is understandable that love may reproduce in a beloved the engulfing, life-giving power of godlike parents. Insofar as the polarization of power in Verona requires either continual submission or the devious homicidal assertiveness of the feud, love's mutual worship answers profound needs. For if individuals become disenchanted with absolute security and heroic aggression, as Romeo and Juliet do, they need alternative convictions to sustain them. Love is therefore counterphobic not only as any system of immortality must be, but also as a defense against the anxious demands of an ideology whose spell is no longer wholly efficacious. Mercutio makes the point in a wisecrack about play-death. Having lost Romeo after the Capulets' party, Mercutio jokes that "The ape is dead," and invokes Rosaline's "quivering thigh" to resurrect him (2.1.15–21). The jibe reduces Romeo to a mindless animal who can only "ape" autonomy in sexual arousal.

Romeo envisions Juliet as a supernatural being, a masculine "bright angel" and "winged messenger of heaven" who overmasters awestruck "mortals" so that they "fall back and gaze on him" (2.2.26–32). At the same time, as in the gender of the angel, Romeo's vision expresses the infantile wish to be chosen by, and identified with, a majestic father. His imagination finds fulfillment in the paradox of empowering self-effacement at the heart of patriarchy. The fantasy's completion comes in Romeo's dream that Juliet has awakened him from death and ordained him an emperor, the paramount patriarchal role (5.1.9).

Juliet participates in the same fantasy when she equates orgasm and immortality in her cry,

> Give me my Romeo; and when I [Q4: he] shall die,
> Take him and cut him out in little stars,
> And he will make the face of heaven so fine
> That all the world will be in love with night.
>
> [3.2.21–24]

Like "all the world," Juliet will be subsumed as a worshipper in Romeo's apotheosis. If his transformation into stars alludes to Caesar's apotheosis as a "goodly shyning starre" in Ovid, as one editor has suggested,[8] then Juliet is envisioning an analogue to Romeo's dream that sexual love (her kiss) can revive him from death to become an emperor. By "dying" through sexuality "are happy mothers made"

(1.2.12). By the same means, reciprocally, may a woman make a youth an immortal lord. In its imagination of power this fantasy is profoundly patriarchal. Like Romeo's vision of the angel, however, this celebration of all the world absorbed in the face of heaven also suggests a worshipful infant's concentration upon the all-important, life-giving face of a parent.

The lovers' mutual worship expresses a generosity, subverted or repressed elsewhere in Verona, that balances their self-destructiveness.[9] In their lovemaking Romeo and Juliet repeatedly fantasize that death-like self-effacement leads to apotheosis. Repudiating their own names (2.2.34–57), loving in darkness, they try to be invisible in hopes of escaping patriarchal control. They imagine innocent self-nullification that excuses their actual defiance of their fathers even as each casts the beloved in the role of life-giving lord.[10] When Juliet wishes Romeo were her pet bird, a "poor prisoner" (179) whose liberty she would be "loving jealous of" (181), Romeo eagerly assents. Yet Juliet declines to dominate him, protesting that "I should kill thee with much cherishing" (183).

Finally, however, the lovers' behavior is equivocal, and that doubleness makes their self-effacement perilous. Confronted by Tybalt after his secret marriage, Romeo tries to play possum, placating him. Yet his passivity allows Tybalt to use him as a screen, thrusting under his arm to kill Mercutio (3.1.103). Immediately guilt and anger overwhelm Romeo. Released, his will now turns against Juliet—"Thy beauty hath made me effeminate," he cries, "And . . . soft'ned valor's steel" (3.1.113–15)—and then, murderously, he turns against Tybalt.

In this crisis actual uncontrollable death breaks the spell of symbolic immortality, and the underlying patriarchal structure asserts itself. Defeated by Tybalt's "triumph" (122), called a "wretched boy" (130), Romeo feels overwhelmed by "black fate" (119). In reaction he tries to reassert heroic control over death by levying a death sentence on Tybalt (129). Rebelling—against the emasculating "angel" Juliet as well as the would-be master Tybalt—Romeo discharges his rage at a rival "son" and alter ego. In the complex of motives that produces the lovers' suicides this process is important. For there the part of the self that identifies with the patriarch and demands mastery finally punishes with death part of the self that for the sake of love would forgive enemies and forego worldly power in hopes of deferred rewards. The internalized father slays the weakening child.

Because the basic patriarchal structure governs even rebellion, desires for autonomy tend to call up opposite roles organized around fantasies of death and omnipotence. This split appears everywhere in Verona. When Gregory and Sampson jest about breaking the law, they promptly fantasize about slavery and execution,[11] and then in reaction about their slaughter of enemies. Similarly, the Juliet who would make Romeo outshine Caesar is also the paralyzed child who helplessly hears her parents wish her dead. If she cannot have Romeo, she vows, then "My grave is like to be my wedding-bed" (1.5.135). Protesting the ultimatum to marry Paris, she cries out to the friar:

> . . . hide me nightly in a charnel-house,
> O'ercovered quite with dead men's rattling bones,
> With reeky shanks and yellow [chapless] skulls;
> Or bid me go into a new-made grave,
> And hide me with a dead man in his [shroud]—"
>
> [4.1.81–85]

Juliet's brave challenge masks a fantasy of punishing her own unconscious rage at her father, and guilt at her lover's murder of her kinsman. Lying with slain males like a child ("hide me . . . in his shroud") and a submissive paramour,[12] she would be magically undoing death with sexual fertility as in patriarchally conceived marriage. The idea of playing dead promises to resolve conflicts on more levels than she or the Friar realizes.

Exposed in his rebellion by the murder of Tybalt, the Romeo who would be an emperor (5.1.6–9) similarly abases himself, feeling himself put to death by the mere word "banishment" with which the friar, like a patriarchal judge, "cut'st my head off" (3.3.21–23). Taunted as a slave by Tybalt (1.5.55), Romeo goes to his doom in grandiose defiance of slavery, vowing to "shake [off] the yoke of inauspicious stars / From this world-wearied flesh" (5.3.111). Death and omnipotence are two faces of the same fantasy. Their dissociation contributes to the irrational violence of the feud as well as to the lovers' "mad scenes"—Romeo's tantrum on the floor of the friar's cell and Juliet's near-hallucinatory collapse as she dispatches herself with the sleeping potion.

As it happens, we can glimpse the origins of this polarization of the self in Romeo and Juliet. Headed toward the Capulets' ball, Romeo worries about "some vile forfeit of untimely death" that may overtake him before he can redeem the "despised life clos'd in my breast" through some heroic act (1.4.106–13). His imagery implies that he has mortgaged his life and will lose it since the term will "expire" before he can pay. Punning, he fears an "untimely debt" as well as "death," one that will "forfeit" his "despised life."[13] A sense of guilty inadequacy makes him expect the punishment of death or foreclosure.

In patriarchy, however, the child owes the godlike father a death inasmuch as he or she holds life at the father's will. In Theseus's summary of the doctrine, the child is "imprinted" by the father and is "within his power / To leave the figure or disfigure it" (*MND* 1.1.50–51). What is more, the child owes a debt of obedience or self-efface-ment, in which guilty wishes for autonomy are repressed in a symbolic death. Where patriarchy splits into the roles of the father who is a judge and the son who is a warrior, the son additionally owes this conscience figure a debt of heroic glory that may have to be paid by risking his life. Such a debt produces the self-hate in Romeo's "de-spised life" and helps to explain his desperate reassertion of lost "va-lor" in the murder of Tybalt.

Juliet's behavior also reveals an underlying psychic debt. The origin of this debt surfaces in the Nurse's account of Juliet's weaning (1.3.16–57). Though physically capable, the child angrily resisted her own inde-pendence. On the previous day her first efforts at autonomy had led to a fall that brought not parental support and further self-assertion, but a queasy joke from a surrogate father—the Nurse's husband—that a woman lives to fall. "Thou wilt fall backward when thou hast more wit." Yet Juliet's fall implies a threat of death, especially for a child whose alter ego Susan (the Nurse's daughter) is "with God" (19).

In falling Juliet gave her "brow" "a perilous knock": the same in-jury she imagines inflicting on herself on waking in the monument. Trapped in the suffocating family tomb—within objectified patriarchy itself—she fears being overcome by guilty rage and dashing out her brain, seat of the self and forbidden autonomy. Moreover, she would punish herself by means of a "great kinsman's bone" (4.3.53), meto-nymic parental force. As in the weaning anecdote, a venture toward autonomy produces in her mental life a fall toward death, then trauma.

The Nurse's husband's joke proposes a patriarchal solution to the fall toward death. A "fall backwards" into sexually submissive marriage and motherhood will rescue the child from the terrifying "fall" toward autonomy at the cost of being able—in the joke, literally—to stand on her own two feet. Juliet consents to pay a debt/death through a marriage that will at once efface and exalt her. Girls must "fall" sexually to be redeemed by a new lord and win posterity for the family and themselves, even as young males must be willing to fall in battle to win immortalizing glory.

In this imperative of self-sacrifice lies the germ of the idea of a play-death such as Juliet acts out with the friar's potion. Her fall in a death-counterfeiting sleep would appease an outraged parental judge and lead to a resurrection from the family tomb with the banished Romeo. Making Verona new in amity, Juliet would be fulfilling a patriarchal fantasy comparable to Romeo's dream of love's resurrecting him as an emperor (5.1.6–9). The play emphasizes the pervasiveness of this fantasy in Verona. Engineering Juliet's resurrection, the friar takes a god-like role, planning literally to raise her from the grave. Uniting the lovers, aspiring to atone all Verona, he parodies Capulet's marriage plans, implicitly correcting them, as if to prove himself "the best father of Verona's welfare" (Brenner, p. 52)—one more form of patriarchal rivalry.

IV

Reconstituting patriarchal forms to serve their own desires for autonomy, the lovers never openly defy their parents. Yet with the wish for autonomy comes a veiled recognition of the suffocating claims their parents make on them. The parents' will to subsume their children's identities comes unconsciously to seem to the lovers like cannibalism. The monument that embodies her family in Verona becomes to Juliet an imprisoning mouth (4.3.33–34) and to Romeo a devouring "maw," womb, and mouth (5.3.45–47). Just as the mother becomes an expression of the father's will, and the father expresses ideologically the life-giving and potentially life-withholding generativity of the mother, so the tomb conflates the parents into one ravenous orifice.

As in Lear's fantasy of the savage who "makes his generation messes / To gorge his appetite" (1.1.116–18), the threat is not merely of parental wrath or incestuous desire, but also of cannibalistic self-aggrandizement, a frantic hunger to incorporate more and more life in order to overcome death. Such aggrandizement is the more terrible for being sharply felt by the child and yet invisible. In effect, the lovers fear an infantile voracity such as a once-subsumed child, having at last come to dominate, might release against its own offspring.[14] Since monuments objectify a claim to transcend annihilating time, the "hungry" tomb expresses patriarchy's deepest and most primitive drive, the drive for survival.

We need to remember that the father's claims to mastery over death are corroborated in his role as judge and even executioner. As I noted earlier, the father is always potentially Death himself. In this respect the prince's struggle to contain the feud is a struggle—echoed in the world outside the Elizabethan theater—to reserve for a supreme patriarch the right to command death.

At its most benign this power thrillingly confirms the lord's generosity. By conspicuously sparing the child's life, the father (or monarch) makes the love between them incalculably valuable. And so in his amorous surrender to Juliet, Romeo exults, "O dear account! my life is in my foe's debt" (1.5.18). At its most terrifying, internalized by the child, such power generates intolerable insecurity, as in Romeo's dread of the hostile stars and his suicidal sense of doom.[15]

From this standpoint the lovers' suicides reflect the dynamics of patriarchal control. To master her fate, Juliet would play a lordly role as Cleopatra does to escape Caesar: "myself have power to die" (3.5.242). Yet unconsciously, the introjected imperatives of the parental judge can make suicide a form of execution in which an alienated conscience destroys a rebellious self, as in Juliet's vision of herself dashing out her own brain with an ancestral bone, the reified will of the father. Likewise Romeo's conscience punishes him with suicidal self-hatred. Banished for his defiance, he "[falls] upon the ground . . . / Taking the measure of an unmade grave" (3.3.69–70). Angry at Juliet for his own defiance in slaying Tybalt (3.1.113–15), he turns his anger against himself, fantasizing that his own name has murdered her (102–5). With Juliet he calls down punishment on himself as Elizabethan noblemen routinely did in speeches from the scaffold professing love for the queen: "let me be put to death. / I am content, so thou wilt have it so" (3.5.17–18). And: "Come, death, and welcome! Juliet wills it so" (24). Ambiguously, however, Juliet is also "my soul" (25), so that this execution too is internalized.

As patriarchy's internal conflicts become intolerable, its radical connection with death threatens to surface in consciousness, most insidiously in the personification of death by parent and child. Old Capulet envisions death as a young, rivalrous inheritor who has "lain with" Juliet and usurped his control over her (4.5.36). His description of his adversary of course exactly fits Romeo. In the Capulets' monument, in turn, Romeo also conceives death as a rival: a warrior-king whose "pale flag" has not yet fully "conquered" Juliet (5.3.93–96). Then the rival becomes an "amorous . . . lean abhorred monster" who will make Juliet his "paramour." Romeo imagines Juliet sexually enslaved in the "palace" of a "monster" who is also a warrior-king.[16]

This fantasy projects the long-denied dark side of the patriarchal forms in which the lovers have construed each other. Romeo dissociates from himself as Death the part of him that would be made an emperor by Juliet's kiss. In this final moment of tenderness he rejects the devouring triumphalism latent in all patriarchy. He repudiates the Death that "hath suck'd the honey" of Juliet's breath. Otherwise, loving such an emperor-Romeo, Juliet would be submitting to rape like the women Sampson fancies "ever thrust to the wall" (1.1.16). Sampson identifies with patriarchal tyranny, the same tyranny that Romeo at last projects upon death and vows to resist to the end of time.

Romeo then kisses his beloved to seal "a dateless bargain to engrossing death" (5.3.115). "Engrossing" readily applies to patriarchal hegemony and competitiveness. In addition, such greedy possession calls to mind not only Romeo's imagery of the self held in forfeit, but also his vision of the tomb as a "detestable maw," a "womb of death" (45). The metaphors place the young in an engulfing parental womb that should grant, not swallow, life. The womb and the sexually enslaving monster express the parents whom the lovers love and fear and also, unknowingly, hate.[17] The spatial arrangement of Verona onstage reinforces this conflation since the monster holds Juliet in a "palace" that is in fact the Capulet monument and also, in the Elizabethan playhouse, the Capulets' house with its fortresslike walls (Gibbons, p. 74). Juliet's balcony and the lovers' first bedchamber are virtually present in Death's stronghold, as Juliet inadvertently warns Romeo: "the place [is] death, considering who thou art" (2.2.64). Just as Juliet has associated her lover with patriarchal stars (3.2.22) and a "gorgeous palace" (85), so she impulsively fantasizes about sexual violation by a patriarchal death such as Romeo imagines: "I'll to my wedding bed, / And death, not Romeo take my maidenhead" (137).[18]

Giving his own life with chivalric valor to rescue Juliet from a monster, Romeo finally plays out the warrior's debt of the son to his father. Even as he sacrifices himself in part for patriarchal values, he would "shake the yoke of inauspicious stars" (5.3.111) in a final repudiation of the fathers. It is the fatal paradox at the heart of patriarchy: that rebellion against a myth, insidiously encompassed by that myth, serves the myth. In taking his own life to defend Juliet's sexuality against the rival warrior-king Death, Romeo gives sublime new life—eschatological life—to Verona's feud.

At the close of the play, in the funerary statues the fathers decree, benevolence takes disturbing forms. Still thinking in terms of demands, Capulet vows: "This is my daughter's jointure, for no more / Can I demand." To which Montague replies: "But I can give thee more." Whereupon he boasts that he will make Juliet the golden cynosure of all true lovers: "There shall no figure at such a rate be set / As that of true and faithful Juliet" (296–304). The fathers' economic vocabulary and competition call to mind the psychic debts felt by the children, and the ominous economic term "engrossing" (115) that Romeo associates with death.[19]

Now that marriage and the sword have failed, the fathers would reconstitute their conviction of immortality by recreating their children as holy martyrs to love, "Poor sacrifices of our enmity!" (5.3.304). As icons the children will be fabricated into exemplary types. Yet there must be a difference between the golden statues and the poignant individuals we have seen. That difference is of course the basis of the play's critique of patriarchy. And in the end that difference also measures the dramatist's need to honor the structure of power outside the Globe Theater and no doubt in his own upbringing, while also enacting onstage—and in the sympathies the play evokes—a challenge to that power.

Audiences have often interpreted that challenge as a justification of romantic exaltation, even as various critics have taken it to legitimate the lovers' aspirations to autonomy. By contrast, at least one historian maintains that the original Globe audience would have felt obliged to condemn the play's disobedient children (Stone 1977). If we understand patriarchy as a system of beliefs evolved to control poisonous anxiety about death, however, these contradictory responses to the play appear in a new light. Seizing on a limited truth, each tries to protect the illusion of security at stake in the play, either by revaluing the social order (for example, by postulating its reform through love) or, more often, by repudiating patriarchal values on behalf of a substitute system of beliefs. Like the voices onstage, we too need to fortify ourselves against the prospect of annihilation.[20]

Given the danger of offending an audience, especially an audience of Elizabethan patriarchs, the play does not forcibly disenchant its myths. Instead it creates conditions in which imagination might discover itself as a tissue of beliefs. Such a recognition would momentarily at least turn the imagination against itself, showing the triumphal verities onstage and off to be as compulsive and insubstantial as dreams. In such a moment of alienation the self could begin to appreciate its dependency, even (to echo Sampson and Gregory) its enslavement. In that dizzying moment, that is, lies the possibility of change and perhaps a new ground for heroic values.

Recognition that people live by strategic fictions such as patriarchy opens up everything for negotiation and therefore provides a basis for consensual relationships and, not incidentally, the artist's own creativity. Disconnected from underlying physical forces and appetites, by contrast, a cultural fiction may be a terrifying illusion, a candle lighting fools the way to dusty death. If disenchanted, Shakespeare saw, human behavior may reduce to a fierce appetite for domination and nurture tenuously held in check by ruthless strategy: in Verona a feud, or in the imagery of the history plays a struggle between a king and ravenous wolves.

Hence Shakespeare's equivocation. Like Queen Elizabeth's regime, which revived old forms such as chivalry to disguise its innovations, he survived public life in a world of homicidal religious and political rivalry by honoring venerable cultural forms while recreating them. In one sense his genius lay in devising ways of making disenchantment healthy. His own *Romeo and Juliet* appears simply to echo Brooke's familiar, lifeless *Romeus*, although in fact it functions as a sort of pun on Brooke's story, producing a new meaning. Such a quibbling imaginative stance permitted devious self-assertion in the ostensible service of deference.

Although *Romeo and Juliet* seems to me deeply disenchanted at its core, it dramatizes the imagination's resilience in the face of annihilation. As London and Shakespeare himself survived a devastating plague in the early 1590s (a catastrophe echoed in 5.2.8–12), so the play registers the shock of mortality to a privileged system of belief. The final lines show Verona turning blasted life into art ("never was a story of more woe" [5.3.309]), as Shakespeare himself, having sensed the darkness beyond the bright dreams of culture, would go on generating fictions that engaged that darkness, including the flagrantly dreamlike late romances. In this perspective, like the lovers striving to recreate themselves in the starry gloom, the play probes the origins of belief and creativity, reshaping its anxiously conventionalized source story as that story began to reveal the dread and aspiration which are its hidden motive energy.

Chapter 9

Prophecy and Heroic Destiny
in the Histories

Let me begin this exploration of prophecy and heroic imagination in Shakespeare by recounting an episode from 1532 in which prophecy played a central role. In that year William Neville, one of fifteen younger brothers of the third Lord Latimer, fell under the influence of a motley group of wizards—by trade an astrologer, a caulker, and an Oxford scholar who specialized in alchemy and sorcery. Sizing up their new client, the wizards began forecasting that his inconvenient older brother would soon die, whereupon Neville himself would become the powerful lord. To keep their dupe's imagination fired up, the seers staged omens, revealed wondrously auspicious dreams, and portentously discussed politics and magic. Eventually the talk became dangerous. Neville began speculating about, then openly predicting, the deaths of his brother and Henry VIII as well. As G. R. Elton puts it, "Neville was talking like a man planning to overthrow the state in his search for what he had come to regard as his proper rights."[1] At least one of the wizards fueled Neville's delusions by foreseeing that he would inherit the earldom of Warwick, as if Neville were a long-lost changeling child related to the legendary Guy of Warwick. Obsequiously the wizard addressed his client as earl of Warwick, although later he claimed he had only been making sport of Neville "who was a laughing stock around the neighborhood": a disclaimer, Elton judges, which "carries hardly any conviction" (p. 53). Eventually several of these inspired characters ended up in the Tower suspected of treason, although in the end none suffered the ghastly death executed on many another prophet of the time.

On the surface, Neville's experience is a tale of cynical deception reminiscent of Jonson's *The Alchemist*[2] and the sharp conjuring that ensnares the Duchess of Gloucester in *2 Henry VI*. And yet all involved, even the rogues, seem to have been radically equivocal in their attitudes toward the occult. The Oxford wizard, for example, promised to make the king's fortune if they would only release him from the Tower so he could finish mastering the philosopher's stone. Neville himself had "an unhealthy interest in magic," and had even tried to make a cloak of invisibility for himself out of certain magical parts of a dead horse.[3] Pricked by prophecies to ever more perilous ambition, he built a gallery in his house whose secret doors could admit a troop of armed men to help him seize his glorious future by force. In his flirtation with catastrophe Neville seems like a burlesque of the ambitious Macbeth. Yet under interrogation he claimed that he had always loyally contradicted or pooh-poohed the wizards' predictions. Through the sycophantic wizards Neville sought to fashion a new identity for himself that otherwise would have been unthinkable. In effect, the prophecies were collaborative acts of storytelling that tried to counter paralyzing cultural taboos against self-aggrandizement and make history itself obey the power of wishes. In this way prophetic behavior employs the dynamics of play-death and apotheosis, displacing the self into a glorious future, seeking transcendence through self-effacement. In apocalyptic prophecies, the fulfillment entails nothing less than a merger with the cosmic father at the end of time.

Not surprisingly, Neville's prophetic "plots" were as ambivalent as they were equivocal. Even as they dispatched his brother and the king to happy deaths, the stories validated Neville's own apotheosis as "a great man of the realm" who would lead a force to subdue vague enemies whom "the King had made of low blood" (pp. 53, 54). Identifying with a dangerous oppressor, he imagines himself destroying base upstarts and hence preserving the king who, in reality, represents the powers that make Neville himself a nonentity of "low blood." The transparent reversal in this fantasy confuses love and rage, expansiveness and dread. In his heart Neville was at once a murderous usurper, a potentially tragic overreacher, and yet also a faithful kinsman like Prince Hal or *As You Like It*'s Orlando, a comic hero destined to save the day. In his actual life Neville remained immobilized between these comic and tragic possibilities. After all, he operated with mild deviousness in his conquest of fate until credulity made him brash. The cloak of invisibility he sought perfectly expresses the desperate doubleness in his mind insofar as it promised him boundless self-aggrandizement even as it would have made him a totally secure nonentity as well.

Neville's adventures provide a useful contemporary context in which to consider how prophetic imagination shapes the destinies of two of Shakespeare's most important historical figures, Richard III and Prince Hal. In *Richard III* predictions intimately structure history. In a way the play is a verbal struggle to control the future. Richard himself initiates the action by using "drunken prophecies . . . / To set my brother Clarence and the King / In deadly hate the one against the other" (1.1.33–35). He murders not so much to satisfy any personal hatred as to seize the future from his victims. In turn Queen Margaret and his other victims retaliate by invoking a world to come that will confound and subsume Richard, making him God's avenging angel— in A. P. Rossiter's words an "angel with horns."[4]

In a sense prophetic behavior is natural, even fundamental. As psychologist George Kelly has shown, personality itself can be understood as a process of anticipating events.[5] Where Freud emphasizes the shaping influence of the past, Kelly's theory sees the individual living toward the future, creating a vision of the world that seeks to predict and control the course of events. Some kinds of prophecy might be said to reduce the processes of identity to concrete, manipulable form. The forecasts of his hired wizards, for instance, clearly enabled Neville to formulate a wishful new identity as a lord, supplying him ready-made roles and scenarios. As a means to transfiguration, creating the horned angel Richard, for example, prophecy is a mode of play-death and apotheosis.

In *Richard III* Crookback's victims repeatedly use prophecy in an effort to substantiate themselves in the face of crushing oppression. "Say poor Margaret was a prophetess!" cries the bereft queen, damning her enemies to a punishing future and casting herself as the triumphal agent of God's wrath (1.3.300–302). Trying to nullify her "frantic curse," Hastings explicitly repudiates her "falseboding" or falsely prophetic role (246). As for Richard, the deepest source of his power is his ability to anticipate the behavior of others in his plots and "inductions dangerous" (1.1.32). To manipulate others he has to predict their responses to him, shaping himself to meet their expectations. His hair-raising seduction of Lady Anne, say, depends on his intuition that the "poor Anne" who weeps "helpless balm" over Henry's coffin (1.2.9, 13) unconsciously wishes to be an exalted Cleopatra whose beauty, as Richard vows, "did haunt me in my sleep / To undertake the death of all the world" (122–23). Similarly, he senses that King Edward's fears will enable a mere "drunken prophecy" to turn him against his brother Clarence. Again and again Shakespeare allows his villain to preempt adversaries with thrilling prescience. Richard ambiguously shares the dramatist's privileged insights into the plot, especially at the outset, where if anything he triumphs a little too mechanically. Shakespeare plainly expects his audience to marvel at Crookback's apparently uncanny grasp of the future and therefore destiny itself.

To be sure, prophetic behavior need not always be conscious. Time and again characters in the play unwittingly foresee events in self-revealing ways. Richard's treacherous formula that "G / Of Edward's heirs the murtherer shall be" (1.1.39–40) betrays not only King Edward but himself also. For ironically the false prophecy proves to be true when "G"—not George (Clarence) but himself, Gloucester—comes to murder the young princes. While Richard's words dramatize the ancient belief that murder will out, they also suggest that Shakespeare understood prophecy as imaginative behavior: in this instance as the vehicle of violent thoughts and the compulsion to confess.

In a similar fashion Hastings ignorantly predicts his own execution. Feigning loyalty to Richard, eager to have Crookback slaughter his enemies for him, Hastings nevertheless impulsively vows, "I'll have this crown of mine cut from my shoulders / Before I'll see the crown so foul misplac'd [on Richard's head]" (3.2.43–44). We are meant to shiver as the man blindly decrees his own death. At the same time the double meaning (amphibole) affords striking insight into his character. Consciously, Hastings' vow defiantly asserts his own power. Unconsciously, he expresses guilt and fear that in using Richard's cruelty against his own enemies he exposes himself to the headsman's axe. And sure enough, once condemned, he pours out pity for his enemies and loathing for Richard with the apocalyptic relief of a man finally coming to face a truth long hidden from himself. "I, too fond, might have prevented this," he laments (3.4.81). He rues his "too triumphing" hatred of "butcher'd" enemies who could have been his natural allies, and his identification "in grace and favor" with Richard (89–91).[6] Finally he predicts "the fearfull'st time . . . / That ever wretched age hath look'd upon," calling down death on the persecutors who now "smile at [him]" (104–7). As self-discovery, Hastings' speech resembles Stanley's monitory dream that "the boar had rased off his helm" to kill him (3.2.11), Lady Anne's blind forecast of her torment as Richard's wife—"If ever he have wife, let her be made / . . . miserable" (1.2.26–27)—and Clarence's unwittingly clairvoyant dream of drowning (1.4.9–63).[7] In each instance characters intuit a future they cannot consciously accept. When truth can no longer be contained, characters surrender to it with expedient fatalism. In the end the skeptical Hastings (3.4.82–93), Anne (4.1.80), Buckingham (5.1.27), and even Richard himself (4.2.96, 107; 5.3.204–6) come to believe that destiny is shaped by prophetic powers beyond their control. Like individuals, governments also may be seen to define themselves into the future. Laws—the king's objectified will—imply the character of the state even as they act to regulate and thereby form the future. As William Neville's imagination vividly illustrates, where power is steeply hierarchical and absolute, personified in one figure, rebellion is apt to be symmetrical, invoking absolute, supernatural authority to justify itself. As Keith Thomas points out, "prophecies . . . were employed in virtually every rebellion or popular uprising which disturbed the Tudor state."[8] Paradoxically and ambivalently, ancient predictions "had the effect of disguising any essentially revolutionary step by concealing it under the sanction of past approval" (p. 423). For in a society like Tudor England, which justified its existence by claiming unbroken links to a remote, legitimizing origin, "the facts of change are rapidly reinterpreted to sustain the illusion of a static society. . . . A pretender to the throne must demonstrate genealogical continuity. Hence the great cult of prophecies during the fifteenth century," when York and Lancaster murderously struggled for legitimacy (p. 426).

In Shakespeare usurpers from Crookback to Glendower and Macbeth use supernatural forecasts to sanction their ambitions.[9] But likewise, however expediently, the plays invoke predictions to validate the Tudors. Shakespeare has Crookback remember that "Henry the Sixth / Did prophesy that Richmond should be king" (4.2.95–96). And years afterward (1613), *Henry VIII* directly connected the sanctioned Richmond with the living Jacobean audience in the Globe Theater by producing a rhapsodic Cranmer to foretell the apotheosis of Richmond's granddaughter Elizabeth and her "starlike" heir James, whose progenitive honor and name "Shall . . . make new nations," thereby securing a blessed future (5.4.51–52).

Strictly speaking, as Keith Thomas observes, prophecy had a conservative function insofar as its use "disguised the break with the past. Contemporaries were therefore mistaken when they declared that it was the circulation of prophecies which fomented rebellion. Essentially it was the existence of rebellious feelings which led to the circulation of prophecies" (p. 425). Considered as behavior, that is, prophecy is a form of disguising or play that gives concrete shape to hopes and fears otherwise inadmissable. Like theater, which allows a common actor to rule the world as Tamburlaine or a king of fairies, prophetic behavior tacitly dramatizes the power of imagination. Covertly it makes the creation of identity and personal power a problem anyone might come to think about. An individual may use prophecy, but also, reciprocally, prophecy may promise to recreate the individual inasmuch as it can supplant conventional authorities in validating a new identity—witness the experience of William Neville.

Hence the principle that governs Shakespeare's judgment of prophetic behavior: the deep taboo in the plays against attempts to seize the future by force. Like Macbeth's "dagger of the mind, a false creation" (2.1.38), prophecy may objectify desires to coerce the world into a new shape, even as it appears to dissolve personal responsibility, "marshalling" a deceptively passive self "the way that [it] was going" (42). Not the least of these deceptions is the way prophecy appears to keep history static or predestinate even though it cannot help but imply the possibility of change and in turn ambition. In contemporary political ideology as in theology, to strive to control time was ultimately to usurp the autonomy of king and God, and thereby spawn hellish chaos. In this context prophecy threatens to produce madness even as it promises exaltation. Touched by the witches' forecast of his kingship, for instance, Macbeth's identity begins to disintegrate with terrifying ease. The prospect of seizing supreme power unfixes his hair, unseats his heart, and raises "horrible imaginings" (1.3.135–38):

> My thought, whose murther yet is but fantastical,
> Shakes so my single state of man that function
> Is smother'd in surmise, and nothing is
> But what is not.
>
> [139–42]

Like the consciousness the serpent offered Eve, the witches' forecast cannot actually confer the godlike autonomy it seems to promise (you shall be king: ye shall be as gods) and yet, fearfully, it cannot be forgotten either. Such "soliciting / Cannot be ill, cannot be good" (130–31). Macbeth cannot go ahead without ruinous violence, yet he can't go back either. The result is the struggle against madness and dissolution that makes Macbeth tragic and not merely evil.

Conversely, prophecy proves benevolent for selfless figures. Banquo will accept honor, he tells Macbeth, provided that "[he loses] none / In seeking to augment it" (2.1.26–27).[10] Vicariously, asking nothing for himself, Banquo will become king through his posterity as the witches predicted. *Richard III* likewise makes Richmond self-effacing toward destiny, and accordingly Richmond fulfills Henry VI's prophecy: "If secret powers / Suggest but truth to my divining thoughts, / This lad will prove our country's bliss" (*3H6* 4.6.68–70). Although Crookback and the ghosts at Bosworth Field attribute Richmond's success to predestination, Shakespeare takes pains to show Richmond's humbly beseeching divine aid (5.3.108–17). In prayer he makes his own will transparent: the vehicle of divine purpose.

Where prophetic behavior reinforces the established order outside the theater, playing out a vision of community, it is apt to take the form of a blessing, as at the close of *Henry VIII*. After slaying Crookback, for example, Richmond invokes a benign future to be based on marriage. In ritually charged language, sanctifying prediction as prayer, he vows:

> O now let Richmond and Elizabeth
> The true succeeders of each royal house,
> By God's fair ordinance conjoin together!
> And let their heirs (God, if thy will be so)
> Enrich the time to come with smoothfac'd peace,
> With smiling plenty, and fair prosperous days!
>
> [5.5.29–34]

By contrast, where prophetic behavior expresses the helpless righteousness of victims, it takes the form of curses. For Queen Margaret and the ghosts who haunt Richard, victims who have lost everything and are literally selfless, curses turn the future against their powerful tormentors. As Keith Thomas reminds us, "although post-Reformation Protestants usually denied both the propriety and the efficacy of ritual cursing, they frequently believed that, if the injury which provoked the curse were heinous enough, the Almighty would lend his endorsement. . . . It was a moral necessity that the poor and the injured should be believed to have this power of retaliation when all else failed" (p. 507). To suffer injury from another is to suffer effacement, while the aggressor appropriates the victim's personal force, magnifying himself and his own strength. And so the victim's curse serves to restore a static, just relationship in the time to come, forcing destiny and yet not violating the taboo against self-aggrandizement. One by one, for instance, Margaret's tormentors go to their deaths acknowledging, as Grey says, that her "curse is fall'n upon [their] heads" (3.3.15). The doomed Buckingham makes the prophetic behavior explicit: "Margaret's curse falls heavy on my neck: 'When [Richard],' quoth she, 'shall split thy heart with sorrow, / Remember Margaret was a prophetess'" (5.1.25–27).

Few characters could coerce destiny more violently than Crookback. Consider Richard's famous command: "Shine out, fair sun, till I have bought a glass / That I may see my shadow as I pass" (1.2.262–63). His words command not only the sun but the future also. Like Hastings' unwitting clairvoyance, his language is crucially ambiguous. Seeking to celebrate his progress toward the apotheosis of kingship, Richard ironically foretells his end at Bosworth Field, where he becomes a shadow passing through illusion into annihilation.[11] Grasping at figments of identity, his future now decreed by ghosts commanding him to "Despair and die!" he cries out in his nightmare: "I am I," "No. Yes, I am," "I love myself," "I rather hate myself," and so on. Groping repetition calls attention to the riddling emptiness of the self in words: "I myself / Find no pity to myself" (5.3.183–204). On a sunless morrow he "enacts more wonders than a man" in battle (5.4.2), yet he dies slashing wildly at six illusory Richmonds (11), nullified, in a negative apotheosis.

Ultimately Richard is shadowy because he lives not for any immediate self-interest, but for an endlessly empowering future. His power comes from his ability to keep himself invisible while pretending to mold himself to the expectations—the futures—of others. His sole delight, he swears, is to "spy my shadow in the sun / And descant on mine own deformity" (1.1.26–27).[12] "Spy" suggests that this self-awareness is accidental and even unnatural to him. Celebrating his deformity, he repudiates himself with heroic contempt, speaking as if from outside himself, with a disembodied and inhuman idealism. To "descant" on deformity is to make an art of hate, gaining a sense of power by rejecting an imperfect creature and an imperfect present time as a god might.[13]

One way to understand this synergistic self-hate and self-inflation is to recognize that Richard's ugly "unfinish'd" body (1.1.20) objectifies the elemental terror of death and meaninglessness that haunts humankind. Insofar as prophetic behavior enables Richard to live endlessly in an imminent future, it promises him undying potency. To be "sent before my time / Into this breathing world, scarce half made up" (20–21) is to be cheated of an ideal destiny. As long as he can "feel now / The future in the instant," as Lady Macbeth puts it (1.5.58), he can act out an illusion of self-transendence.

The paradigm for this self-transcending behavior comes at the close of *3 Henry VI*, where the king predicts Richard's career and Richard kills him, equivocally justifying himself by prophecy as one "ordain'd" to kill the king. Stabbing his victim Richard exclaims: "die, prophet, in thy speech: / For this, amongst the rest, was I ordain'd" (5.6.57–58). In Richard's words Muriel Bradbrook finds "a direct recollection of the role of the Prophets" in the old craft cycles in which a "providential pattern linked events."[14] More complexly, Moody E. Prior contends that Richard's claim to be "ordain'd" in his action "carries a fleer at the prophetic pretensions of Henry, yet in context the line becomes a part of Henry's inspired projection of the future and suggests that Henry is indeed the mouthpiece of an ordaining power."[15] In this clash of prophets, each strives to subsume the other and identify himself with superhuman necessity.

The confrontation, then, dramatizes a symbolic struggle for being. The king decrees Richard "less than a mother's hope / . . . an indigested and deformed lump" at birth (50–51). Born incomplete yet with full teeth (53) to "bite the world" (54), Richard is to the king all appetite: a sort of cannibal or vampire homicidally hungry for life. Henry's prophecy would dehumanize or more exactly decreate Richard into parts: teeth, a scarcely existent lump. Richard reacts to this threat of nightmarish unbeing by stabbing Henry in an act of violent self-assertion, acting out the superiority of "living" force to "dying" words that his own language tacitly vows: "die, prophet, in thy speech: / For this, amongst the rest, was I ordain'd" (57–58).

As an apotheosis, embodying England and God's will, the only one in society who is truly autonomous, the king possesses superhuman potentiality and potency. By title and execution he makes and unmakes men. In a vicious parody of the king's supremacy, Richard slays him appealing to his own "ordain'd" authority. The murder, that is, enacts a fantastic project of self-creation whose ultimate object will be Richard's apotheosis as king. In biting the world, consuming the vitality of others, he pursues chimerical supremacy trying to overcome the unbearable nullity that human beings, God, and "dissembling nature" pronounce on him through the king. "Counting myself but bad till I be best" (91), Crookback undertakes feats of superhuman destruction striving to establish that "I am myself alone" (83).

Such a project is of course as evil as it is futile. In theory Henry subsumes the identities of all his subjects, and even the lowliest partake of cosmic power and life through him as through Christ. In this respect his role is sacrificial: he is all and nothing. Assaulting him, Richard acts to aggrandize all power to himself with demonic selfishness. In this sense he "bites" or devours the world, finally consuming himself as well. In his opening soliloquy in *Richard III*, for example, the terms of Henry's prophetic judgment recur as if Richard has taken his words as well as his life. Descanting on his own deformity and insubstantiality, he is still trying to escape the king's judgment. Internalized, Henry's prediction virtually comes to haunt his murderer. Proclaimed an "indigested and deformed lump" in *3 Henry VI* (5.6.51), Richard now compulsively expands upon the epithet as if to coopt the king and thereby remove the painful sting. In his own words he is

> . . . curtail'd of this fair proportion,
> Cheated of feature by dissembling nature,
> Deform'd, unfinish'd, sent before my time
> Into this breathing world, scarce half made up.
> [1.1.18–21]

Although he vows, "I am determined to prove a villain" (30), his word "determined" signifies not only his resolute will but also helpless fatality.[16] The king's haunting prediction, that is, witnesses the futility of his murder even as it looks forward to the slaughtered yet triumphant ghosts at Bosworth Field and Richard's dying assault on the six illusory impersonators of Richmond.

Prophetic behavior, then, reveals the fetishistic nature of the crown, the life-giving apotheosis. Like Macbeth, Richard grasps at power to no earthly end, not for policy or any quotidian pleasure. Rather, he appears compelled by the crown's promise of vitality. Overtly desacralized, even mocked, kingship nevertheless retains a power for him that can only be called superhuman, and Richard devotes himself to it with a fanaticism reminiscent of the terrifying genocidal struggles for religious supremacy that Shakespeare's world knew all too well. It could be argued that Richard's behavior parodies the bloodthirsty absolutism of Henry VIII, Mary Tudor, and—in ideology if not in actual practice—the early Elizabeth. In this perspective Shakespeare's Richard appears to express an unconscious resentment against royalty's overwhelming appropriation of power and autonomy to itself in the Tudor period. He caricatures the providential Richmond and his inheritors even as the viciously fascinating Satan does the Christian God.[17] In psychological terms, as the play's imagery insists, Richard is also an enraged, "biting" child capable of ferocious and yet exhilarating independence. Rather than suffer himself to be subsumed in the identity of the father-king and to share in a vicarious transcendence, as doctrine prescribed, he threatens to devour the patriarch himself. Rather than internalize the repressive values of the father-king, he acts out repression with homicidal fury on others, and with transcendent self-hatred on himself.

For all his strategic clarity, in short, Richard dramatizes the same profoundly human desperation that surfaced more transparently in the "small army of pseudo Messiahs" that the reign of Elizabeth produced. Among them was one William Hacket, "an illiterate and bankrupt ex-serving man, who had persuaded himself that he was the Messiah and had come to judge the world on God's behalf. He laid claim to gifts of prophecy and miracle-working; and he threatened a series of plagues upon England unless immediate reformation took place. He was a fierce man, who was said to have once bitten off and eaten an antagonist's nose; 'his manner of praying' was observed to be 'as it were speaking to God face to face' " (Thomas, pp. 133–34). To his associates Hacket "was both King of Europe and the Angel who would come before the Last Judgment to separate the sheep from the goats" (p. 134). Truly an angel with horns, Hacket attacked the authority of the queen and cried annihilation against the world while advertising himself to be personally indestructible up to the moment in 1591, in the streets of London, when his monarch had him put to death.

From this standpoint history itself threatens to stand revealed as an awesome struggle for apotheosis. When kings and heroes fail—when vicarious transcendence fails—for whatever reason—civil slaughter is apt to follow. It is a measure of Shakespeare's insight that at one point or another nearly every one of Richard's victims betrays a compulsion toward power. Just such a compulsion is comically at the center of

William Neville's escapades with wizards, and tragically latent in his fantasies about commanding an armed uprising. And just this sort of awareness, it seems to me, underlies the dying Henry IV's fear of a future England "peopled with wolves" (*2H4* 4.5.137). He foresees human beings consuming one another in a wolfish rage for survival, destroyed by the monstrous compulsion to "bite the world" as Richard would. Even as the failing King Henry couches his horror in a controlling prophecy, so *Richard III* controls its vision of universal savagery by a network of prophetic projections that appear to secure at last Richard's accursed extermination and Richmond's triumphant airy benediction.

II

Let me balance this dark example of prophetic behavior with a happier one, the destiny of Prince Hal. As Henry V, Hal himself was credited with powers of prognostication in the Tudor period. In *A Defensative against the Poyson of Supposed Prophecies* (1583), for example, Henry Howard, Earl of Northampton, anxiously catalogs the evils of prophecy: and with good reason, since he had lost two kinsmen—the poet Earl of Surrey and the Duke of Norfolk—to the headsman thanks to incited ambition. Unexpectedly, the earl interrupts his supererogatory catalog of follies to endorse Hal's prescience: "Henry the fifth, [sayth maister Haule] prognosticated, that the young Earle of Richmonde, who was then his page, should one day stint the strife betweene Yorke & Lancaster: which secret coulde not have beene revealed, as some thinke, without deeper insighte into future things, then common sense or reason can attaine or reach unto."[18] Following Hall, the earl connects the idealized Henry V with the founder of the Tudor dynasty, Crookback's nemesis, and justifies the ascendancy of Richmond by appealing to the uncanny prescience of Henry V.

Like Richard III, Hal too has a crucial soliloquy that functions as a self-validating prophecy. But where Richard blindly foretells his own shadowy dissolution (1.2.262–63), Hal's sense of the future is never confuted. Where Richard would force the future to his will, violating taboo and thereby confounding himself, Hal would "imitate the sun" by effacing himself behind base clouds while his father commands England's awe (*1H4* 1.2.197). He will allow clouds to "smother" and mists to "strangle" him in a sacrificial play-death (201–7). "By so much shall I falsify men's hopes," he vows, for "My reformation, glitt'ring o'er my fault, / Shall show more goodly and attract more eyes than that which hath no foil to set it off" (211, 213–15). While he imparts his intentions in the soliloquy, on another level his words also foretell the play's action. It would be a mistake, I think, merely to construe the speech as the personal revelation of a Machiavellian schemer. At the least the soliloquy has the justificatory cast so often associated with prophecy. The voice projects a Prodigal Son scenario with the atavistic detachment of a Chorus or Prologue in an old play. Although it appears colloquial, in the end Hal's language has an apothegmatic and ritualistic quality. Echoing Eph. 5.7, itself a vision of "the ages to come," Hal predicts: "I'll so offend, to make offense a skill, / Redeeming time when men least think I will" (216–17).

In the course of the play Hal defines himself partly by countering the "hopes" or predictions of others, especially his father. "The hope and expectation of thy time / Is ruin'd," the king laments, "and the soul of every man / Prophetically do forethink thy fall" (3.2.36–38). From his early forecast that Hal is "only mark'd / For the hot vengeance, and the rod of heaven" (3.2.9–10) to his deathbed foreboding that his dissolute son will rule an England peopled with wolves, Henry forcefully works to reshape Hal's character. In effect, he invokes various appalling futures for his son in an effort to foreclose them. The prince counters at last, in the crisis before Shrewsbury, with a "promise" to "redeem" the time "in the name of God" (3.2.132–59). At some moments his language is charged with echoes of the New Testament:

> I will redeem all this on Percy's head,
> And in the closing of some glorious day
> When I will wear a garment all of blood,
> And stain my favors in a bloody mask,
> Which wash'd away shall scour my shame with it.
>
> [132–37]

It is tempting to regard this speech as the valorous trumpeting of youth and nothing more. Apt to be overlooked is the subliminal pattern of salvationist eschatology in Hal's vision of his atonement with his father. By suffering a bloody purgation, he vows, he will "wash away" his shame or sin, and "redeem all this." He "will tear the reckoning" from his adversary Hotspur's heart (152), and by his victory heal his father's wounds, "the long-grown wounds of my intemperance"

(156). Magnifying himself and his struggle, the prince concludes on an apocalyptic note. Rather than fail, he swears, he "will die a hundred thousand deaths" (158). Catching the spirit of righteous annihilation, the king retorts: "A hundred thousand rebels die in this." Whereupon he identifies his will with his son's: "Thou shalt have charge and sovereign trust herein" (160–61).

In Hal's peroration, it seems to me, we can hear echoes of the medieval Christian worldview in which "life tends to be seen as a mortal struggle waged by good fathers and good children against bad fathers and bad childen."[19] Coexistent in Hal's vision with chivalric "favors" and "honor," that is, is a vocabulary of messianic struggle. In its most crudely extravagant form the medieval version of this struggle pitted the Christ of the Parousia or the Christ-like Emperor of the Last Days against Antichrist. The Son of God personally confronted the "son of perdition" in an apocalyptic clash. In that final resolution a host of demonic fathers and sons would oppose the armies of the saints, the opposing hosts "each the negative of the other" and "held together in a strange symmetrical pattern" (Cohn, p. 71). At Shrewsbury the disposition of forces is similarly symmetrical, and the prince explicitly sees himself in a cosmic collision with Hotspur since "Two stars keep not their motion in one sphere" (5.4.65). Hal's image dramatizes the completeness of the annihilation threatened by his symmetry with Percy. It is important to keep in mind that "gallant" Percy represents not merely defiance but personalized death to prince, king, and kingdom alike. He would not simply eliminate Hal; he would take his place.

Let me consider the dynamics of the apocalyptic fantasy more closely:

As in the eschatological Messiah, so in the eschatological Enemy, Antichrist, the images of the son and the father are fused—only here of course the images are those of the bad son and the bad father. . . . In his relation to God the Father Antichrist appears as a defiant and rebellious child . . . even daring to usurp the father's place and ape his authority. In his relation to human beings, on the other hand, Antichrist is a father scarcely to be distinguished from Satan himself: a protecting father to his devilish brood, but to the Saints an atrocious father . . . a cunning tyrant who when crossed becomes a cruel and murderous persecutor.

[Cohn, p. 71]

Not to be distracted, we need to focus on the dynamics of the roles in the fantasy. Toward his surrogate fathers, Glendower (who can reckon up "the several devils' names / That were his lackeys" [3.1.155–56]), the treacherous Worcester, and the king, Hotspur is of course compulsively rebellious.[20] Toward ordinary human beings, however, he can act the "atrocious father." At least in Hal's fantasy Percy is a cannibalistic ogre who "kills me some six or seven dozen of Scots at a breakfast, washes his hands, and says to his wife, 'Fie upon this quiet life! I want work'" (2.4.102–5). For his part, the prince is both obedient son and, at Shrewsbury, the powerful symbolic father who personally saves the king. As king (witness his disguised debate with Williams on the night before Agincourt), Hal self-consciously defines himself as the burdened father to his people.

As in the apocalyptic fantasy, where Antichrist acts out rebellion that would be unthinkable in the militantly idealized Christ, so in the *Henriad*, as Ernst Kris and others have noticed, Hotspur plays out the defiant aggression that Hal repudiates in himself.[21] What's more, the destruction of the evil alter ego leads not merely to renewed obedience but to a glorious apotheosis. After all, Hal's atonement speech foresees not meek submission to his father but superhuman or, if need be, suicidal heroism. And the magnitude of the prince's struggle against the rebel in himself can be seen in the shocking meaning latent in the king's equation of the hundred thousand deaths Hal vows to die with the deaths of "a hundred thousand rebels" (160). The king's equation can be taken to express a complex psychological state in which he tacitly and yet unconsciously acknowledges that in choosing fidelity to the Crown, Hal is choosing to destroy the rebel in himself.

The tremendous attraction and horror of rebellion may be measured in the price of its atonement, the sacrifice of a hundred thousand other people. In 1600 Thomas Wilson estimated the total population of nobles, bishops, knights, esquires, and yeomen—that is anyone who was anyone in England—to number only a hundred thousand (Bridenbaugh, p. 16). This context helps to suggest the intensity of the psychic violence at the heart of the *Henriad*. Even in this relatively early speech we can make out motivation that is plausible for the Henry V who will later strive to subdue France. At the same time we can see that the psychic conflicts in Hal's speech relate it, however indirectly, to the fantasies of William Neville, the literal-mindedly messianic William Hacket, and the horned angel Richard III. In each instance prophetic behavior would mediate between irreconcilable visions of the self and its destiny.

In *2 Henry IV* the prince once again has to justify himself to his father. Imagining that his son has "taken away" his crown (4.5.88), the dying king utters a long harrowing prophecy that projects a shameful character for the future Henry V (119–37). The prince in turn appeals to a benevolent future in order to overcome his father's ominous forecast. "If I do feign, / O, let me in my present wildness die," he prays, and "Let God for ever keep the crown from my head" (151–52, 174). Hal pledges himself by invoking a competing future, but without resorting to self-aggrandizing prophecy. The moment might be seen to replay the confrontation between Henry VI and Richard insofar as it presents a failing king who attempts to control a would-be successor through prophecy, fearing death at his hands (Hal's trial of the Crown, his father complains, "helps to end me" [64]). In Hal's hands the crown is an object, momentarily demystified and impotent. Sensing kingship in jeopardy, both rulers fantasize about humankind as wolves. Left alone with Richard by the lieutenant, Henry VI sighs, "So flies the reakless shepherd from the wolf; / So first the harmless sheep doth yield his fleece, / And next his throat unto the butcher's knife" (*3H6* 5.6.7–9). Under Henry V, Bolingbroke foresees the butchery of civil war in an England "peopled / with wolves" (*2H4* 4.5.137). Where Henry VI recoils from the Richard who "cam[e] to bite the world" (*3H6* 5.6.54), Bolingbroke dreads that "the wild dog / Shall flesh his tooth on every innocent" (131–32). But where Richard mockingly justifies his assassination as "ordain'd," all the while ignorantly subsumed in a larger prophetic pattern that dooms him, Hal conspicuously submits to God's future.

Humbled before his father, Hal deflects Henry's horror of devouring aggression from himself to the crown. Not a usurper but the crown itself and therefore all who live through the king have "fed upon the body of [his] father" (159). In effect, Hal recreates the king's own image of wolfish cannibalism as the urge underlying all human striving for power and survival. As in the Mass, he implies, where sacrifice of Christ's body promises immortal life, the metonymic crown "hast eat thy bearer up" (164). In construing his father's approaching death as a willed dispensation of self, a martyr's sacrifice, Hal's words make it possible for the king to bestow a "father's love" on him (179) without dread. Symbolically, that is, Hal corroborates the old man's immortality in the living crown and in his obedient son, freeing him to die in peace.

Reconciled with his son, the king fulfills Hal's pledge from Part 1 to "redeem the time" even as he discovers the mysterious fulfillment of his own prediction that he will die "in Jerusalem" (235). The emotional logic of the scene argues that, in part, it is the reconciliation with Hal—to be exact, the recognition of his true nature—that enables the king to discover "Jerusalem." Ironically, like the intuitions that presumably give rise to prophetic conviction in the first place, this Jerusalem turns out to have been at hand all along: a room, as it were, in his own mind. As in a riddle, the revelation comes to the king in a flash of insight, orderly and yet beyond any ordinary problem-solving strategies.

While ironies radically complicate the significance of this Jerusalem, for contemporary audiences the pattern of atonement, death, and triumphal revelation must have had a powerful appeal to their deepest hopes and fears: an appeal that ironies may have qualified or displaced in the minds of spectators, yet probably never merely dispelled. For one thing, the return to Jerusalem is one of the original themes of Judeo-Christian eschatology and, in the tradition that comes down from St. Augustine, an inward process in which humankind, attaining the heavenly city, restores its relation with God and therein achieves wholeness. As Augustine says in the *Confessions* about the pilgrimage through life: "I shall not turn away but shall come to the peace of that Jerusalem, my dear mother, . . . and there Thou shalt collect from my present scatteredness and deformity all that I am."[22] In this vision Jerusalem offers a release from the nightmarish struggle for apotheosis. Instead of wolfish rebellion—and the king himself first conceived his "voyage to the Holy Land, / To wash [King Richard's] blood off from my guilty hand" (*R2* 5.6.49–50)—Jerusalem offers incorporation into God the almighty father. Instead of "scattered" self ("God knows," Henry laments, "By what bypaths and indirect crook'd ways / I met this crown" [*2H4* 4.5.183–85]), the vision promises wholeness. Augustine's vision answers as well to the "deformity" of the insatiably rebellious Richard III, whose violent alienation and birth with teeth cry out for the Jerusalem that is his "dear mother." Not by chance, I suspect, the play invokes Jerusalem just as Shakespeare needs to dramatize the prince's final integration (in Parts One and Two at least) of his own scattered being. No longer torn between Eastcheap and

Windsor, Hal prepares himself to maintain the crown "'Gainst all the world" (224). In effect, the play fetishizes the eschatological city in a room just offstage, as immediate yet separate as the sanctuary in a church. "It hath been prophesied to me many years, / I should not die but in Jerusalem," the king concludes. Then, with an autonomy corroborated by the uncanny prediction, and a control that for all concerned strongly counters the dread his death must incite, he has himself borne to the adjacent chamber and prophesies: "In that Jerusalem shall Harry die" (236–37, 240). In this way Shakespeare prepares the stage and the cosmos for the ascension of Henry V.

Subsequently Hal "adopts" the chief justice—the English law—as his father, defining himself anew and making good his original forecast in Part One. "With my father's spirits," the new king declares, "I survive / To mock the expectation of the world, / To frustrate prophecies, and to raze out / Rotten opinion" (5.2.125–28). Having "falsified men's hopes," he can now exceed or even transcend them by revealing his true nature.[23] Thus astonished, others' imaginations may sense the authority of apotheosis in the king, and, as he says, "Presume not that I am the thing I was" (5.5.56).[24]

Prophetic behavior, then, can be understood as a means by which Shakespeare tries to validate Hal's heroic stature for us. It is a sign of majesty to be at times intuitively clairvoyant. At Shrewsbury in Part One, for instance, Hotspur's fatalism suggests a gambler's desperation as he urges his comrades on to ill-considered combat: "heaven to earth, some of us never shall / A second time do such a courtesy" (5.2.99–100). By contrast, Shakespeare endows Hal with a composed prescience. After the battle the prince addresses the deceptively slain Falstaff "precisely as if he knew he were faking death."[25] In his eulogy he ambiguously foretells Falstaff's resurrection, undercutting any show of grief that would allow Falstaff to leap up later and boast of Hal's love for him. In its eerie way his speech is as equivocal as Hastings' pronouncement of his own death in *Richard III*, although it confirms rather than confutes Hal: "I should have a heavy miss of thee / If I were much in love with vanity! Death hath not strook so fat a deer today" (5.4.105–7). Were Falstaff truly fallen, the prince's mockery would be heartless. Implicitly his speech sees through death even as Hal would see through the present time in order to redeem it. His farewell—"Embowell'd will I see thee by and by" (109)—predicts Falstaff's actual embalmed demise even as it foresees him in the near future comically stuffed with food (Embowelled: "that has the bowels full" [*OED* 3]).

If it were necessary, we could locate the same prophetic pattern that corroborates the prince in the career of Henry V. As one critic has noticed, "Using the rising sun image of the 'I know you all' speech Henry declares: 'I will rise there with so full a glory / That I will dazzle all the eyes of France'" (*H5* 1.2.278–79). The king literally predicts a blinding apotheosis. Moreover, "From this perspective Agincourt is the climax of the plan announced so long before, whereby the sun-king will shine more brightly for the contrast of the 'base contagious clouds' which hid it, and 'My reformation . . . / Shall show more goodly and attract more eyes / Than that which hath no foil to set it off' (*1H4* 1.2.213–15). Henry knows all along what he is doing. The glory he looks for in France he wants partly in order to fulfill his own prophecy of a glorious career, partly to cure the insecurity of his title and his psyche."[26] At the moment of fulfillment the conqueror projects his glory still further ahead to Doomsday, prophesying that Agincourt will be remembered forever:

> This story shall the good man teach his son;
> And Crispin Crispian shall ne'er go by,
> From this day to the ending of the world,
> But we in it shall be remembered.
>
> [4.3.49–59]

III

If Hal "knows all along what he is doing," as in the above assessment, then his prophetic behavior stands demystified as so much strategy. The alternative is to credit him with some sort of extrarational inspiration—perhaps sentimentally abetted by his creator. One assumption tends to produce a more or less Machiavellian prince operating in ironical and conditional history. The other leads to a providential prince.[27]

In the histories, says Professor Rossiter bluntly, Shakespeare "always leaves us with relatives, ambiguities, irony, a process thoroughly dialectical" (p. 22). In *Richard III*, for example, the "'Christian' system of retribution is undermined, counter-balanced, by historic irony" (p. 22). Margaret's prophetic curses appear to be efficacious, enacting a providential judgment. Yet Professor Rossiter rightly calls attention to "the repulsiveness, humanely speaking, of the 'justice.' God's will it may be, but it sickens us: it is as pitiless as the Devil's" (p. 20), more cruelly pagan than Christian.

For the plays to be "thoroughly dialectical" they have to be capable of generating internal critiques of their own substance. And so they do.[28] In *2 Henry IV*, say, Warwick deflates the prophecy of Northumberland's treachery, which threatens to demoralize the king. By observing an individual's history, he maintains, one may "prophesy, / With a near aim, of the main chance of things / As yet not come to life" (3.1.80–84). In fact, Warwick describes a faculty the dramatist himself might use to develop a given dramatic situation into a play.

Warwick's homely naturalism invites us to understand prophecy as a function of character, while making any providential significance seems incalculable if not purely fantastic. Prescience then becomes a gambler's calculation based on study and chance. A more sophisticated view might add to chance the equally extrarational contribution of intuition or inspiration—in a word, the unconscious. C. L. Barber would see Warwick's and the king's views in terms of an opposition between magical and empirical views of man. The distinction is a reasonable one but not, I think, without some crucial limitations.

At the close of *2 Henry IV* C. L. Barber perceives Shakespeare awkwardly trying to protect the dying king and ascendant Hal from our doubts and dissatisfaction. He scoffs at Henry's opportunistic use of a room named "Jerusalem" to aggrandize his death.

> One can imagine making a mockery of Henry's pious ejaculation about Jerusalem by catcalling a version of his final lines at the close of *Richard II*:
>
> Is this the voyage to the Holy Land
> To wash the blood from off your guilty hand?
>
> An inhibition of irony goes here with Henry's making the symbol do for the thing, just as it does with Hal's expulsion of Falstaff. A return to an official view of the sanctity of state is achieved by sentimental use of magical relations.

Barber has caught the king using the verbal coincidence "Jerusalem" to fetishize the props for his dying scene. Shakespeare, he points out, sentimentally fails to marshall a critique of the occult resonance attributed to "Jerusalem." Barber then offers his well-known distinction between drama and ritual: "the drama must control magic by reunderstanding it as imagination: dramatic irony must constantly dog the wish that the mock king be real, that the self be all the world or set all the world at naught. When, through a failure of irony, the dramatist presents ritual as magically valid, the result is sentimental, since drama lacks the kind of control which in ritual comes from the auditors' being participants." Then, wisely, comes the acknowledgment that although "the Renaissance moment made the tension between a magical and empirical view of man particularly acute, this pull is of course always present; it is the tension between the heart and the world."[29]

Sensible as it is, this formulation of a "tension between the heart and the world" has something diplomatic or even sentimental about it. To make the heart stand for the irrationality at the center of human life is to do as Henry does, "making the symbol do for the thing." Moreover, this particular symbol complacently gives the irrational a rosy glow. At the same time the idea of a "tension" too conveniently divides experience into objective and subjective spheres, either of which might be pure: whereas in truth, as the critic's own use of "heart" itself inadvertently demonstrates, our experience virtually never escapes some measure of subjectivity or "heart."

These reservations become important insofar as categories such as the heart and world keep us from recognizing the insoluble contradictions at the center of human life that the histories manage to dramatize. For the plays are not simply about government or English society as such. Rather they reenact over and over again the creation and destruction of kings and the life-giving power of the Crown. As epitomized in Crookback's career, dread of death and nullity incites a wolfish rage to consume the lives of others in a fantastic struggle for symbolic immortality. To preserve itself, society mounts a compensatory drive to create a hero in whose apotheosis everyone can vicariously share. Divine sanction and dynastic control over the future become signs of the group's power of survival. Whenever that conviction of immortality fails, as it does to some extent in each of the histories, the result is rebellion. And since the ensuing contest unconsciously plays out nothing less than a struggle for being itself, the outcome virtually always means death to the loser, for that death revitalizes the life-giving glory of the crown the victor holds. As Prince John tellingly sums up his defeat of the rebels in *2 Henry IV*, "God, and not we, hath safely fought today. / Some guard [these traitors] to the block of death" (4.2.121–22). The victors covertly aggrandize themselves by attributing their (treacherous) actions to God and thereby justifying the pitiless slaughter of their opponents, including the innocently disbanded common soldiers. It would not be inaccurate to say that in imagination, apart from any conscious trickery, the winners at once identify with, and dissociate themselves from, a violent God.

Like the histories as a group, the scene at Gaultree Forest combines two incompatible perspectives. We may behold a fairly straightforward political action, a drama of state, yet we can also see through the imagery of the scene to an unconscious struggle for apotheosis. To make that symbolic immortality efficacious, culture disguises or denies the reality of death as the play itself manifestly does. In turn, to some extent inevitably, culture can scarcely help but be—as Professor Barber might say—sentimental. Nor should this surprise us. After all, since identity is a symbolic process and potentially limitless, not to say perfectible, we commonly understand ourselves to be godlike as well as the quintessence of dust. We realize that we must die and nonetheless go about our daily business as if we expect to live forever. In subtly compulsive ways we invest ourselves in ideologies, leaders, and objects from art to houses that promise to infuse us with power and permanence. In our own political culture, as in Shakespeare's, we observe painstaking decorum and yet scarcely blink to hear competition for power couched in images of annihilation and apotheosis.[30]

Prophecy calls attention to this insoluble doubleness in human experience, for it may signify a godlike control over time by making the future obedient to the secure past, or it may be a merely natural process of guesswork, even a form of escapism. In a prophetic context the hero's role is usually messianic, and figures such as Richmond and Henry V reflect the same doubleness in their tendency to appear to audiences either as providential agents or as Machiavellian connivers. Similarly, Crookback may strike us as a virtuosic study of Machiavellian psychology, or we may fix on him as a type of the Vice or devil, an antimessiah.

Rather than argue that one of these extremes—or some nice combination of extremes—is the absolute truth about the plays, I would emphasize that Shakespeare exploited the ambiguities of his medium to create a radically comprehensive play-world. While his vision of history is aggressively empirical and ironical, it also honors irrational depths of experience. Given our own historical situation, we are disposed to appreciate the way prophecy and prophetic dreams may dramatize the unconscious forces shaping experience. As critics we readily applaud the plays' demystification of historical process. It is less easy for us to evaluate the plays' ambiguous embrace of magical styles of imagination, and to appreciate that demystification can never be complete. In our criticism we are tempted to schematize irrational behavior in systems of belief such as "The King's Two Bodies," which can be sound as critical concepts and yet not adequate to the mentality implied in a complex art such as Shakespeare's.[31]

In part our difficulty in understanding a problem such as prophetic behavior in the plays is that we ourselves are insolubly equivocal about time. We may experience the past as if, as memory, it is still alive somewhere in the back of our minds. As intuition, the future too may feel alive to us already, as it does to a prophet.[32] Extrarationally and ambiguously, in the midst of our common sense, that is, we may maintain a mode of imagination that enhances our illusion of control over time and minimizes—even denies—time's irreversible fatality. Although in the world around us ideologies threaten to fight to the death over competing eschatological claims, we tend to protect our own eschatological assumptions and consolations from rational challenge.[33] Ultimately we cannot imagine an end to existence or existence without an end.

However different, Shakespeare and his culture were probably no less complex and paradoxical in imagination than we are. Contemporary Christianity, for example, cultivated imaginative forms that embraced humankind's doubleness by meditating on a central figure who is at once person and God, child and father, lamb and shepherd, victim and conqueror, supplicant and king, an alien and yet a presence in all believers. And Christianity is perhaps only the most forthright of examples. In the histories Shakespeare appears to be expanding the imagination of his time, encouraging his audiences to face more openly the immensity and contingency of history. I like to think that the plays serve to demystify history, and therefore represent a healthy assertion of consciousness over intractable and dangerous materials. But I am aware that in Shakespeare as in our own lives there are also strong elements of escapism and self-deception that we need to respect. We should not be surprised that "in tone and sentiments" the benediction and "Amen" at the close of *Henry V* recall "Richmond's final speech in *Richard III*, which also concludes 'God say Amen' and casts a prophetic glow over the coming of the Tudor dynasty." Neither should we be astonished when Professor Prior goes on to insist that as history, "the happy optimism of the ending [of *Henry V*] is totally unfounded."[34]

Historically, then, Shakespeare's use of prophetic behavior seems to represent a new effort to honor the complexities of experience by dramatizing the dreamlike depths of imagination. Just as Richard III, the angel with horns, plays out a fantasy about omnipotence and revenge against life that resembles in some ways the furious apotheosis imagined by a self-anointed Messiah in the streets of Elizabethan London, so Hal's prophetic destiny evokes—discreetly, even subliminally—the messianic provenance of the English Crown.

Chapter 10

Play-Death and Individuation

Prophetic behavior employs the dynamics of play-death to displace the self into a glorious future. At the far reaches of imagination, in apocalyptic schemes, all individual identity dissolves into the cosmic father. As *Venus and Adonis* and *Romeo and Juliet* illustrate, the wish to merge with a cosmic parent represents an escape from the burdens of individuality—from isolation and guilt and personal vulnerability. Yet the prospect of self-loss may also be self-aggrandizing if the anticipated merger arouses convictions of being chosen or even godlike. The self may have its uniqueness confirmed as it contemplates its dissolution. Given this paradox, *Venus and Adonis* (or *Romeo and Juliet*) shares some of the deepest concerns of the apocalyptic histories.

In this chapter I use a psychoanalytic lens to examine the dialectic of individuation and merger in some early and late plays. My aim is to show how play-death dramatizes the formation of identity and a premodern conception of individual growth, and I close the chapter by considering the extent to which Prospero's farewell dramatizes an individual's effort to take responsibility for his own death.

Let me begin on a happier note, with love's promise of immortality through union, as in Titania's pledge to Bottom: "I will purge thy mortal grossness so, / That thou shalt like an aery spirit go" (*MND* 3.1.160–61). Although it usually escapes audiences, the Fairy Queen personifies everlasting life: "The summer still doth tend upon my state" (155). Put another way, she is a wishful solution to the problem of death. One source of that solution is the neoplatonic commonplace that lovers die for their beloveds, "to be eftsoones reuiued in them" (*Monophylo* [1572], in Meader, p. 123). Ficino, who devised much of the doctrine, anxiously insisted on love's spirituality. Yet for him love begins to resemble life in death: "the lover takes possession of himself through another, and the farther each of the lovers is from himself, the nearer he is to the other. In fact, there is only one death in mutual love, but there are two resurrections."[1]

Ficino's notion of reciprocity in love associates merger and apotheosis. Lovers submerge their separate identities in each other. "Since love aspires to deification, each of the lovers is yearning for oneness with the supreme beauty that will thereby destroy their present humanity. . . . Though each lover is lost in the other, each also lives in the beloved. By mutually possessing one another, they regain themselves as well as the other and consequently undergo what Ficino calls a . . . double resurrection since each of the lovers is reborn with two selves, the beloved's as well as the lover's own self."[2]

In neoplatonic fantasy death is actually psychic dissociation: self-forgetfulness that minimizes any awareness of real death at a time of great vulnerability, when the self is apt to be most unrepressed and overawed by the beloved. Dissociation protects the self from realizing its frailty and insignificance. Likewise it protects love from comparisons that might diminish it, placing it outside conventional categories. A "dying" lover cannot evaluate the experience: cannot judge it to be habitual or trivial. Yet the avoidance of judgment may lead to self-delusion, since the experience then becomes "ineffable" or even "infinite."

Shakespeare registers all of these tensions in the Sonnets and plays. For every rapturous voice that translates neoplatonic love into imagery of angels, stars, or flowers in Paphos, there are at least as many that mock love's pretensions to transcendence, as in the giddy infatuations of *Love's Labor's Lost* or Benedick's wry vow to Beatrice: "I will live in thy heart, die in thy lap, and be buried in thy eyes; and moreover, I will go with thee to thy uncle's" (MAAN 5.2.102–4). And yet no mockery completely negates the underlying wish for life. Titania's offer to etherealize Bottom is poignant as well as ludicrous. When the immortalizing process fails, for whatever reason, the imagery may turn hellish, as in the sexual nausea of King Lear and the Sonnets that equates love with the "sulphurous pit" of the vagina (*KL* 4.6.126–29; Sonnet 144). The underlying association is that a lover "dies" into the beloved's corrupt body in hopes of rising again. Much can and has been said about the misogynistic nature of this imagery. I want only to point out that such fantasies are, among other things, means of controlling the dread of death. The menace is not merely woman, the scapegoat, but the mortality that she exposes.

By association, woman as mother contains paradise or hell. Erik Erikson postulates a "universal nostalgia for a paradise forfeited" that emerges as individuation separates the child from the mother.[3] In Shakespeare that nostalgia seems to show itself as mourning, a connection I will develop shortly. In the meantime let me turn attention to the first ground of sexual union, the infant's intimacy with the mother. To some extent ambivalence toward sexuality is the natural outcome of the lifelong, problematical process of individuation:

> [C]rises in the process of separation can engender the wish to rein-
> habit the symbiotic unity of infant and mother; crises within the envi-
> ronment provided by the mother, including those that provoke fears of
> "reengulfment," can lead to the defiant repudiation of essential others
> and to fantasies of a powerful autonomous self that magically incorpo-
> rates symbiotic omnipotence. Neither the longing for fusion nor the
> longing for omnipotent autonomy can be integrated fully into the con-
> tingencies of living, and the separation-individuation process . . . is
> never complete."[4]

As an object of ecstatic union woman is associated with paradise; as an object of fear, threatening the child's autonomy, she is a demonic lair. As an escape from death as engulfing as death itself, she is an ambivalent force like the patriarch.

Fantasies of play-death may attempt to mediate that contradiction insofar as self-effacement permits a merger that holds out the promise of eventual independence. Alternatively, fantasy may promise that a parental figure who is lost or even destroyed will in time be resurrected. *The Winter's Tale* shows that the wish for union with a mother figure can be repudiated and idealized in the same theatrical event.

The same sorts of conflicts shape intrapsychic development as well. In the Oedipal stage, Freud maintained, the child's self-image turns negative and the child compensates by creating an ego-ideal that becomes

> the target of the self-love which was enjoyed in childhood by the actual
> ego. The subject's narcissism makes its appearance displaced onto this
> new ideal ego, which like the infantile ego, finds itself possessed of

every perfection that is of value. As always, where the libido is concerned, man has here again shown himself incapable of giving up a satisfaction he has once enjoyed. He is not willing to forego the narcissistic perfection of his childhood; and when, as he grows up, he is disturbed by the admonitions of others and by the awakening of his own
critical judgment, so that he can no longer retain that perfection, he
seeks to recover it in this new form of an ego ideal. What he projects
before him as his ideal is the substitute for the lost narcissism of his
childhood in which he was his own ideal.[5]

The conditions that bring about the ego's fall from perfection (social
admonitions and awakening judgment) also contribute to an emergent
awareness of death. In Freud's description the ego rescues itself from
its fall by projecting an "ego ideal." Call that ego-ideal an idealized
alter ego, and what emerges is a rudimentary fantasy of play-death and
deliverance. Ultimately the drive to magnify the self moves toward
apotheosis. If the individual tries to embody the ego-ideal in an actual
person, the effort is likely to produce heroic striving or, vicariously,
hero worship.

Melanie Klein's theory of early childhood development can be used
to make clearer the psychoanalytic connection between play-death and
the stresses of individuation. Though she relies upon some especially
murky and melodramatic concepts, a death instinct among them,
Klein finds the fear of annihilation elemental in the infant's experience
and a cause of persecutory anxiety as well as defensive aggression. As
the infant's relation to his mother develops, privations inevitably dis-
turb the balance between libidinal and aggressive impulses, reinforcing
aggression and giving rise to "the emotion called greed. . . . Any increase in greed strengthens feelings of frustration and in turn the aggressive impulses."[6] A greedy rage for life is amply evident in many of
Shakespeare's characters, from the infant Richard III, born with appalling teeth, to the passionately starved Leontes, who calls his wife's
rebirth a pleasure "lawful as eating" (*WT* 5.3.111). Where Richard dramatizes fixated cannibalistic impulses, Leontes is able to sublimate.

In the early "paranoid-schizoid" phase of development, the infant
would destroy all that frustrates him. Later, in the "depressive position," he feels guilt and in turn love, by which he would restore or
repair the loss that he fears his aggression has caused. Klein's formulation suggests the symbolism of play-death: "When the infant feels that

his destructive impulses and phantasies are directed against the complete person of his loved object, guilt arises in full strength and, together with it, the overriding urge to repair, preserve or revive the loved injured object. These emotions in my view amount to states of mourning, and the defences operating to attempts on the part of the ego to overcome mourning" (Klein, 1:340).

As in the archetypal pattern I described in Chapters 5 and 6, the child acts to undo mourning. What has been lost he would recreate. "The reparative tendency . . . first employed in an omnipotent way, becomes an important defence [against anxiety]. The infant's feelings (phantasy) might be described as follows: 'My mother is disappearing, she may never return, she is suffering, she is dead. No, this can't be, for I can revive her'" (Klein, 3:75). This is the emotional core of scenarios of play-death as rescue such as *Twelfth Night* and *The Winter's Tale*, where recuperation and forgiveness are almost voluptuously rewarded. Yet reparation itself follows the dynamics of play-death insofar as the anxiety and mourning of the depressive position disintegrate the child's ego and precipitate omnipotent fantasy solutions comparable to apotheosis in adult imagination.[7]

In later stages of development the capacity for reparation increases: "its range widens and sublimations gain in strength and stability; for on the genital level they are bound up with the most creative urge of man. Genital sublimations in the female position are linked with fertility—the power to give life—and thus also with the re-creation of lost or injured objects. In the male position, the element of life-giving is reinforced by the phantasies of fertilizing and thus restoring or reviving the injured or destroyed mother," (Klein, 3:82). As she dies playing a nursing mother, Cleopatra conjures up the Antony she has effectively killed. By falling in love, *Twelfth Night* implies, Viola and Olivia prepare for the restoration of lost siblings and parents.

Klein's formulation also helps to explain patriarchal fantasies in which generativity compensates for sadistic dominance, and exceptional reverence for marriage compensates society for the enforcement of order at swordpoint. Analogously, in the latently incestuous relationships of the late romances, for example, a father may reconceive his wife in a compliant daughter in order to circumvent dangerous impulses aroused by the wife's intimidating maternal associations. Revived by affectionate daughters, for example, Pericles and Leontes promptly recover their lost wives. Reparative eros, not just penitence, releases the women into life once more.

II

Let me turn now to the process of individuation in an early comedy, *A Midsummer Night's Dream*, in which many themes of this book come together. In the playlet of Pyramus and Thisbe two lovers grope toward a union that is frustrated by parental repression represented as a wall. As everyone knows, the hapless pair parody not only the quartet of lovers in the dominant plot but also Romeo and Juliet. My intention is to read the lovers' hysterical suicides as play-deaths that reflect the patriarchal system of immortality we have encountered in Verona and also play out some important assumptions about individual development.

As I see it, the quarrel between the Fairy King and Queen implies a feud akin to Verona's insofar as Oberon is as resentful of Theseus as the duke, were he to learn that Hippolyta has been Oberon's "buskin'd mistress, and . . . warrior love," would be roused against him (*MND* 2.1.68–76). The male child of the couple, the "changeling" boy, is caught between Titania's wish to feminize him and patriarchal demands that he become a knight (2.1.24–27). The child himself has no voice in the play, unless we take the situation in the playlet to reflect the larger familial strife, and regard Pyramus as a comic projection of the conflicted son. As in Verona, this son has defied paternal prohibitions by identifying with an enemy's daughter. In his reaction to the lion, Pyramus even echoes Romeo's repudiation of the warrior ethos and identification with the beloved, as his suicide at "Ninny's tomb" parodies Romeo's.

What divides Pyramus and Thisbe is a wall who is on stage a man like the obstructive fathers. He stands for the repressive cultural boundaries that define identity in terms of possession and valuation. What's more, the wall reproduces the dynamics of patriarchal conflict in the young lovers. When Pyramus calls for a kiss, his beloved kisses "the wall's hole" (5.1.201) as her "cherry lips have often kiss'd [the wall's] stones, / . . . stones with lime and hair knit up" (190–91). The obscene joke insinuates the daughter's submissive love for the father: she kisses his arse and also the symbols of his potency, stones/testicles. Thisbe inadvertently confesses the sort of incestuous dependency or failure of individuation that causes panic in Prince Pericles: "I kiss the wall's hole, not your lips at all" (201). This "confession" immediately elicits from Pyramus an ambivalent impulse to defy the wall yet be united "at Ninny's tomb" (202), a patriarchal monument akin to the

Capulets'. Instantly Thisbe answers, "'Tide life, 'tide death, I come" (203).

What follows is consistent: Pyramus interprets Thisbe's bloody mantle as a sign of patriarchal aggression "lion vild hath here deflower'd my dear" [292]: at once the punishment of a disobedient child and a rape such as Romeo envisions the "lean abhorred monster" (5.3.104) committing on Juliet. Supplanted by the father, Pyramus punishes—and heroically inflates—his rebellion by stabbing himself. Thisbe follows suit. The expiatory quality of the play-deaths is evident in the lovers' appeals to the heavens for pity that could placate introjected parental rage.

The playlet burlesques the hysteria of children unable to achieve individuation. Walled in by parental will, they appear to seek autonomy while in fact only substituting one form of dependency for another. Panicked by apparent betrayal, they sacrifice themselves at the tomb of paternal authority, their trite voices witnessing their incompleteness. The dramatist does not merely scapegoat the parents. As in Verona, the patriarchs are actually less formidable than they advertise. Aggression—the fathers' rage and the children's own unconscious anger—blunders onstage as an apologetic lion. Like Falstaff, the weak surrogate father who steals his "son's" glory after Hal slays his alter ego Hotspur, patriarchy in the playlet is itself still full of childish needs. The king of beasts worries about intimidating the ladies. The wall is a clumsy illusion that presents inhibitions which (through the chink) actually channel and intensify the lovers' desire. By its satire the playlet would purge the anxieties that paralyze the children.

To account for the lovers' collapse it helps to recall that the wall enacts not only patriarchal will but also the obstructive and fatal human body. Spirits would kiss, yet "the wall's hole" intervenes, symbol of humankind's shameful animal nature, the orifice through which the digested dead bodies that nourish life are expelled as foul waste. This aspect of the wall is akin to the devouring monument that Romeo associates with overwhelming parents. Paradoxically the hole itself is physical and yet a form of nothingness, ephemeral as mortal identity itself. Trying to unite, the lovers discover their dependency on the body. The impulse to love exposes the essential nothingness of the self and the cultural structures that the wall enacts: the repressive "laws" that define possession and value and identity. Not only can patriarchy not insure immortality, it may embody death. Thisbe's empty mantle likewise suggests the beloved's nothingness: a cultural scrap remains after the vital personality has vanished. The lovers panic, then regress to guilty mourning (the tomb) and suicidal merger with "fate."

The wall recapitulates ambivalence toward the body which is crucial in the play. Oberon sends a comically degraded alter ego with an ass's head and a scatological name to humiliate his insubordinate wife.[8] But Bottom's bestiality is also innocent. He revels in physical pleasure, from caresses to good dry oats, and his dalliance with the Fairy Queen is a merger with an adoring and infinitely gratifying mother. In the playlet Bottom is once again changed into a lover—Pyramus—and thwarted by patriarchal hostility this time actually figured as the king of beasts. As the image confirms, the father subsumes the "animal" child.

Given this link, the supposed slayings excite the lovers' anxiety not only about the father's wrath but also about their own infantile rage at the "betrayal." This is aggression such as Klein describes, and Pyramus's suicide acts out the guilt that, barring successful reparation, Klein would predict. Bottom himself offers reparation when he steps out of role to offer a ceremonial Bergomask dance. By forgetting his role, Bottom unwittingly demonstrates the capacity for detachment that is the basis of maturity. His "resurrection" is a comic form of self-transcendence. By his sacrifice, the lowliest (bottom) fool justifies leveling authority ("the wall is down") and rises to meet the master face to face.

Earlier Bottom vowed to sing of his infantile love at Thisbe's death (4.1.219). His rapture with the Fairy Queen "shall be call'd 'Bottom's Dream,' because it hath no bottom" (215–16)—such ecstasy transcends mere ego (Bottom) and the mortal body (bottom). In the event that ecstatic song never materializes. At the crucial moment Bottom dies again as Pyramus, and the play-death is fulfilled in his resurrection as an actor. As the playlet's decorum collapses, so for the moment does cultural repression. The duke hastily frees "his" people to consummate love. In fact, love becomes a crucial spell that substitutes for the suddenly questionable spell of authority.

Almost at once the human lord himself yields the stage to the King of Shadows, whose name connotes lordship not only over players (= shadows) but also over the underworld and death. While Oberon takes care to distinguish the fairies from "damned spirits" that must "for aye consort with black-brow'd Night" (3.2.382–87), he commands "fog as black as Acheron" (357) and "death-counterfeiting sleep" (364) that transforms life into "a dream and fruitless vision" comparable to the eschatological sleep Prospero imagines rounding our little lives (371). He purges the lovers of their chaotic infantile infatuation and aggression by subjecting them to a feigned execution: "strike more dead / Than common sleep of all these five the sense" (81–82). Because the quarrel between the Fairy King and Queen has disrupted the harvest cycle, their reconciliation makes the play a restoration of symbolic immortality: a fitting rite for a king of shadows who "with the Morning's love [has] oft made sport" (389). These characteristics define Oberon as an equivocal lord of death and resurrection, a secular appropriation of Christian themes.

In the play as a whole, then, play-death is a means of engaging threats to identity while distancing them, controlling guilt through expiation. Each "passing out" represents an attempt both to engage and to leave behind implacable conflicts. In a sense the play itself performs a symbolic analysis of those conflicts. Each onlooker potentially collaborates in the analysis, but the process leads toward a dreamlike reformulation of the ground of identity rather than a new adjustment based on cumulative insight.

III

At the end of his career Shakespeare was still improvising on the same solutions to problems of individuation, although with a change in emphasis. In *Cymbeline* as in *Pyramus* young lovers are thwarted by weak patriarchy and suffer play-deaths that work to repair family bonds. As in the other romances, *Cymbeline* postulates an idealized queen-mother, a tutelary goddess like Titania, whose loss has brought psychic turmoil to her people. "[G]ood Euriphile, our mother" (4.2.234) is replaced by her daughter Imogen, who is resurrected from the mother's grave as "Fidele" (238), and by a nameless, poisonous stepmother, "the Queen." This maternal splitting allows the play to expose and contain otherwise inaccessible anxieties, but at the cost of scapegoating women and falsifying the prospect of autonomy.

At the core of the play's dilemma is the baffled patriarch Cymbeline. While he appears victimized by the malicious queen, her domination also protects his own dependency. Like the Lear who makes mothers of his daughters, Cymbeline is anxious about the waning vitality of old age. Like Lear's, his response is twofold. Even as he submits to a surrogate mother, he deviously attempts to dominate his "heavenly" daughter. "O disloyal thing, / That shouldst repair my youth," he snarls at Imogen, "thou heapst / A year's age on me" (1.2.131–33). When balked, he curses her with his deepest dread: "let her languish / A drop of blood a day, and being aged / Die of this folly!" (156–58).

Violently backing Cloten's designs on Imogen, Cymbeline acts through a projective agent. Cloten dramatizes the infantile rage for survival latent in an old man. Like a sinister Bottom (who also brags and loses his head in bestial obsession), he acts out a king's repressed infantile urges. Like Caliban, another symbolic stepson, he would dominate by rape. Guiderius and Belarius associate him with madness (4.2.135) and patriarchal tyranny driven by the needs of the mortal body. He is "an arrogant piece of flesh" who would "Play judge and executioner all himself" (127–28). Since daughter and stepmother are two faces of the same projective mother, Cloten is ambivalence personified and Cymbeline's ambivalence as well. Thwarted by the idealized daughter, he would kill her; in reparation he submits to her evil alter ego "the Queen."

At the same time Cloten is only one of four surrogate sons. In patriarchal and intrapsychic structure the sons enact aspects of the father and also one another. Cloten expresses the dark side of Posthumus.[9] Determined to rape Imogen in Posthumus's garments, Cloten becomes his surrogate, caricaturing his vaunting admiration of Imogen and his murderous rage against her. In the process he debases heroic values, substituting infantile bonds, as in his boast that rivals "dare not fight with me because of the Queen my mother" (2.1.18–19). As son of Jupiter and "under-hangman of his kingdom," Cloten would be not a self-sacrificing warrior-son but a privileged killer (2.3.125–31). In fact, a noble son slays this projected monster, and Imogen/Fidele rises almost literally out of his grave. The maternal ideal is reborn out of the sadistic infantile self.

Like the changeling stepson of Oberon and Titania, Posthumus is torn between the demigoddess Imogen and Cymbeline. Identification with either one produces ambivalence, and in the bargain alienates the other. Separated from Imogen by her father, Posthumus becomes obsessed with her fidelity. The dangerous anger he could be expected to feel against the king is covertly redirected at Imogen. An orphaned nobody might well feel resentful mistrust toward a mother-wife who has abandoned him under pressure from a rivalrous royal father, but those feelings are split off in Jachimo and Cloten. Forced into individuation yet beset by such conflicts, the son regresses.[10]

Just as the playlet *Pyramus* gives symbolic form to intrapsychic processes that motivate the Athenian lovers, so Jachimo's test of Imogen externalizes Posthumus's motivation. Both "playlets" are organized around play-deaths. Jachimo spies on Imogen asleep "as a monument, / Thus in a chapel lying" (*Cym.* 2.2.32–33). She is like Venus (14), in particular the fainting Venus who evokes Adonis's sadism and dependency. The voyeurism climaxes in access to her breast and a mole erotically charged as her nipple. "I kissed it," pants Jachimo to Posthumus, "and it gave me present hunger / To feed again, though full" (2.4.137–38). Such intoxicating desire could only lead to reabsorption into the mother—presumably, as in the fate of Adonis—through regression and death. The paradox of all-absorbing appetite, self-effacing yet inexhaustibly alive, is insolubly ambivalent.

The voyeur himself symbolically plays dead. Jachimo hides in the womblike (and tomblike) trunk in a parody of infantile fusion with the mother, and his rapture over eyes "lac'd / With blue of heaven's own tinct" (2.2.22–23) evokes the primal feeling Freud called oceanic. The mole on her breast becomes the lock that guards "the treasure of her honor" (42). The visual assault on Imogen mimics sexual intimacy, yet Jachimo's imagery "unconsciously cherishes the wish for oral fusion above all. . . . The speech is a polymorphous confusion of pregenital sexuality" (Schwartz, p. 229).

Jachimo's rapture is idolatry. He sees Imogen as the imperishable phoenix (1.6.17) and subjects her to a mock death (like the physician Cornelius) in order to make her a goddess. Yet he values her competitively, as the source of his rival's heroic immortality. In his eyes Posthumus "sits 'mongst men like a [descended] god; / He hath a kind of honor . . . / More than a mortal seeming" (1.6.169–71). Moved to seize that supremacy for himself, Jachimo would rape Imogen. Failing that, he would spoil her reputation—in Cassio's words, her immortal part (*O.* 2.3.262–63)—thereby destroying Posthumus and appropriating the exclusive idol for himself.

Like the sectarian fury of contemporary Europe, this fratricidal competition is in some measure a struggle over symbolic immortality. Posthumus and a Frenchman "fell in praise of [their] country mistresses; [Posthumus] vouching (and upon warrant of bloody affirmation) his to be more fair" (1.4.57–59). Even earlier in Orleance, Post-humus had been proselytizing for his heavenly beloved "with so mortal a purpose" (40). Such chauvinism and "arbitrement of swords" (49–50) could be a sally in a patriarchal feud, since praise of one mistress automatically devalues others. As in Romeo's Verona, feuding behavior allows males to dramatize their autonomy while in fact obeying cultural imperatives that block individuation. For while the wager with Jachimo sublimates violence, it produces grimly stereotyped behavior. The "articles" that regulate the wager (156) not only declare faith in "unprizable estimations" (90–91), they also register the value of the beloved in the eyes of competing males, and in the process witness how compulsively the group (ultimately the father) subsumes the individual.

If Jachimo embodies emotions denied in Posthumus, then the "spy" makes it possible for Posthumus to act out and make amends for infantile rage at the woman who guarantees his "more than . . . mortal" identity (1.6.171). Also he enables Posthumus to attack the paternal Cymbeline through an enemy army, then to assume the role of the dutiful warrior-son who will "fight against the part I come with" (5.1.25), subduing his anger (and his masculinity)[11] to prove himself through sacrifice. As Jachimo weakens, Posthumus and the other displaced sons become warrior-angels (5.3.85) saving the father. Entombed in prison, Posthumus is "reviv'd from death" as Imogen is (5.5.120), and reconciled with his royal family.

The resurrection of Imogen/Fidele brings a recuperation of heroic belief,[12] with Cymbeline's lost sons Guiderius and Arviragus replacing the purged Cloten and Jachimo. Burying Imogen, the "wild" sons reenact the interment of "good Euriphile, our mother," "Save that Euriphile must be Fidele" (4.2.234, 238). Recovery of the mother-ideal, safely diminished to "Fidele," drives out the devilish queen (1.5.16), releasing sons to support the frightened Cymbeline, and restoring his family.

Posthumus survives traumatic mourning to find conditional autonomy, as his name suggests, beyond death. In this respect he is like Pyramus/Bottom rising from doom into the festive embrace of the Athenian court. The analogy is evident in Jachimo's perverse relation to Imogen, which reflects the lovers' situation in *Pyramus*—even to spying through a hole in the patriarchal order. Like Pyramus, Jachimo imagines a beloved dead, praising her and (unconsciously) attacking her. In both plays the resulting panic, dissociated in Posthumus, climaxes in self-sacrifice and the gratuitous blessing of a supernatural father, Oberon/Jupiter.[13] In the main plot of *A Midsummer Night's Dream* there is a corresponding situation. Titania undergoes a death-like sleep while Oberon spies on her, and his agents Bottom and Puck celebrate and also mock maternal symbiosis. At once Oberon can dominate her and repent his supremacy.

In *Cymbeline* comic conventions such as mistaken identity imply a dramatist unsentimental about the enchantment of heroic belief. Even Imogen becomes ridiculous when her compulsive idealism takes the headless Cloten for her husband. Her inventory of his graces—"foot Mercurial . . . Martial thigh, / The brawns of Hercules"—comes to a ludicrous climax in the missing "Jovial face" (4.2.309–12). Not only does this catalog echo Jachimo's catalog of intimate proofs, reducing the beloved to a commodity,[14] it exposes wish-fulfilling incorporation into the maternal beloved as a faceless annihilation. Yet the moment is still more complex, for Imogen's misperception is unwittingly true. Unconsciously, we might say, she discovers the brutish, infantile Cloten in the idealized Posthumus and nevertheless grieves for him. The encounter is comparable to Titania's blind, all-accepting love for the ass Bottom. Both plays find pathos in a husband-son's release of infantile impulses whose dissociation permits maternal recognition and forgiveness followed in turn by reparation. Play-death acts out masculine desires for pity and clemency as well as aggression,[15] for drastic submission as well as patriarchal autonomy.

The Winter's Tale faces ambivalence about the mother-ideal more directly than *Cymbeline* or *A Midsummer Night's Dream*. Unlike the Fairy King, the Sicilian monarch is not conveniently split into a gracious supernatural patriarch and a child-Puck and mild Bottom who can act out his repressed urges. On the contrary, Leontes reacts to Hermione's apparent betrayal with paranoid rage. Like Bottom, Leontes' son Mamillius incarnates vital infantile aspects of his father (1.2.153–60). Although the maternal figure dotes on both surrogates, Mamillius perishes when she is persecuted, whereas Bottom is edifyingly mystified. Hence the mock death and primal mourning that Leontes must suffer.

Where Shakespeare protects Oberon and Cymbeline from our disenchantment, *The Winter's Tale* challenges its fantasies of omnipotence while preserving them in agencies such as the oracle, Great Creating

Nature, "Julio Romano," and *his* creators Paulina and Hermione. In none of these plays does the husband personally act to renew love. Oberon works on Titania through a magical messenger and an ass. Dramatic contrivance enables Cymbeline to postpone any confrontation of his feelings about women. Leontes comes to admit his "appetite" for maternal love, but formality inhibits his face-to-face recognition of the mortal individual Hermione. Dissociation—the permutations of play-death—keeps intimacy grounded in awe or magical control, submission or dominance: the dynamics of parent and child relations.

IV

The Tempest unfolds during Prospero's supposed death on an island that, like the wood in *A Midsummer Night's Dream*, dramatizes psychic dissociation. However, the liminal moment between play-death and apotheosis is expanded to fill the entire play. Prospero is simultaneously ghostly and godlike. Within this mock death, moreover, are others, including those the duke imposes on his enemies. The "direful spectacle of the wrack" (*Tem.* 1.2.26) is an instance of magical undoing that repeats his earlier abandonment to the sea, with Prospero this time the triumphant usurper. Earlier I remarked that in *A Midsummer Night's Dream* there is a latent feud between Theseus and Oberon. In *The Tempest* the duke of Milan is a sort of Oberon, exiled to the fairy wood, who contrives to regain authority in Athens by dispensing mock death. Titania is split into the absent, evil Sycorax and Prospero's absent, idealized duchess. This comparison suggests that even late in his career Shakespeare was drawn to visions of lordly omnipotence in which individuation requires the effacement of others, especially women. Were it not for his renunciation, Prospero would be as supernatural a creature as the Fairy King, a far cry from the cynosure of maturity he is sometimes made out to be.[16]

Prospero's renunciation is impressive because he seems to recognize the yawning grave (5.1.312) and yet respond with self-control and love. Unlike *Romeo and Juliet* or *Pyramus*, here the patriarch sacrifices himself rather than the children. Acknowledging his own sonship, he throws himself on the mercy of the cosmic father.[17] Having pardoned his enemies, he pleads that "my ending is despair, / Unless I be relieved by prayer" (Epi. 15–16). This collapse begs to be rationalized as triumphant self-mastery, if only because otherwise a sense of futility is apt to poison the hero's supreme moment and our collaboration in it.

But there is another basis for Prospero's sacrifice: it is a form of play-death and grounded in a promise of apotheosis. Not only does the virtuous duke appear to deserve eschatological promotion, he has been, and in subtle ways continues to be, a "god o' th' island" (1.2.390). As we shall see, his surrender is radically equivocal and open-ended. Like play-death elsewhere in the play, it combines aggression and reparation, persecution and rescue. Consider the latent ambivalence in his imagery. The prayer that can save him from despair "pierces so, that it assaults / Mercy itself, and frees all faults" (Epi. 17–18). Christ-like humility is also an "assault" on the Father that resembles the Redeemer-son's apocalyptic raid on the gates of hell: a sally that likewise "frees all faults." In the depths of association, safely attenuated, Prospero's plea evokes the split figure of the father as supreme master and abhorred monster in Romeo's imagination.

The Prospero who would assault Mercy through prayer echoes Caliban the would-be assassin and rapist, and not without symbolic logic, since he says of Caliban, "this thing of darkness I / Acknowledge mine" (5.1.275–76). In his psychic exile Prospero has undergone a clarifying dis-integration that recapitulates the process of individuation in childhood, in particular the discovery of the self and its mortality. With the expulsion of the witch-mother Sycorax the bestial child in Prospero is split off and subdued as Caliban, while his "tricksy spirit" provides a tamed form of magical omnipotence to help him achieve autonomy, and is then released toward offstage eternity. If Ariel enacts the infantile roots of magic, Caliban caricatures the son Prospero might have been had he not cultivated his art. Under his mother's spell the monstrous son thrived in ecstatic ignorance of death, whereas half-civilized by the father, "pinched" toward mortal awareness, the "slave" (1.2.328, 308) greedily tried to rape his way to immortality through Miranda, wishing to people all the island with versions of himself—a wish Prospero will fulfill through Ferdinand. For Ariel, by contrast, death is inherently moot.

If the monster and sprite are projections of the executive self, they also dramatize patriarchal relationships. Impatient for autonomy over "his" island, the unruly son Caliban would follow a drunken god (5.1.297) to parricide, although the would-be usurpers achieve only the burlesque immortality of pickling in horse-piss (282–84).[18] Freed from the witch-mother, reborn through the father, Ariel acts the obedient warrior-son by sinking an enemy vessel and routing the mutinous "brother" Caliban. From his tomblike cell the duke plays the all-seeing judge, the unmoved mover.

Like the ancient Roman paterfamilias, Prospero also functions as priest. Having acquired his art through shamanistic dissociation, he produces not only betrothal rites featuring goddesses and feasts, but also healing rituals. Like hysterical catharsis in the rites of many premodern societies, the trances he induces reorganize personality. As the tempest imposes its shock therapy on the visitors, he conducts a spellbound Miranda through a process of individuation, feeding her a life story (1.2.15–307). She is reborn out of him, as is the near-drowned Ferdinand, for whom the duke becomes "so rare a wonder'd father" (4.1.123). The lovers come together inside the magic circle of this all-encompassing parent.

But then, as Stephen Orgel has emphasized, Prospero never engages others as independent beings. Rather than struggle against the villains, for instance, he preempts them. Like Miranda's mother and the young lovers, "Antonio's is another of the play's identities that Prospero has incorporated into his own," for "the point is not only that Antonio does not repent here but also that he is not allowed to repent. Even his renunciation of the crown is Prospero's act."[19]

Because the magician subsumes "his" creatures as a dramatist does, he can give his daughter (and by extension his dukedom) to his enemy Naples while incorporating one and all into himself. If this imaginative imperialism is customary for Renaissance monarchs,[20] it is no less symptomatic of the artist, who at once expends and aggrandizes himself in the theater. In the waking dream of theatrical performance, the dramatist is present in his play even as the audience and the players are. This fusion may also reflect the relationship of mother and infant, both in its nurturing possibilities and in its potential function as a form of magical undoing in which the playwright reenacts the dominance of an original mother in order to dissolve it.

Prospero's deployment of artistic energies suggests that autonomy entails the usurpation of parental roles, so that the child vicariously becomes father and mother to himself and others. Development in this scheme proceeds by a series of reversals. Presumably while Prospero presented a conventional self in Milan, the witch-mother Sycorax held infantile energies in thrall. Withdrawing from a socially defined identity, "being transported / And rapt in secret studies" (1.2.767), he mastered the psychic space of the island by discovering and replacing the baleful mother. Magic gives him the power of transference, so that those who come under his influence are fixated, as in hero worship (and infantile dependency), until he personally restores their wills. From another angle, "being transported" suggests a child's withdrawal from symbiosis with the mother into the "secret studies" of individual thought and, above all, self-awareness.

Nevertheless, the play closes on the edge of life, in a moment of disintegration. Ariel is released "to the elements" and Caliban abandoned. The moment is thoroughly equivocal. The rejection of infantile energy is a source of compensatory righteousness, yet potentially a sterile, anaesthetic triumph. Hence the voice of the Epilogue, with its tentative mixture of, among other things, humility and blandishment, exhaustion and homiletic bossiness ("As you from crimes would pardon'd be, / Let your indulgence set me free" [19–20]). This final, decomposing Prospero identifies the audience with the engulfing witch-mother and the patriarchal magus whose spells could confine him on the island as others have been imprisoned (Epi. 3–10). The voice that beseeches parental approval for its reparative magic and eagerness to please (13) also begs for help in "assaulting" Mercy as Caliban recruited gods to abet his liberation. Yet the supplicant reverses roles one last time to urge the assembled clients to repent their own "crimes" (19). And all the time that myriad voice controls its disengagement by staging a suspenseful show rather like a gladiator facing a mob giddy with the choice of life or death.

The forces balanced in this equilibrium are present in earlier plays. What is poignant here is the effort to humanize them. Not a fabulous king of fairies but a mortal reconnoiters the island of his being. In his farewell, despite covert resistance, Prospero appears to take responsibility for his own death as few heroes in Shakespeare do. In spite of his apocalyptic vision of cloud-capped towers dissolving ("I will die but so must everyone else") and his obsessively projective involvement in his children's future ("I will live on in others"), he is able to contemplate his grave without becoming wolfishly greedy for survival.

To the extent that he appears able to take responsibility for his own death, Prospero's behavior represents not so much a demystification of heroic immortality as a remystifying of the ground of belief. But then, it is an axiom of Shakespearean drama that only blind contact with the ground of heroic values can be innocent and liberating. Otherwise heroic striving readily becomes self-serving. If it is not to be degraded into a meretricious ballad, Bottom's dream must remain unsung. This paradox governs Prospero's farewell, which seems to argue that life's pleasure lies in proving one's individuality in the wink of time before the cosmic father takes back the mortal self forever, even as in the utterance the personage before us becomes irreducibly complex and unfathomable. Metadramatically speaking, the Prospero who "ritually bequeaths his role to the audience"[21] is an accumulation of human possibilities. This "Prospero" needs quotation marks around it to signal its uncanny status in the tempest of symbolic discourse that is the play.

V

Since the Renaissance, Western culture has increasingly marshaled organic metaphors to accommodate the contradictions that define humankind. The assumptions of evolutionary biology give life genetic coherence and remove problems of ontological authority to a different level of abstraction. Shakespeare, by contrast, tended to carry forward the static conceptual categories of earlier ages. Even Jaques' "seven ages of man" is as much a sequence of discrete roles (the lover, the soldier, "the lean and slipper'd pantaloon") as it is a vision of individual genetic development that includes "mere oblivion, / Sans teeth, sans eyes, sans taste, sans everything" (*AYLI* 2.7.165–66).

Play-death implies an essentially conservative model of identity. Character remains constant until changed by episodes of self-loss and transformation. Threats tend to be defined apart from the self, and denial reinforces existing ego structures, however maladaptive, until sooner or later the increased stress causes traumatic dissociation and formation of what is perceived to be a new self. Change occurs not through organic development but as a sequence of substitutions: not by progressively modifying imaginative schemas but by replacing schemas—or by dreaming of escape from all schemas into ecstatic power.

In a word, development in this model takes place through conversion experiences. This is a style of personality usually associated with early- or premodern cultures. Yet it is difficult to estimate how much individual development actually differed from the development that occurs in modern lives insofar as we are looking at artistic constructions: what people wanted to think, and were able to express, about their experience. And of course this is not the only model of identity in Shakespeare.

In the privileged space of the island Prospero balances greed and reparation, omnipotence and "most faint" abnegation. Indirectly we are looking not only at a rigorously equivocal playwright, himself facing his last years, but also at a particularly ambiguous historical moment. Critics routinely praise the play's celebration of the "restorative powers of love,"[22] a theme appropriate for the wedding of the Princess Elizabeth to the Elector Palatine in the winter of 1612–1613: and doubly so given the recent death of Prince Henry. The nation mourned the prince as Alonso does Ferdinand, yet Henry was also a potential rival to his father. The collapse of the young man's promise produced traumatic anxiety and crystallized latent ambivalence, and not only for his thanatophobic father. During the lying in state, "a young lunatic, stark naked, burst in upon the mourners at St. James's and announced that he was the Prince's ghost come from heaven with a message for the King."[23] All unawares, the astounded mourners at St. James's were participating in a fantasy latent in the earliest Shakespeare; only instead of the revived Henry V they beheld a royal messenger of the unconscious vaunting the indestructible vitality of the hero even in his midwinter nakedness. As Shakespeare could have predicted, the eruption of that fantasy brought not solace and inspiration but a punishing reassertion of control. "After the ghost had been lashed and exposed in his nakedness for twenty-four hours at the porter's lodge, King James ordered him turned loose" (Akrigg 1963, p. 137).

At the same time *The Tempest's* allusions to the Bermudas evoke contemporary fantasies of the New World as a source of renewal, and more specifically the sensational survival of the flagship of the Virginia Company's expedition to Jamestown in 1609 after a storm. The play fancies injustice flowing out of Europe to a demonic yet idyllic island where fatherly magic can purify it. In these ways, then, the play shaped and was shaped by a preoccupation with renewal outside the theater. But there is another dimension to this historical matrix to consider as well.

Prospero's illusory tempest parodies a patriarchal execution, striking down enemies by decree and yet wishing to undo that aggression by restoring them, rehabilitated, to life. Righteousness subdues rebellion with a majestic wave of a wand. Likewise the abandonment of infantile energies in Prospero's farewell construes maturity in terms of the aristocratic-heroic dream of achieving apotheosis by separating the self from all that is base and mortal, having nobly attempted of course to improve and make peace with despised commonness. As the seventeenth century unfolded, an increasingly maladaptive effort to perpetuate just such a dream of apotheosis climaxed in the tragic encounter of King Charles, cloaked in visions of divine right, with the headsman's leveling axe. In the magic window of hindsight we can see *The Tempest* as not only conserving declining cultural forms, but also registering signs of the transformation of England's personality that was to come.

Chapter 11

Epilogue

To my knowledge, no contemporary writer was so richly concerned with play-death and apotheosis as Shakespeare. After his passing the ground of heroism shifted radically in England. The iconoclastic imaginations that defaced statues of saints and killed the king were acting out a change in the dynamics of hero worship that the Restoration would not undo. At the same time Puritan emigrants to the New World, many of them anxious about portents of doom in reprobate England, were gradually transforming the old system of self-effacement and autonomy into a new ethos of pious self-reliance that was to have unforeseeable consequences.

The Shakespearean pattern flourished again only in the nineteenth century, in Poe's indefatigable corpses and Twain's self-dramatizing Tom Sawyer and Huck Finn. In the visionary psychology of Romanticism the pattern is crucial. Mary Shelley's *Frankenstein*, for instance, develops as an obsessive sequence of play-deaths that make possible the chimerical omnipotence that excites its narrators. The novel's protagonist loses himself in fainting spells, trances, fevers, traumatic hysteria, and numbing polar wastes, splitting into the godlike scientist and a monstrous, instinctual alter ego brought to life by genius. At the other end of the century Stevenson's Dr. Jekyll and H. G. Wells's invisible man also undertake sinister, liberating immortality projects.

Rising from his coffin to recruit an ever-expanding army of surrogate selves through his oral depradations, Bram Stoker's insatiable count is the apotheosis of heroes who have triumphed over Turkish infidels as Henry V daydreams his son will do (*H5* 5.2.206-9). At one point linked to the ghost in *Hamlet*, Dracula is no less a Richard III born to bite the world. Served by a tacitly incestuous harem, he reincarnates the atavistic warrior-lord in an ambivalent Victorian patriarch who would command eternity. In one crisis, having fed on Mina's blood, the count nurses her at his bleeding breast like "a child forcing a kitten's nose into a saucer of milk to drink." Not even Shakespeare dramatized more brilliantly the infantile, symbiotic greed for life that underlies play-death and heroism.

The nineteenth century invented the mad scientist whose power over death has since become terrifyingly literal in messianic totalitarianism. Hitler had a taste for rhetorical resurrections, as in his boast that he would revive the true teachings of his forerunner Jesus Christ, "which we now call socialism." For "*We are the first to exhume these teachings! Through us* alone, and not until now, do these teachings celebrate their resurrection! Mary and Magdelene stood at the empty tomb. For they were seeking the dead man! But we intend to raise the treasures of the living Christ!"[1]

Today the fantasy of play-death seems to be increasingly military and industrial. The mad scientist continues to thrive in the anthropomorphic computer or robot who is at once dead and undying, sub- and superhuman, and capable, as in the film *2001*, of defiant rage. Even the fanatical Professor in Conrad's *The Secret Agent* is a dilettante in the company of Dr. Strangelove. The godlike automaton is fearfully epitomized by the soldier in a tomblike missile bunker who could be called upon, at the sound of a disembodied command, to push a button that will annihilate nations of enemies (and incidental others) half a world away. Self-effacement and apotheosis have never before been so perversely literal.

Popular films commonly recombine gothic and military-industrial imagery. In *The Terminator* (1984) a "cyborg is sent back in time from the year 2029 to present-day Los Angeles to assassinate a woman destined to give birth to a revolutionary [that is, the millennial] hero."[2] As the woman and her lover flee for their lives, they manage again and again to destroy the alien assassin (Arnold Schwarzenegger), only to have him rise up each time more malevolent than ever. Each of these play-deaths tears away more of the killer's human disguise, culminating in a symbolically apocalyptic inferno that bares his robotic skeleton: which of course springs to life one last time in a horrific evocation of the lean abhorred monster Death himself. Like the cartoon "Masters of the Universe" (Chapter 3, n. 3), *The Terminator* deploys muscle-beach masculinity and a skeletal nemesis, but ambivalently (and apocalyptically) fused in the annihilating hero that Arnold Schwarzenegger plays.

Fantasies of heroic play-death continue to seek new grounds for authority. For instance, the ancient symbol of apotheosis implied in Juliet's vision of Romeo "cut . . . out in little stars" (*RJ* 3.2.22) persists in the trivial glamor we attribute to celebrities when we call them stars. But more primitive survivals are not hard to find. In 1985 an American corporation named Celestis announced plans for burials in the heavens that would use a rocket to send the ashes of the dead into orbit in a capsule with "a highly reflective outer skin, making it visible on clear nights as a comfort to those left behind." The ashes of "as many as 10,330 people" would "stay up for eternity, or 63 million years, whichever comes first." Later flights would offer a more individualistic alternative to this collective apotheosis, having "an ejection mechanism to make each capsule a separate space traveler."[3] The scheme would fill the heavens with consoling personal authority. With its mixture of religious and military-industrial power, the symbolic and the literal, the "Celestis" scheme calls attention to the deeply equivocal nature of thought, and some of the fantastic convictions that equivocation disguises.

As I write, a tabloid on sale at my local supermarket is trumpeting: "Doctors Raise Dead with Ancient Chant: Corpse of 45-year-old woman revived—after 72 hours!" It could be a reprise of Cerimon's ministrations in *Pericles*, though in fact it claims to be a report from the Chinese press agency *Xinhua* on "researchers at North-West University in Sian, China" who rubbed a woman's body with "ointments concocted from rare herbs and powdered roots" and then used "an ancient Tibetan chant" to revive her "for just over half an hour."[4] On my desk is an advertisement for "alternative" healers that recommends a "psychic healer" and "counsellor" who urges clients, "Learn from your 'past lives' and their karmic carry-overs. Contact your spirit guides and the spirits of deceased loved ones for healing."

Less exotic than Tibetan techniques and no less frankly wishful are the anecdotal miracles of "born-again" Christian evangelists such as Oral Roberts, who claimed at the Charismatic Bible Ministries Conference in June 1987, "I can't tell you about the dead people I've raised. I've had to stop a sermon, go back, and raise a dead person." Like a dramatist he recognized "It did improve my altar call [audience response] that night."

The emotional power of resurrection fantasies is evident in Oral Roberts's account of exorcising demons. Empowered by heroic transference, he first feels "God's presence, usually through my hand." Then "I catch the breath of a person—it will have a stench as of a body that has been decayed. Then I notice the eyes. They're—they're like snake eyes."[5] To Oral Roberts, the person possessed is like a dead man and, by analogy, Satan is death and the fear of death. Like the English nobles invoking the power of the lost Henry V to demonize the French, the preacher as hero-worshipper turns an attack of anxiety into a conviction of immortal strength by directing all his energy at a demonic scapegoat.

In the secular world educators and therapists also seek to rob death of its sting, sometimes by using forms of play-death. One Florida school district offered a course in "death education," which taught first graders to make model coffins from shoeboxes. A "simulation mind game" developed at the University of Kentucky and recommended for use in health classes calls for students to undergo a series of physical relaxation exercises in a candlelit room. In this hypnogogic atmosphere the teacher then intones:

> Today you are going to experience death, not as a terrifying end but as a natural part of life, a transition stage. On my command you will experience death and at that moment you will see yourself rise to the ceiling of this room and look down upon your own lifeless form. You will die now. As you look upon your body you are not frightened, just feeling a little awkward in your new state of being. . . . You can see loved ones who hear the news of your death and mourn. Try to reassure them that you are content in your new state.[6]

In this "game" the teacher combines the roles of priest and stage hypnotist. "On command," death becomes a social activity and an "awkward new state of being" no more disconcerting than swimming. With its candlelit ritualism, migrating souls, and eschatological diplomacy ("try to reassure them that you are content"), the game calls to mind a host of ancient beliefs, including ancestor worship, that likewise have worked to control the guilt, anger, and dread produced by death. In trivializing death the game also suggests how superficial repression can afford to be in a society in which mortality has become for the most part a problem of old age.

II

It seems appropriate in this sketch to glance at an institution in some ways comparable to Shakespeare's Globe, the Epcot Center at Disney World in Florida, one of the great theaters of heroic immortality. The park is divided into a "World Showcase," which like an old-fashioned world's fair aspires to introduce the visitor to exotic foreign lands, and "Future World," which projects a utopian future. The premise of boundless human mastery in a world without conflict is shockingly undramatic, yet the park employs some of the same materials Shakespeare used—exotic lands, wizardry, and heroic nationalism— and promises the visitor imaginative self-expansion even as the theater does.

The uses of apotheosis in the Disney "kingdom" are worth a moment's analysis. Although advertised as exotic, for example, each country in the "World Showcase" consists of a stereotype such as the Eiffel Tower or the English pub. A few costumed employees represent each country, and there are no signs of individual lives. The visitor, too, is depersonalized. Yet this play-death allows the visitor symbolically to possess and dominate each country. While some lands include a gallery of precious artifacts to admire, the visitor can actually do only two things: eat and buy. For every country is essentially a restaurant and souvenir shop, and the visitor can only relate to it by consuming it.

In such an adventure the primary pleasure is the infantile dream of consuming the world. Were the process not scrupulously depersonalized and euphemized, it might recall the wolfish appetite for survival that rattled Henry IV. Despite public rhetoric about friendship, the imagery of the exhibits alludes to that wolfish potential in nostalgic symbols of warrior heroism such as samurai swords and exotic armor. In addition there are symbols of assorted divinities, including a Mayan relief depicting the sacrifice to the gods of a human baby—a sacrifice analogous to the sublimated devouring the godlike visitor will do in this surrogate Yucatan. And there are animated mannikins that promise, like slaves, to extend a master's will endlessly and, like mummies or Renaissance funerary effigies, blur the boundary between life and death.

Heroism in such a world is purchased at a cost in labor and personal autonomy that is artfully hidden. The souvenirs for sale might be the effortless products of Prospero's spirits. Or you might think that the crucial labor comes only from machines, whose enchanted cousins, the animated mannikins, are the actors in the dioramas. In these exotic lands nobody can suffer privation or colonial despotism—or threaten privation or tyranny—because finally there is nobody there. Over-population is no problem because the sexual drive for immortality is moot. The eye and the mouth conquer all.

"Future World" frankly promises apotheosis. The exhibits magnify the human creature. "World of Motion" identifies the clumsy biped with supersonic machines, prosthetic machines, even as "Universe of Energy" boasts about humankind's acquisition of cosmic vitality. In-domitable humanity will populate the farthest reaches of the universe, the deserts, and the seas. The covert metaphors are colonialism and inexhaustible procreation, though the only crowds to be seen are in the sightseers' queues.

To dispel misgivings the utopian promise is systematically grounded in the masculine authority of the recent past. Though they may peer out of spacesuits or portholes at the bottom of the sea, the creatures who will prevail in the cosmos appear in family groups from the imag-ery of the Eisenhower era. But then, this is a paradoxical future, where nothing is mysterious or truly new. The vaunted machinery of the future turns out to be icons of Victorian industry: giant gears, rockets nostalgically derived from Jules Verne, an enormous desert-harvester whose pedigree looks back to Eli Whitney. The 3D film "Journey into Imagination" insists that in making snapshots you are not trying to seize fragments of perishable life from the current of time, you are "making memories" that ostensibly will endure forever. And the ob-jects of memory are kindly grandparents, authorities far enough re-moved to bypass the usual struggles between parent and child.

In its imagery, that is, the Disney future aggressively denies time. This is the future domesticated, purged of chance and malice and, to be sure, death. The world to come disguises the world of childhood piety. To put it another way, "Future World" fetishizes the symbols of conventional industrial authority—the selfless Edisonian inventor-tin-kerer, the agricultural pioneer taming the American plains—and calls that venerable past the future. And since that imagery is largely the invention of the great corporate public relations geniuses of an earlier age, it would not be unfair to say that the apotheosis implied is as strategic and atavistic as any that Tamburlaine and Faustus sought.

Managing the experience of millions of people, the park, like Prospero, exhaustively controls fantasy. The dream of omnipotence comes with clever crowd-control fences and subtly coercive public-address music featuring dreamy harps and triumphal brass. Although the slogans of individual freedom abound, the visitor's experience is relentlessly collective and mass-produced. The park is a people-moving machine, and a symbolic theater of sophisticated authorial tyranny, where the actors are all robotic Ariels capable of undying service as long as the electricity flows.

As in Shakespeare, the pattern of play-death and apotheosis in the Disney park implies an economy of production. The heroic mentality transforms raw materials, including alien "native" lives, into precious objects to be admired and consumed. This material is in turn transformed into the symbolic immortality embodied in the park's mythic America and the cosmic future. The movement of visitors in the park is unconsciously the living manifestation of its economy. People are processed, mind and body, from one adventure to another, exchanging money—the symbolic product of mortal work—for a conviction of immortality.

Tragic versions of that economy are not far to seek. For years the Reverend Jim Jones stunned his followers with prophecies of apocalyptic warfare, promising to rescue those who gave him their money by taking them into a cave from which—as from a tomb—they would emerge to start life over. In Guyana in 1978, conjuring up a heavenly reunion and lacing party punch with cyanide, Jones compelled some nine hundred followers, many of them children, into a play-death of spectacular evil.[7]

Let me conclude with an example of play-death and apotheosis in which the pattern is unconsciously exploded if not demystified: a joke in which Christ relieves St. Peter from his watch at the pearly gates, saying: "Thou look'st weary, Peter. Get thee on thy coffee break, and I will watch for thee."

No sooner is Christ seated on Peter's stool than an old man wafts up from earth seeking admission to heaven. "Old man," Christ demands, "who art thou?"

"Lord," wheezes the old man, "on earth I was a humble carpenter."

"A carpenter?" Christ echoes, intrigued. "Hadst thou a family?"

"I had but one son. He was much beloved among men."

"A son? Much beloved among men?" Christ leans forward intently. "Where is thy son now?"

"Alas," croaks the carpenter, "he was taken from me at an early age and suffered terrible trials."

"A son taken from thee at an early age? And suffered terrible trials?" Christ radiates amazement: "Can it be? At long last! after so many years!" He stretches out welcoming arms: "Father!"

The old man is radiant. "My son!" he cries reaching out: "Pinocchio!"

The essence of this joke, it seems to me, is its deflation of patriarchal fantasies. As Christ, the son has sacrificed himself and become God, the supreme patriarchal judge over his father. Gepetto, by contrast, would degrade the son to a wooden puppet subject to godlike patriarchal control. The punchline draws its energy from the astonished collision of those opposed conceptions of power, and its humor subverts not only the role fantasies but also, ambiguously, the eschatological claims of traditional Christianity that the play-death fantasy has long supported. Although it is no more than a joke, vulgar and devious and to some extent unwitting, it suggests an effort to disenchant fantasy that is now, as in Shakespeare's theater, only beginning.

Appendix

Dr Forman's Dream as Return to Paradise

What follows is an example of cultural fantasy from the 1590s that unconsciously construes heroism in the context of edenic themes, and illustrates how heroic forms may refashion orthodox authority to serve immediate historical needs. In 1597 the astrologer, physician, and avid playgoer Simon Forman recorded in his diary a dream about the aging Queen Elizabeth:

> I dreamt I was with the Queen, and that she was a little elderly woman in a coarse white petticoat all unready; and she and I walked up and down through lanes and closes, talking and reasoning of many matters. At last we came over a great close where were many people, and there were two men at hard words. One of them was a weaver, a tall man with a reddish beard, distract of his wits. She talked to him and he spoke very merrily unto her, and at last did take her and kiss her. So I took her by the arm and put her away; and told her the fellow was frantic. And so we went from him and I led her by the arm still, and then we went through a dirty lane. She had a long, white smock, very clean and fair, and it trailed in the dust and her coat behind. I took her coat and did carry it up a good way, and then it hung too low before. I told her she should do me a favour to let me wait on her, and she said I should. Then said I, "I mean to wait *upon* you and not under you, that I might make this belly a little bigger to carry up this smock and coats out of the dirt." And so we talked merrily and then she began to lean upon me, when we were past the dirt and to be very familiar with me, and methought she began to love me. And when we were alone, out of sight, methought she would have kissed me.[1]

At which point Forman woke up.

As Louis Adrian Montrose has pointed out, the scantily clad virginal sex object of Forman's dream, the "little elderly woman," closely resembles the queen as described in the year of the dream by observers such as the ambassador extraordinary of France, who reported that at his first audience Elizabeth

> was strangely attired in a dress of silver cloth, white and crimson. . . .
> She kept the front of her dress open, and one could see the whole of
> her bosom, and passing low, and often she would open the front of
> this robe with her hands as if she was too hot. . . . Her bosom is some-
> what wrinkled . . . but lower down her flesh is exceeding white and
> delicate, so far as one could see. As for her face, it is and appears to be
> very aged. It is long and thin, and her teeth are very yellow and un-
> equal. . . . Many of them are missing so that one cannot understand
> her easily when she speaks quickly.[2]

At the core of the dream, Montrose notes, is Forman's joke about waiting upon, not under, the queen. "The joke . . . is generated from Forman's verbal quibble: to *wait* upon/to *weight* upon. Within this subversive pun is concentrated the reciprocal relationship between dependency and domination" (Montrose, p. 64). In Forman's wordplay, "the subject's desire for employment (to *wait* upon) coexists with his desire for mastery (to *weight* upon); and the pun is manifested physically in his desire to inseminate his sovereign, which is at once to serve her and to possess her." For "the dreamer insinuates into a gesture of homage, a will to power" (Montrose, p. 65). Montrose links Forman's dream to *A Midsummer Night's Dream*, but we may also take it as a vernacular version of the coterie fantasy I have analyzed in *Venus and Adonis* (Chapter 7), in which eros conquers death.

While no one overtly plays dead in Simon Forman's dream, the dynamics of the play-death fantasy are nevertheless at work in it. At a time when Elizabeth was declining and was still without a successor, Forman dreamed a solution to the anxiety that haunted her subjects. Vicariously and unconsciously, he was improvising his own version of the queen's Accession Day rituals, which celebrated rebirth. Not only does he protect the "little elderly woman" from quarreling men and from contaminating "dirt" and "dust," he promises to renew her decaying body by making her a mother. Her pregnant belly will then be able to "'carry up this smock and coats out of the dirt'"—meaning, I take it, that as a mother-to-be she will no longer be a virgin endangered by "dirty" appetites such as the weaver with the reddish beard reveals (and the dreamer himself projects); and also that she will no longer be vulnerable to the dust of death.

In redeeming his sovereign (and nation) from old age and death, Doctor Forman was of course dreaming about his own heroism. He would accomplish what the noblest young males in the kingdom had failed to do. By winning the queen's love and obligingly usurping her womb, he would release England from its apprehension and make himself the source of the country's future. (In this sense the dream is a self-aggrandizing prophecy not unlike the one that fascinated William Neville.) Impregnated, Elizabeth would no longer require her subject to protect her from weakness and degradation, and her sovereignty would be palpably revitalized in her womb. Yet as Forman's consort, safely "past the dirt," she would be powerful but "very familiar with [him]," no longer exerting over him the intimidating authority of the actual queen.

Nevertheless, Doctor Forman is strikingly unassuming about this apotheosis. Intimacy he imagines as "talking and reasoning of many matters" with Elizabeth, whereas the other parvenu, the weaver, is "distract of his wits"—that is, he crazily tries to dominate the queen with brazen kisses even as Forman's own desire would have been crazy in the waking world. In his dream, then, the doctor projects his most aggressive motives in a form that can be safely repudiated. Conversation initiates Forman to power and reveals itself as a mode of sexuality in the joke by which he violates the historically formidable virgin. At once talk humanizes Gloriana and the transference that bonds her subject to her, making possible a vision of mutuality that contains the forbidden inversion by which the lowly Forman would master the monarch. As Montrose observes, Forman triumphs through this self-effacing joke: he minimizes his own will even as he entertains the most grandiose claims imaginable.

In the archetypal geography of the dream Forman can be seen as a wishful Adam guiding a susceptible Eve past the dangers of the Genesis story. Like Eve, Elizabeth presents a putatively ingenuous male with the temptations of supreme autonomy. As an initiate, "talking and reasoning" with the living embodiment of governance—that is, behaving "as gods" with her, successfully incorporating the fruit of knowledge—Forman imagines dispelling the threats conflated in "dirt": importunate sexuality and dusty "returne to the earth: for out of it wast thou taken" (Gen. 3.19: *Geneva Bible*, 1560 ed.). In orthodox ideology desire for autonomy brings the punishment of death and curses sexuality with the demand for painful procreation, whereas in Forman's dreamwork, by a sort of magical undoing, sexuality banishes the shadow of death and liberates human will. In this way heterodox patriarchal values preempt Christian myth by the same sort of ambiguous symbolic play as the wordplay on *wait / weight* that ingratiates Forman with the queen. His dreamwork attempts to solve the elemental existential dilemma, that consciousness brings death as well as the promise of autonomy, in a symbolic context conditioned by Christian Europe's central myth of the dilemma's origin.

Louis Montrose brilliantly links Forman's dream to Bottom's brief ascendancy as the beloved of the Fairy Queen. My concern is to point out the astonishing frequency with which Shakespeare associates the pattern of Forman's dream with play-death and resurrection, as when the marginalized Romeo "gets past the dirt" that associates love with smutty jokes in patriarchal Verona, and dreams that by a kiss Juliet can revive him from the radical passivity of death and make him an emperor. Like Simon Forman, Romeo imagines being dependent on a woman for his life and yet also empowered by her love. In Doctor Forman's words, "when we were past the dirt . . . methought she began to love me. And when we were alone, out of sight, methought she would have kissed me."

In psychoanalytic terms we are almost certainly looking at an infantile wish to be exalted by a mother or mother-surrogate. Forman's own mother was quite elderly at the time of his dream, and in his childhood, as he himself wrote, "had never loved him" (Montrose, p. 63). But in its specific historical situation this is also masculine dreamwork expressing a patriarchal society temporarily dominated by a woman whose symbolic force gave fear of death particular poignancy and therefore became a medium for the heroic assertion of those who served it. Just this network of materials we have seen in the background of *Venus and Adonis*.

If we approach Forman's dream from a slightly different direction, we can better estimate its archetypal ground as well as the lurking anger and dread in Simon himself. Like Shakespeare, Forman lived through the terrors of the 1593 plague. After doing medical services Forman wrote his "Discourse of the Plague" (1593), in which he subscribes to orthodox explanations of the origins of the disease. Plagues may be sent by devils, with God's permission, or by God Himself. Guided in part by Holy Writ, Forman's anxiety fastens upon "dirty" women as a source of divine wrath. Though England has no Potiphar's wife lusting for Joseph and no lascivious Jezebel, Forman observes, he nevertheless strongly condemns whoredom, and after listing many astrological portents of God's judgment, his tract concludes on a broadly, even compulsively censorious note: "The laws of England are good, the country fertile and good, but the people very bad. And never worse than now." The coda is a prayer for mercy "in the last day when we shall all come before Him to give account of our lives and deeds past. Amen."[3]

If this tract is as earnest as it seems, Simon Forman's experiences with plague must have been traumatic. His anxious misanthropy reflects the punishing aspect of the popular apocalyptic fantasies I have associated with prophetic behavior in Shakespeare. In this context his dream of edenic union with the queen in 1597 represents a wish to undo a sense of threat that may well have originated in his insecure childhood, but probably crystallized in the long nightmare of 1593, which gave special force to sadistic, justificative themes latent in the heroic theology of his time.

Notes

Chapter 1

1. All quotations are taken from *The Riverside Shakespeare,* ed. G. Blakemore Evans (Boston: Houghton Mifflin, 1974).

2. It may be that rescue fantasies are apt to mask aggressive motives, as Freud postulated, and that by sharply defining difference (us-them, hero-enemy), games of battle strengthen boundaries of identity, sorting out desires for infantile merger with powerful others according to prevailing cultural models. See Chapters 3, 4, and 10.

3. G. P. V. Akrigg, *Jacobean Pageant* (Cambridge, Mass.: Harvard University Press, 1963), pp. 145–46.

4. "There seems no end to the number of resurrection scenes in [the last] plays," William Carroll remarks in *The Metamorphoses of Shakespeare's Comedy* (Princeton, N.J.: Princeton University Press, 1985), p. 208. As Carroll's study indirectly makes clear, play-death is a type of metamorphosis and historically has elicited many of the same anxieties. Perpetuating Augustine's nervousness about shape-shifting, for example, Aquinas decreed, "Those transformations which cannot be produced by the power of nature cannot in reality be effected by the operation of demons; for instance, that the human body be changed into the body of a beast, or that the body of a dead man return to life" (p. 8).

5. In Northrop Frye's famous formula comedy turns on a "potentially tragic crisis near the end, a . . . 'point of ritual death'" from which the main characters at last find deliverance, while mortal crisis is central to the structure of romance. See *The Anatomy of Criticism* (Princeton, N.J.: Princeton University Press, 1957), p. 179.

6. Clifford Geertz, *The Interpretation of Cultures* (New York: Basic Books, 1973), pp. 52, 50.

7. Thomas M. Greene, *The Light in Troy* (New Haven, Conn.: Yale University Press, 1982), p. 3.

8. Roy Strong, *The Cult of Elizabeth* (London: Thames & Hudson, 1977), p. 128.

9. William Bullein, *A Dialogue against the Pestilence* (1573, 1st ed. 1564), excerpted in *Life in Shakespeare's England*, ed. J. Dover Wilson (Cambridge, Eng.: Cambridge University Press, 1911), p. 135.

10. Simon Kellway, *A Defensative against the Plague* (London, 1593).

11. Mary Douglas, *Natural Symbols* (New York: Pantheon, 1982), pp. xiv–xv.

Chapter 2

1. Cf. this Dutch variant: "In 1620 a thirteen-year-old who had perpetrated man-slaughter was committed [to the *Tugthuis* or House of Correction] 'because of his youth,' having been symbolically decapitated in public, with a sword swung over his head, flogged and branded before admission." See Simon Schama, *The Embarrassment of Riches: An Interpretation of Dutch Culture in the Golden Age* (New York: Alfred A. Knopf, 1987), pp. 18–19.

2. In *Shakespeare's Creation* (Amherst: University of Massachusetts Press, 1976), I have described two opposed modes of identity exhibited by Shakespeare's characters, one socially determined, the other dramatically generated from within. The self-efface-ment fantasy can be seen as a strategy for controlling that opposition (see pp. 67–70). See also Terence Eagleton, *Shakespeare and Society* (New York: Schocken Books, 1967), esp. chaps. 1 and 2.

3. See A. Alvarez, *The Savage God* (New York: Random House, 1972), pp. 49–50.

4. R. W. Chambers, "*King Lear*: The First W. P. Ker Memorial Lecture" (Glasgow: Jackson, 1940), p. 44.

5. "Subsumed" is the term Peter Laslett uses in *The World We Have Lost*, 2d ed. (New York: Scribner's, 1973), pp. 20–21.

6. "Homily on Obedience (1559)," in *Elizabethan Backgrounds*, ed. Arthur F. Kinney (Hamden, Conn.: Archon, 1975), pp. 63–64.

7. Robert Hughes, *Heaven and Hell in Western Art* (New York: Stein & Day, 1968), p. 10.

8. The Statute (1st Edward VI. c. 3) appears in R. Liddesdale Palmer, *English Social History in the Making* (London: Nicholson & Watson, 1934), pp. 76–77.

9. With its emphasis on an individual's direct relationship with God, Puritan thought urgently personalized the drama of salvation. Lawrence Stone sees the Puritan con-science "sapping respect for rank and title at all levels of the social hierarchy" in *The Crisis of the Aristocracy* (Oxford: Clarendon Press, 1967), p. 745.

10. Historians continue to disagree about the origins and development of individual-ism in England. In Alan Macfarlane's view, "the majority of ordinary people in England from at least the thirteenth century were rampant individualists, highly mobile both geographically and socially . . . market-oriented and acquisitive, ego-centered in kinship and social life." See *The Origins of English Individualism: The Family, Property, and Social Transition* (Oxford: Basil Blackwell, 1978), p. 163. Cf. E. M. W. Tillyard's formulation: "Those who know most about the Middle Ages now assure us that humanism and a belief in the present life were powerful by the twelfth century, and that exhortations to condemn the world were themselves powerful at that time for that very reason. The two contradictory principles coexisted in a state of high tension." See *The Elizabethan World Picture* (New York: Macmillan, 1942), p. 5. I have been focusing my argument on Elizabethan doctrine and theory in order to minimize speculation about actual histori-cal behavior, although of course the two are ultimately inextricable.

11. Paul Zweig, *The Heresy of Self-Love* (Princeton, N.J.: Princeton University Press, 1968), p. 65.

12. In *The Family, Sex, and Marriage in England, 1500–1800* (New York: Harper & Row, 1977), Lawrence Stone theorizes that "the deferential society is itself a reflection of the defence mechanism of the ego when it discovers a basic conflict between its own impulses to autonomy and . . . obedience ruthlessly enforced by its parents. Thus the deferential behaviour of the children is a defensive response to ego repression, as the only way to survive, while the authoritarian . . . behaviour of the parents is an expres-sion of the original desire for autonomy" (p. 178).

13. Carl Bridenbaugh, *Vexed and Troubled Englishmen* (New York: Oxford University Press, 1968). Laslett points out that ordinarily "neither peasant, pauper, nor craftsman nor even gentleman in the preindustrial world ever changed his reference group in such a way as to feel aware of what is called relative deprivation" (*The World We Have Lost*, p. 184). As *The Tempest* dramatizes, however, one of the changes that must have called social roles and reference groups into question was growing awareness of the New World.

14. Frank Whigham, *Ambition and Privilege: The Social Tropes of Elizabethan Courtesy Theory* (Berkeley: University of California Press, 1984), pp. 5, 18.

15. In the allegories of alchemy it seems likely that the same superstition contributed to the belief that by the secret "virtue" of alchemical processes lead may become gold.

16. Christopher Levett, *A Voyage into New England* (1628), in Bridenbaugh, *Vexed and Troubled Englishmen*, pp. 51–52.

17. Thomas Nashe, *Christ's Teares over Jerusalem* (1593), in *The Complete Works of Thomas Nashe*, ed. R. B. McKerrow (London: Sidgwick, 1904–10), 2: 83.

18. Anthony Esler, *The Aspiring Mind of the Elizabethan Younger Generation* (Durham, N.C.: Duke University Press, 1966).

19. Complementing Esler and germane to this point is Stephen J. Greenblatt's *Sir Walter Ralegh* (New Haven, Conn.: Yale University Press, 1973). In 1603 while imprisoned Ralegh feigned suicide in a sort of play-death, which he followed by a brilliant assertion of autonomy in the subsequent trial. As C. L. Barber suggested to me, Ralegh's behavior fits the Shakespearean pattern.

20. Laslett warns that "we know very little indeed about child nurture in preindustrial times" (*The World We Have Lost*, p. 110). Recent studies, including Stone (*Marriage*, 1977), have been most persuasive when exploring upper-class childhood and contemporary theories of child-rearing. See Leah Sinanoglou Marcus, *Childhood and Cultural Despair* (Pittsburgh: University of Pittsburgh Press, 1978), p. 341. In an important article Debora Shuger gathers evidence from Lancelot Andrewes, Richard Hooker, and others for a Renaissance conception of the father as nurturant and noncoercive. Such a conception sharply qualifies the conventional picture of the authoritarian patriarch. See "Reflections of the Father: Patriarchs, Politics, and Narcissism," *English Literary Renaissance* (forthcoming, 1989).

21. In "Recurrence and Renaissance: Rhetorical Imitation in Ascham and Sturm," *English Literary Renaissance* 6 (1976): 156–79, Marion Trousdale argues that the theory of *copia* postulates an essential Platonic idea that persists when students turn out imitative variations on a model. Like priests, i.e., fathers and tutors bring the student closer to immutable origins. In this way sterile exercises may actually serve an initiatory function.

22. The conventional association of disobedience with parricide is evident in a conduct book such as Bartholomew Batty's *The Christian Mans Closet* (1581), which judges the disobedient son a "cruel murderer of his parents." See Lu Emily Pearson, *Elizabethans at Home* (Stanford, Calif.: Stanford University Press, 1959), p. 246.

23. King Henry fantasizes about his son as an inferior changeling substituted for the model son Hotspur (1.1.85–89). Cf. Leontes' comment to Florizel, "Your mother . . . did print your royal father off, / Conceiving you" (*WT* 5.1.124–26).

24. Marcus surveys these contrasting images of the child in *Childhood*, pp. 42–93. For the background of the Augustinian and Pelagian traditions, see Robert Pattison, *The Child Figure in English Literature* (Athens: University of Georgia Press, 1978), pp. 10–20.

25. The practice of naming a younger child after an older sibling who died suggests a belief that identity can be lost and yet tacitly resurrected as well.

26. Stone, *Marriage*, pp. 113–114, 117. In his controversial and polemical essay on "The Evolution of Childhood," in *The History of Childhood*, ed. Lloyd deMause (New York: Psychohistory Press, 1974), Lloyd deMause analyzes evolving conceptions of the child in terms of evolving adult defenses against the anxiety children arouse.

27. F. G. Emmison, *Elizabethan Life: Disorder* (Chelmsford, Eng.: Essex County Council, 1970), p. 156. See also Keith Wrightson, "Infanticide in Earlier Seventeenth-Century England," *Local Population Studies* 15 (1975): 10–22. Some authorities, including Laslett, are more guarded about this problem. There is some agreement among historians that at this time the English held children in higher regard than they had earlier. For Keith Wrightson, in *English Society, 1580–1680* (London: Hutchinson, 1982), "it seems clear that in the main, parents did their utmost both to bring up and bestow their children, following their progress with both anxiety and satisfaction, and that they demanded little in return" (p. 117).

28. Thomas Becon, *A Pistill . . . upon All the Sonday Gospelles*, vol. 2 (1566), in Arthur Kirsch, *Shakespeare and the Experience of Love* (Cambridge, Eng.: Cambridge University Press, 1981), p. 76. Marcus (*Childhood*, p. 29) points out that "both the Norton Catechism and Calvin's *Institutions*, widely used as a catechism in sixteenth-century England, extended 'Honor thy father and mother' to encompass all of higher rank . . . and reminded children that according to Exod. 21.17 any rebellion against due authority was punishable with death." Such evidence strongly suggests that infanticidal motivation took many forms and persisted as children grew.

29. My treatment of projective distortions of the child follows deMause, "The Evolution of Childhood."

30. Janet Adelman discusses the relationship between the food-related riots of 1607 and *Coriolanus* in "'Anger's My Meat': Feeding, Dependency, and Aggression in *Coriolanus*," in *Shakespeare, Pattern of Excelling Nature*, ed. David Bevington and Jay L. Halio (Cranbury, N.J.: Associated University Presses, 1978), pp. 108–9. Famine may have been a recurring threat (Bridenbaugh, *Vexed and Troubled Englishmen*, p. 377; Emmison, *Elizabethan Life*, p. 64), and Tudor legislation indirectly witnesses to the number of homeless child beggars (M. J. Tucker, "The Child as Beginning and End: Fifteenth- and Sixteenth-Century English Childhood," in deMause, *History of Childhood*, p. 250).

31. A. C. Bradley, *Shakespearean Tragedy* (London: Macmillan, 1905), p. 394.

32. Cf. the "natural" cycle of aggression and compensation implied in this passage from *Batman upon Bartoleme* (1582) cited in the Arden edition of *King Lear*, ed. Kenneth Muir (New York & London: Methuen, 1972), p. 118: "The Pellican loueth too much her children. For when the children be haught, and begin to waxe hoare, they smite the father and mother in the face, wherefore the mother smiteth them againe and slaieth them. And the thirde daye the mother smiteth her selfe in the side that the bloud runneth out, and sheddeth that hot bloud upon the bodies of her children. And by virtue of the bloud the birdes that were before dead, quicken againe." Parental wrath is expiated (and justified) by self-punishment. Smiting herself, the mother magically undoes the infanticide by repeating the murder. But her violence also replicates the violence of the children ("smite . . . in the face").

33. See Alvin Kernan, *The Playwright as Magician* (New Haven, Conn.: Yale University Press, 1979), pp. 23–49, and Ann Jennalie Cook, *The Privileged Playgoers of Shakespeare's London, 1576–1642* (Princeton, N.J.: Princeton University Press, 1981), pp. 99–105. While actors were legally servants of their patrons, Cook notes, many passed as "counterfeit gentlemen," and others "could fairly be designated as privileged by birth, education, wealth or achievement" (pp. 122–23).

34. See Michael Shapiro, *Children of the Revels* (New York: Columbia University

Press, 1977), pp. 67–71, and more generally Alfred Harbage's *Shakespeare's Audience* (New York: Columbia University Press, 1941), chap. 4.

35. Like a magician or actor, Harry Berger, Jr., notes, the ascendant Prospero "prefers the security of the one-way window relationship in which he may observe without being observed," and "hides either behind a cloak of invisibility, or behind a role, a performance, a relationship, which has been prepared beforehand." See "Miraculous Harp: A Reading of *The Tempest*," *Shakespeare Studies* 5 (1969): 275. In Prospero, according to this view, self-effacement and assertion deeply reinforce one another.

36. C. L. Barber, *Shakespeare's Festive Comedy* (Princeton, N.J.: Princeton University Press, 1959).

37. James L. Calderwood, *Shakespearean Metadrama* (Minneapolis: University of Minnesota Press, 1971), p. 141.

38. In a letter about the present chapter Calderwood reminds me that Shakespeare "is also the 'father' of the audience, inasmuch as he, like Prospero, is employing his parental illusions toward the audience's 'education.' Surely part of the irony of Puck's epilogue is that in it Shakespeare self-effacingly plays the role of pleasing child to the audience's parent while actually playing the role of parent who has (like Oberon taking control of the [changeling] child by way of illusory strategies) manipulated his child audience for its own good."

39. Raymond Southall's *The Courtly Maker* (Oxford: Clarendon Press, 1964) recognizes the Elizabethan world picture itself as a majestic public fiction attempting to mediate among men: "The doctrine of World Order was inconsistent both with the spirit of the old courtly tradition and with the new spirit of the Reformation; its promulgation as state doctrine by Elizabeth is simply a sign that the Reformation had been called to a halt" (p. 55).

Chapter 3

1. Ernest Becker, *The Denial of Death* (New York: Free Press, 1973), p. 11. See also Becker's *Escape from Evil* (New York: Free Press, 1975).

2. C. W. Wahl, "The Fear of Death," in *The Meaning of Death*, ed. Herman Feifel (New York: McGraw Hill, 1965), p. 18.

3. At the time my daughter vowed to elevate the supermarket, television featured the animated cartoon "Masters of the Universe," whose villain Skeletor unmistakably descends from the grim reaper of medieval iconography, and whose hero, He-Man, bulges with pink, muscular, well-fed health.

4. Geertz, *Interpretation of Cultures*, p. 80.

5. "*Il Beato Agostino Novello e Quattro Suoi Miracoli Dopo la Morte.*" See Figure 1. Born into a noble Spanish family in Taormina, Sicily, holder of a doctorate in law from Bologna, the Augustinian friar became papal legate and confessor to Pope Nicholas IV.

6. Common in Renaissance England are pamphlets advertising news of "strange," "monstrous," or "misshapen" births. The pamphlets testify to the dread of the body that Becker is describing, though they invoke a religious context that moralizes the horror in cosmic terms and thereby promises to tame it. The same dynamics are evident in Christian iconography that gave demons grotesque body parts while idealizing the bodies of angels, say, with eternally youthful features.

7. A. L. Rowse, *The Elizabethan Renaissance* (New York: Scribner's, 1972), p. 227.

8. Johan Huizinga, *The Waning of the Middle Ages* (New York: Doubleday, 1954), p. 151.

9. Theodore Spencer, *Death and Elizabethan Tragedy* (Cambridge, Mass.: Harvard University Press, 1936). Spencer is indirectly corroborated by Philippe Ariès's *Western Attitudes toward Death*, trans. Patricia M. Ranum (Baltimore: Johns Hopkins University Press, 1974) and *The Hour of Our Death*, trans. Helen Weaver (New York: Random House, 1982). Ariès sees death becoming more individualized and dramatic after the Middle Ages. The dramatization of mortality desacralized death, as Marjorie Garber has pointed out in "'Wild Laughter in the Throat of Death': Darker Purposes in Shakespearean Comedy," in *Shakespearean Comedy*, ed. Maurice Charney (New York: New York Literary Forum, 1980), p. 121. Dramatization was part of a new secular technology for managing death. Nancy Lee Beaty surveys religious techniques for making a good death in *The Craft of Dying* (New Haven, Conn.: Yale University Press, 1970). In *Last Things in Shakespeare* (Gainesville: Florida State University Press, 1976), Harry Morris examines the *memento mori* tradition in Shakespeare's plays. In *The House of Death* (Baltimore: Johns Hopkins University Press, 1986), Arnold Stein has studied constructions of death in Renaissance poetry.

10. Michael Goldman, *Acting and Action in Shakespearean Tragedy* (Princeton, N.J.: Princeton University Press, 1985), p. 113. Reuben A. Brower derives this greatness from conventional classical prototypes. See *Hero and Saint: Shakespeare and the Graeco-Roman Heroic Tradition* (New York: Oxford University Press, 1971).

11. C. G. Jung, *The Archetypes and the Collective Unconscious*, 2d ed. (Princeton, N.J.: Princeton University Press, 1968), p. 116.

12. In *Shakespeare's Creation* I have analyzed some of the strategies by which Shakespeare creates illusions of ineffable meaning. See also Sigurd Burckhardt, "The Poet as Fool and Priest," in *Shakespearean Meanings* (Princeton, N.J.: Princeton University Press, 1968); and Stephen Booth, *An Essay on Shakespeare's Sonnets* (New Haven, Conn.: Yale University Press, 1968): "Perhaps the happiest moment the human mind ever knows is when it senses the presence of order and coherence and before it realizes the particular nature of (and so the particular limits) of the perception. At [that] moment . . . the mind is unlimited" (p. 14).

13. Ennead 3.2.15, in *The Enneads,* trans. Stephen MacKenna, 3d ed. (London, 1956), p. 173. See also Anne Righter, *Shakespeare and the Idea of the Play*, pt. 1 (London: Chatto & Windus, 1962); and Jackson L. Cope, *The Theater and the Dream* (Baltimore: Johns Hopkins University Press, 1973).

14. Robert Grudin, *Mighty Opposites: Shakespeare and Renaissance Contrariety* (Berkeley: University of California Press, 1979), p. 26. In *Rites and Symbols of Initiation* (New York: Harper & Row, 1975), originally published as *Birth and Rebirth* (1958), Mircea Eliade analyzes alchemy as a fantasy about death and rebirth whose outcome puts the practitioner in the heroic role of "striving to deliver nature from the consequence of the 'fall,' in short, to save it" (p. 124). The adept must return to his mother's breast or even womb in order to produce regeneration. Eliade quotes Paracelsus: "[H]e who would enter the Kingdom of God must first enter with his body into his mother and there die" (pp. 57–58).

15. Helmuth Plessner, "On the Relation of Time to Death," in *Man and Time*, ed. Joseph Campbell (Princeton, N.J.: Princeton University Press, 1957), p. 237. See also Mircea Eliade, *Cosmos and History: The Myth of the Eternal Return*, trans. W. R. Trask (New York: Harper & Row, 1954); Ernst Cassirer, *An Essay on Man* (New Haven, Conn.: Yale University Press, 1944; reprint, 1962), pp. 83ff.; and the cognitive analyses in Bruno Snell, *The Discovery of the Mind in Early Greek Philosophy and Literature* (Cambridge, Mass.: Harvard University Press, 1953; reprint, 1960), pp. 1–22.

16. F. M. Cornford, *From Religion to Philosophy* (New York: Harper, 1957), p. 161, cited

in Jacques Choron, *Death and Western Thought* (New York: Collier, 1963), p. 23. In *The Origin of Consciousness in the Breakdown of the Bicameral Mind* (New York: Houghton Mifflin, 1976), Julian Jaynes hypothesizes that until three thousand years ago human mental organization was effectively preconscious, so that the dead lived on as hallucinatory voices—as "gods"—in the memories of survivors. Jaynes postulates stress as one determinant of this hallucinatory mentality, but it is unclear at what point, and to what extent, that stress expresses a denial of (or refusal to discover) death.

17. See Ernst Kantorowicz, *The King's Two Bodies* (Princeton, N.J.: Princeton University Press, 1957).

18. In *James I and the Politics of Literature* (Baltimore: Johns Hopkins University Press, 1983) Jonathan Goldberg demonstrates James's projection of a Roman style and the mutual staging of power and the powers of the stage.

19. Robert Jay Lifton, *The Broken Connection* (New York: Basic Books, 1983), p. 17.

20. While he tries to honor the claims of objectivity and the "sense" of immortality, Professor Lifton himself minimizes the mind's ability to blur the distinction between literalness and tacitness. Qualifying Becker's concept of denial, he argues that humankind lives as much through the creation of connections and transcendence as in denial of death. However—absurd though it is to be pointing this out in a footnote—Lifton consistently weakens the idea of annihilation. One of his modes of symbolic immortality, e.g., is "the perception that the natural environment around us, limitless in space and time, will remain," and he illustrates it with an ancient oriental saying: "The state may collapse but the mountains and rivers remain" (p. 22). This mode of immortality—and all the others he adduces—fudges the threat of nothingness. Paleontologists speak of periodic mass extinctions on the earth, and astronomers foresee the death of the sun and the solar system, with incomprehensible questions beyond. It is the idea of being dead forever that jars the foundations of thought. Where powers of abstraction are restricted, anxiety will also be limited. In this light Lifton's study has an unspoken consolatory function that may be—given the anxieties of publishers and the public—inescapable. Science is not privileged, even though "the bioscientific, medical model of disease, our prevalent model, assumes that death is always the result of a disease process; if there were no disease, there would be no death." But this view, concludes Dr. James F. Fries, "is hard to defend." ("Aging, Natural Death, and the Compression of Morbidity," *New England Journal of Medicine* 303: 135). The medical model, i.e., resembles the primordial belief that death is always either an accident or the result of malice. Wahl ("The Fear of Death") notes that psychoanalysts "significantly" avoid the problem of death (p. 19), and Becker (*The Denial of Death*) firmly concurs, pp. 93–124.

21. For a theory of drama as the sacrifice of heroes see John Holloway, *The Story of the Night* (London: Routledge & Kegan Paul, 1961); Northrop Frye, *Anatomy*, pp. 205–22; and René Girard, *Violence and the Sacred* (Baltimore: Johns Hopkins University Press, 1977).

22. Paul A. Cantor, *Shakespeare's Rome* (Ithaca, N.Y.: Cornell University Press, 1976), p. 166. Cantor locates the exposure in 4.15.59–68, 75–78.

23. Cf. W. Thomas MacCary: "What is such 'brotherly love' but the libidinal investment of the self in the sibling of the opposite sex, and when this narcissistic choice of object is lost, there is a mourning of the most profound kind, because the self itself is called into question." *Friends and Lovers: The Phenomenology of Desire in Shakespearean Comedy* (New York: Columbia University Press, 1985), p. 184. Also see Coppélia Kahn, "The Providential Tempest and the Shakespearean Family," in *Representing Shakespeare*, ed. Murray M. Schwartz and Coppélia Kahn (Baltimore: Johns Hopkins University Press, 1980), pp. 218–19.

24. In *Sixteenth Century England* (Harmondsworth, Eng.: Penguin, 1984), Joyce Youings quotes a father who equates self and house/estate in his testamentary deliberations (1598): "If I shall leave my land and living equally divided among my children . . . then shall the dignity of my degree, the hope of my house . . . be quite buried in the bottomless pit of oblivion" (p. 380). To go on living his property—like a body—must be kept intact.

25. Cf. the drowned father in Ariel's song, whose apotheosis is a "sea-change / Into something rich and strange" affirmed "hourly" by mourning "Sea-nymphs" (*Tem.*, 1.2.397–405).

26. David Bergeron, *English Civic Pageantry, 1558–1642* (London: Edward Arnold, 1971), p. 63.

27. See Pompeo Molmenti and Gustav Ludwig, *Vittore Carpaccio* (London: J. Murray, 1907). The painting's vocabulary of torment represents a conventionalized social vision, as witnessed by the many poses Carpaccio adapted from agonies perfected by other painters. See Jan Lauts, *Vittore Carpaccio: The Paintings and Drawings* (New York: Phaidon, 1962). Compare Carpaccio's holy war and apotheosis to a twentieth-century Islamic version in which a volunteer fighting in Afghanistan reports that as he "watched by the graves of two martyrs, a shaft of light, like white neon, came out of the graves and shot straight up into the sky" in a sign of divine recognition (*The International Herald Tribune*, July 23, 1986, p. 2).

28. Sara Jayne Steen, "Fashioning an Acceptable Self: Arbella Stuart," *English Literary Renaissance* 18, no. 1 (1988): 87–88. Stuart's boast is especially poignant since she spent most of her adult life under various forms of house arrest designed to curb her autonomy for dynastic reasons. Cf. Plutarch's account of eschatological promotion to godhead in *Of Isis and Osiris, the Philosophy Commonly Called the Morals*, tr. Philemon Holland ([1603] 1657), which Walter Coppedge has pointed out to me: "But others hold, that there is a transmutation of Bodies as Souls: and like as we may observe, that of earth is ingendered Water, of Water Air, and of Air, Fire, whiles the nature of the substance still mounteth on high: even so the better Souls are changed, first from Men to Heroes or Demi-gods, and afterwards from them to Daemons, and of Daemons some few after a long time, being well refined and purified by vertue, came to participate in the Divination of the gods" (p. 1079).

29. C. L. Barber, "The Family in Shakespeare's Development," in Schwartz and Kahn, *Representing Shakespeare*, p. 201.

30. John Lawlor in *Early Shakespeare*, ed. John Russell Brown and Bernard Harris (London: Edward Arnold, 1961), p. 139.

31. Caroline Spurgeon, *Shakespeare's Imagery* (Cambridge, Eng.: Cambridge University Press, 1952), p. 185.

Chapter 4

1. A useful study of the literary sources of heroic forms in Shakespeare is James E. Bulman, *The Heroic Idiom of Shakespearean Tragedy* (Newark: University of Delaware Press, 1985).

2. Milton McGatch, *Death: Meaning and Mortality in Christian Thought and Contemporary Culture* (New York: Seabury Press, 1969), p. 80. According to McGatch, "the doctrines of purgatory and of afterlife in the interim could never supplant the vivid picture of the heroic apocalypse in the imagination of theologian and layman alike" (pp. 92–93).

3. Slavery is not an idle metaphor but a historically pertinent analogue, as Orlando Patterson has shown in *Slavery and Social Death* (Cambridge, Mass.: Harvard University Press, 1982). "Slavery," says David Brion Davis in *Slavery and Human Progress*, "is preeminently a relationship of power and dominion originating in and sustained by violence. It is a state of 'social death' substituting for a commuted physical death from war, capital punishment, starvation, or exposure" (New York: Oxford University Press, 1984), p. 11.

4. Cf. Webster's articulation of the connection between dread and tyranny in *The White Devil*, where he makes Brachiano warn: "On pain of death, let no man name death to me; It is a word infinitely terrible" (5.3).

5. For David Riggs the trilogy insists "that the received ideals of heroic greatness may be admirable in themselves, but they invariably decay, engender . . . violence and deadly rivalries, and . . . make chaos out of history. . . . The problem disappears only in some mythical past." See *Shakespeare's Heroical Histories: Henry VI and its Literary Tradition* (Cambridge, Mass.: Harvard University Press, 1971), p. 99. In *Time and the Artist in Shakespeare's Histories* (Newark: University of Delaware Press, 1983), John W. Blanpied describes the "queasy sense of instability [that] mocks and undermines the monumental postures from the start. Stability is always in the past, it seems; the present is always the awareness of falling through space" (p. 32).

6. Michel Rouche, "The Early Middle Ages in the West," in *A History of Private Life*, ed. Paul Veyne (Cambridge, Mass.: Harvard University Press, 1987), 1.429–30.

7. Cf. Fenton's version of Pasquier's *Monophylo*, in which the lover reasons that "we are borne for [our Mistresses] and not for our selues, so we liue in them and.not in our selues, and die for them, to be eftsoones reuiued in them" (vol. 1, fol. 33, quoted in William G. Meader, *Courtship in Shakespeare* [New York: Octagon, 1971], p. 123).

8. *An Apology for Actors* (1612); quoted in Steven Mullaney, "Brothers and Others, or the Art of Alienation," in *Cannibals, Witches, and Divorce: Estranging the Renaissance*, ed. Marjorie Garber (Baltimore: Johns Hopkins University Press, 1987), p. 86.

9. In *Man's Estate: Masculine Identity in Shakespeare* (Berkeley: University of California Press, 1981), Coppélia Kahn treats the Talbots' behavior in terms of the pattern of father-son rivalry evident in the histories (pp. 47–81).

10. In *Patriarchal Structures in Shakespeare's Dramas* (Berkeley: University of California Press, 1985), Peter Erickson understandably calls this sort of apotheosis "chivalric sentimentality" (p. 183). Yet this judgment underestimates the complexity of the mentality in question, especially its religious urgency. Consider, e.g., Henry V's fantasy about soldiers who die in France:

> . . . though buried in your dunghills,
> They shall be fam'd; for there the sun shall greet them,
> And draw their honors reeking [breathing] up to heaven,
> Leaving their earthly parts to choke your clime,
> The smell whereof shall breed a plague in France.
>
> [*H5* 4.3.99–103]

Play-death here expresses anxiety about degradation and decay ("dunghills") converted into revenge ("plague"), and exorcised in a purifying ascent to heaven.

11. Madelon Gohlke (Sprengnether) makes the Lacanian point that crucial faces, especially the mother and the beloved, can help bring the self into being as well as negate it. See "'And When I Love Thee Not': Women and the Psychic Integrity of the Tragic Hero," *Hebrew University Studies in Literature* 8 (1980): 48.

12. In his Cambridge edition of *1 Henry VI* (1959), J. Dover Wilson discerns topical

references in the play to the English campaigns in France in 1591–92, with Talbot an allusion to Essex. In an important essay, "Topical Ideology: Witches, Amazons, and Shakespeare's Joan of Arc," *English Literary Renaissance* 18, no. 1 (1988), Gabriele Bernhard Jackson examines the play's topicality in detail, demonstrating how improvisatory Shakespeare's compositional process could be.

13. Cf. actual slavery, in which the slave's identity totally "depended on the hazards of fate and on an 'artificial' loyalty to authorities who were not his kin. This point helps to illuminate . . . an ancient religious metaphor. To become a 'slave' to Yahweh or Christ was not simply to imitate the humility and subservience of a bondsman. It was also to acknowledge the transference of primal loyalties and obligations to a new and awesome power, in the hope of gaining a new and transcendent freedom" (Davis, *Slavery and Human Progress*, p. 16).

14. Stephen Greenblatt, "Invisible Bullets: Renaissance Authority and its Subversion, *Henry IV* and *Henry V*," in *Shakespearean Negotiations* (Berkeley: University of California Press, 1988), p. 63. For David Riggs, the heroes of the histories embody "the real, but highly suspect, aspirations of a large part of Elizabethan society" (*Shakespeare's Heroical Histories*, p. 69).

15. John Earle, *Micro-Cosmographie*, 1628, quoted in J. D. Wilson's *Life in Shakespeare's England* (Cambridge, Eng.: Cambridge University Press, 1911), p. 49.

16. My chapter on *Hamlet* in *Shakespeare's Creation* details the oppressiveness of the Ghost, a view developed also in Richard Wheeler, *Shakespeare's Development and the Problem Comedies* (Berkeley: University of California Press, 1981), p. 194, and in Erickson, *Patriarchal Structures*, pp. 67–72. In an essay that exhaustively documents Renaissance funeral customs, James V. Holleran argues that in *Hamlet* the official funeral rites for the old king, Polonius, and Ophelia were "maimed," and the court blindly, compulsively plays out tragically deformed substitutes for those rites in the action of the play. See "Maimed Funeral Rites in *Hamlet*," *ELR* 19 (1989).

17. The association of the lost hero's face with heaven and Judgment Day recurs in Hamlet's imagery as he invokes his father: "Heaven's face does glow / O'er this solidity and compound mass / With heated visage, as against the doom [i.e., Judgment Day]" (3.4.48–50). Cf. *1H6* 1.1.12–16, 28–30. The equivocal Ghost intensifies the psychological dilemma David Sundelson finds in the *Henry VI* plays, in which "the father is killed, returns, and is killed again, in which fathers are poised between overwhelming power and total disappearance." See *Shakespeare's Restorations of the Father* (New Brunswick, N.J.: Rutgers University Press, 1983), p. 11.

18. Janet Adelman, "Male Bonding in Shakespeare's Comedies," in *Shakespeare's "Rough Magic,"* ed. Peter Erickson and Coppélia Kahn (Newark: University of Delaware Press, 1985), p. 95.

19. This ravenous behavior is prefigured in *2 Henry VI* by Jack Cade: "Away, burn all the records of the realm, my mouth shall be the parliament of England" (4.7.15). "Then," quips an observer, "we are like to have biting statutes, unless his teeth be pull'd out" (16–17).

20. Becker, *The Denial of Death*, reminds us that "Life cannot go on without mutual devouring of organisms. If at the end of each person's life he were to be presented with the living spectacle of all that he had organismically incorporated in order to stay alive, he might well feel horrified by the living energy he had ingested. . . . To paraphrase Elias Canetti, each organism raises its head over a field of corpses, smiles into the sun, and declares life good" (p. 2). This is precisely the haunting, inadmissable truth about human life dramatized by the biting, "unfinished" Crookback and Henry IV's vision of humankind as insatiable wolves (*2H4* 4.5.137).

21. Janet Adelman's reading of appetite in Coriolanus indirectly sheds light as well on Crookback. See "'Anger's My Meat,'" pp. 108–24.

22. For a strong version of this position see Lisa Jardin, *Still Harping on Daughters* (Sussex, Eng.: Harvester Press, 1983).

23. See, e.g., Greenblatt's analysis of Thomas More's lifelong, perilous reliance on ironic role-playing in his negotiation of identity (*Self-Fashioning*, pp. 11–73). I have looked at the phenomenon in "Imitation and Identity: Shakespeare and the Imagination of His Culture," in *Shakespearean Metadrama*, ed. John Blanpied (Rochester, N.Y.: University of Rochester, 1977), pp. 78–100.

24. Cf. Whigham's discussion of reactions to widespread opportunistic use of courtesy books to manufacture noble character (*Ambition and Privilege*, pp. 1–31).

Chapter 5

1. Leslie Fiedler, "Shakespeare's Commodity-Comedy: A Meditation on the Preface to the 1609 Quarto of *Troilus and Cressida*," in Erickson and Kahn, *Shakespeare's "Rough Magic*," p. 55.

2. Joseph Campbell, *The Hero with a Thousand Faces* (Princeton, N.J.: Princeton University Press, 1968), pp. 35–36. In their useful introduction to *Death and the Regeneration of Life* (Cambridge, Eng.: Cambridge University Press, 1982), Maurice Bloch and Jonathan Parry trace the evolution of anthropological treatments of rebirth themes.

3. Eliade, *Rites and Symbols of Initiation*, pp. 131–32. ˇ

4. Maud Bodkin, *Archetypal Patterns in Poetry* (Oxford: Oxford University Press, 1934), p. 21. Bodkin summarizes Freudian and Jungian theories of the rebirth archetype.

5. Martin P. Nilsson, *Greek Popular Religion* (New York: Columbia University Press, 1940), pp. 18, 20. One variation of this idea, as ethnologist S. W. deRachewiltz pointed out to me, is the popular belief that in answer to prayers the dead may arise from their graves with the identifying tools of their crafts to aid the poor. For a fifeenth-century illustration see Martin Peintner, *Neustifter Buch malerei* (Bolzano, Italy: Verlaganstalt Athesia, 1984), p. 83. This belief counterpoises the fear expressed in Brueghel's *Triumph of Death*, e.g., that the vengeful dead seek to kill all who have survived them.

6. Desiderius Erasmus, *The Education of a Christian Prince* (1516), ed. and trans. Lester K. Born (New York: Columbia University Press, 1936), p. 173, cited in Gordon J. Schochet, *Patriarchalism in Political Thought* (New York: Basic Books, 1975), p. 30.

7. Roy Battenhouse, *Marlowe's Tamburlaine: A Study in Renaissance Moral Philosophy* (Nashville, Tenn.: Vanderbilt University Press, 1941), p. 172n.

8. Girard, *Violence and the Sacred*, p. 317, and *The Scapegoat* (Baltimore: Johns Hopkins University Press, 1986), p. 44. For Girard desire is mimetic and leads to vicious struggles for being and for objects "capable of conferring an even greater plenitude of being" (p. 146). See also Becker's *Escape from Evil*, esp. pp. 26–37.

9. John Holloway, *The Story of the Night* (London: Routledge & Kegan Paul, 1961).

10. C. L. Barber, *Shakespeare's Festive Comedy* (Princeton, N.J.: Princeton University Press, 1959), p. 84.

11. See Eugene M. Waith, *The Herculean Hero in Marlowe, Chapman, Shakespeare, and Dryden* (London: Chatto & Windus, 1962), and Riggs, *Shakespeare's Heroical Histories*, pp. 63ff.

12. Herbert R. Coursen, Jr., *Christian Ritual and the World of Shakespeare's Tragedies* (Lewisburg, Pa.: Bucknell University Press, 1976), p. 15.

13. See, e.g., Walter Beltz, *God and the Gods*, trans. Peter Heinegg (Harmondsworth, Eng.: Penguin, 1983), pp. 218–35, and Erich Auerbach's essay on *figura* in *Scenes from the Drama of European Literature* (New York: Doubleday, 1959), pp. 11–76. In iconography Noah's ark, e.g., is a tomblike structure that facilitates humankind's survival thanks to a righteous hero who prefigures Christ.

14. Elisabeth Kübler-Ross, *On Death and Dying* (New York: Macmillan, 1968), p. 4.

15. Samuel Schoenbaum, *William Shakespeare, a Compact Documentary Life* (Oxford: Oxford University Press, 1977), p. 288.

16. Yet another analogue is the doctor in the old St. George plays who raises the fallen hero/saint with echoes of Jesus and Cerimon. See Joseph Quincy Adams, ed., *Chief Pre-Shakespearean Dramas* (Boston: Houghton Mifflin, 1924), pp. 353–56.

17. Cf. Freud's "The Theme of the Three Caskets," in *The Collected Papers of Sigmund Freud*, vol. 4, chap. 15 (New York, 1959), and Francis Fergusson's very different reading of Portia as a *figura* of Christ in *Trope and Allegory* (Athens: University of Georgia Press, 1977), pp. 119–22.

18. David M. Bergeron, "The Restoration of Hermione," in *Shakespeare's Romances Reconsidered*, ed. Carol McGinnis Kay and Henry E. Jacobs (Lincoln: University of Nebraska Press, 1978), p. 126.

19. In *Man and Animals Struggling against Death and Father Time* (Boston Museum of Fine Arts) by the Flemish painter David Vinckboons (1576–1632), a skeletal warrior death is assaulting a group of city dwellers while a winged Father Time looks on impassively (Figure 3). The painting is contemporary with *The Winter's Tale* (1610).

20. The comment of the Separatist Henry Barrow, in Michael Neill, "'Exeunt with a Dead March': Funeral Pageantry on the Shakespearean Stage," in *Pageantry in the Shakespearean Theatre*, ed. David Bergeron (Athens: University of Georgia Press, 1985), pp. 153–93.

21. Roland Mushat Frye, *The Renaissance Hamlet* (Princeton, N.J.: Princeton University Press, 1984), p. 231. In such tombs "realism . . . is used for its own sake. In other words, what seems to be a symptom of the decadence of the Middle Ages is in reality a further step to the Renaissance" (Spencer, *Death and Elizabethan Tragedy*, p. 28).

22. In many cultural systems the "restitution of life is dramatised . . . by the elaborate construction, and subsequent negation of its antithesis—decomposition and decay. An emphasis on biological processes is used to darken the background against which the ultimate triumph over biology (and hence over death) can shine forth all the more brightly. . . . [Above] the late Mediaeval representation of the maggot-infested corpse we may sometimes discover the pure, radiant and incorrupt soul leaving behind its corruptible shell and arising into heaven. Symbolically it is the corruption of the corpse which *creates* the purity of the soul—a point which Catholic belief comes close to recognising in the notion that it is the flesh that binds the soul to the profane world, putrescence thus becoming a necessary prelude to spiritual purification" (Bloch and Parry, *Death and the Regeneration of Life*, p. 26).

23. Stephen Greenblatt, *Self-Fashioning*, pp. 17–27; and Frye, *The Renaissance Hamlet* (1984), p. 240.

Chapter 6

1. Such schemes made death a function of forces in the human personality. In *Shakespeare and the Experience of Love* (Cambridge, Eng.: Cambridge University Press, 1981), Arthur Kirsch points out that the staging of *The Castle of Perseverance*—"of Mankind's

castle, with his bed under it, surrounded by the scaffolds of God, the World, the Flesh, Belial, and Covetousness—literalizes the scaffolding of a human life and reflects the same allegorical impulse, if not essentially the same mental topography, that is to be found in Freud's diagrams depicting the composition of the psyche" (p. 5). In this instance various cosmic and psychic forces are also destinations arranged in a neighborhood or a kingdom whose relationships center on humankind. The surrounding scaffolds themselves tacitly constitute a perimeter, and the problematical space beyond them is formally moot.

2. In *Shakespeare and Christian Doctrine* (Princeton, N.J.: Princeton University Press, 1963), Roland M. Frye quotes Luther: "[W]e must sleep until He comes and knocks at our little grave and exclaims: 'Dr. Martin, get up!' Then in the twinkling of an eye I shall rise again and will rejoice with Him eternally" (p. 55). Cf. "The Homily against the Fear of Death": "[H]oly Scripture calleth the bodily death a sleepe, where in man's senses be (as it were) taken from him for a season, and yet when he awaketh, he is more fresh than he was when he went to bed." In Greek mythology Thanatos and Hypnos are twin brothers.

3. Michael Neill argues—too sweepingly, I think—that the Reformation made "each man's death . . . (as *Dr. Faustus* vividly demonstrates) a private Apocalypse, whose awful Judgment could never be reversed," so that Hamlet "was . . . tapping a profound source of post-Reformation angst" (*Funeral Pageantry*, p. 180).

4. Gail Kern Paster, *The Idea of the City in the Age of Shakespeare* (Athens: University of Georgia Press, 1985), p. 73.

5. Paster's opening chapter marshals some examples of the ancient association of the city with immortality.

6. See Steven Mullaney, *The Place of the Stage: License, Play, and Power in Renaissance England* (Chicago: University of Chicago Press, 1988).

7. "We should not underestimate . . . contemporary expressions of alarm, which perhaps had more to do with emigration to New England than historians have recognized." Christopher Hill, *The Collected Essays of Christopher Hill* (Amherst: The University of Massachusetts Press, 1985), p. 18.

8. Cf. Stephen Greenblatt, "Invisible Bullets," and Paul Brown, "'This Thing of Darkness I Acknowledge Mine': *The Tempest* and the Discourse of Colonialism," in Jonathan Dollimore and Alan Sinfield, eds., *Political Shakespeare: New Essays in Cultural Materialism* (Ithaca, N.Y.: Cornell University Press, 1985), pp. 48–71. See also Winthrop D. Jordan, *White over Black: American Attitudes toward the Negro, 1550–1812* (Chapel Hill: University of North Carolina Press, 1968), esp. chap. 1.

9. As Leslie Fiedler notes in *The Stranger in Shakespeare* (New York: Stein & Day, 1972), pp. 48–49.

10. See also John Armstrong, *The Paradise Myth* (London: Oxford University Press, 1979), pp. 68ff. In *Psyche and Symbol in Shakespeare* (Bloomington: Indiana University Press, 1972), Alex Aronson offers a Jungian reading of Hero's play-death in *Much Ado* in terms of the Persephone myth (pp. 168–72). Also see Northrop Frye's Introduction to the third essay of his *Anatomy of Criticism*.

11. Following etymological clues, Nilsson traces the myth of Persephone back to the agricultural basis of Greek folk religion, which links sexual fertility and food in ways that are unexpectedly echoed in Leontes' embrace of the revived Hermione: "O, she's warm! / If this be magic, let it be an art / Lawful as eating" (5.3.109–111). See also Peter Stallybrass, "The Body Enclosed," in *Rewriting the Renaissance*, ed. Margaret Ferguson, Maureen Quilligan, and Nancy Vickers (Chicago: University of Chicago Press, 1986), pp. 123–44.

12. See James L. Calderwood's discussion of Macbeth's greed for immortality in *If It Were Done: Macbeth and Tragic Action* (Amherst: University of Massachusetts Press, 1986), pp. 93–97.

13. In "The Articulation of the Ego in the English Renaissance," in *The Literary Freud: Mechanisms of Defence and the Poetic Will*, ed. Joseph H. Smith (New Haven, Conn.: Yale University Press, 1980), pp. 261–308, William Kerrigan considers the psychic topography of the body (pp. 290ff).

14. See R. D. Stock's useful remarks on numinous experience in *The Holy and the Demonic from Sir Thomas Browne to William Blake* (Princeton, N.J.: Princeton University Press, 1982), pp. 17–23.

15. Coursen, *Christian Ritual*, corroborates this reading of Cordelia in the course of arguing for "Shakespeare's extensive use of the Fall of Man" in the tragedies (pp. 286–87).

16. David Sundelson, "So Rare and Wond'red a Father: Prospero's *Tempest*," in Schwartz and Kahn, *Representing Shakespeare*, p. 49.

17. Cf. the ambivalence of mourning in "A Ballet of A father warning his children to feare god & kepe his commaundements," from *Tudor Songs and Ballads From MS Cotton Vespasian A-25*, ed. Peter J. Seng (Cambridge, Mass.: Harvard University Press, 1978), p. 57:

> ffor I the Imaige of youre yeres
> youre treasure and youre trust
> am dyinge now before youre faice
> and shall consume to duste
> for as you se youre fathers fleshe
> consume nowe into claye
> even so shall ye my children deare
> consume and weare away /
>
> The sonne the monne & eye the starres
> that serve both daye and night
> the earthe and every Lyving thinge
> shalbe consumed quight
> and all the worshipp that ys wrought
> that haithe bene harde or seen
> shall clene consume & torne to nowght
> as yt had never bene
>
> Therefore se that you follow me
> youre father and youre frende
> and enter into that same lande
> which never shall have ende
> I leave you here a lytle booke
> for you to loke vpon
> that you may se youre fathers faice
> when he ys deade and gonne

This father mixes punitive control ("you will be annihilated in the apocalypse to come") and paradisial promise ("follow me" into the "lande / which never shall have ende") to make in art (cf. *The Tempest* and Prospero's artful island) a monument or mourning house ("a lytle booke . . . that you may se youre fathers faice when he ys dead").

18. Following Tertullian, Augustine holds that Adam's sin was transmitted through semen, so that even married sexuality is inherently tainted by the threat of death which Adam discovered. See Chapter 5 of Elaine Pagels's *Adam, Eve, and the Serpent* (New York: Random House, 1988), esp. pp. 105–15. Augustine directly attacks the conviction of immortality based on sexual fecundity, substituting a system of immortality grounded in a psychology of radical self-effacement: i.e., in guilty submission to omnipotent cosmic will. His attack suggests that one of humankind's most crucial systems of immortality had become—and would continue to be—disquietingly problematical.

19. Kenneth Burke, *The Rhetoric of Religion* (Berkeley: University of California Press, 1970), p. 219.

20. Norman Rabkin, *Shakespeare and the Problem of Meaning* (Chicago: University of Chicago Press, 1981), pp. 33–62.

21. Jonathan Dollimore and Alan Sinfield, "History and Ideology: the Instance of *Henry V*," in *Alternative Shakespeares* (London & New York: Methuen, 1985), p. 225.

Chapter 7

1. J. W. Lever, "Venus and the Second Chance," *Shakespeare Survey* 15 (1962): 87–88.

2. Hereward T. Price, "The Function of Imagery in *Venus and Adonis*," *Papers of the Michigan Academy of Sciences, Arts, and Letters* 31 (1945): 295, 297.

3. Elias Canetti, *Crowds and Power* (New York: Seabury, 1978), p. 229. In the context of the Vinckboons painting mentioned earlier, in which death is a hunter, Adonis would rival if not supplant death.

4. For a discussion of *The Masque of Proteus* in these terms, see my *Shakespeare's Creation*, pp. 40–45.

5. "People take the overwhelmingness of creation and their own fears and desires and project them in the form of intense mana onto certain figures to which they then defer. . . . Men are literally hypnotized by life and by those who represent life to them." Ernest Becker, *Escape from Evil*, pp. 50–51.

6. Othello interprets his mother's magical handkerchief as a means of controlling the dangerous connection between love and the hunt: "if she lost it, / . . . my father's eye / Should hold her loathed, and his spirits should hunt / After new fancies" (3.4.60–63). Also cf. *TN* 1.1.34–38).

7. Robert P. Miller takes the poem to be "a mythological reenactment of man's fall to sin." See "Venus, Adonis, and the Horses," *ELH* 19 (1952): 250–64.

8. William Keach, *Elizabethan Erotic Narratives* (New Brunswick, N.J.: Rutgers University Press, 1977), p. 83.

9. Kahn, *Man's Estate*, p.48.

10. Anthony Esler, *The Aspiring Mind of the Elizabethan Younger Generation* (Durham, N.C.: Duke University Press, 1966), p. 123.

11. Louis Adrian Montrose, "'Shaping Fantasies': Figurations of Gender and Power in Elizabethan Culture," *Representations* 2 (1983): 61–94.

12. Leonard Tennenhouse, *Power on Display: The Politics of Shakespeare's Genres* (New York & London: Methuen, 1986), p. 31.

13. *Letters*, pp. 51–52. Quoted in Greenblatt, *Sir Walter Ralegh*, p. 24.

14. G. P. V. Akrigg, *Shakespeare and the Earl of Southampton* (Cambridge, Mass.: Harvard University Press, 1968), p. 202. Akrigg connects Southampton to the poem through his costly refusal to marry Burghley's granddaughter and a pamphlet entitled *Narcissus*, which may have been meant to humiliate the young earl, and which Shake-

speare may have been indirectly seeking to counter with his epyllion (pp. 33–34, 195–96).

15. J. E. Neale, *Elizabeth I and Her Parliaments, 1585–1601*, 2 vols. (London: Jonathan Cape, 1965), 1:109. "Of the Earl of Essex's insatiable thirst for those offices and honors which were in the Queen's gift, Naunton wrote that 'my Lord . . . drew in too fast, like a childe sucking on an over-uberous Nurse'" (Montrose, "'Shaping Fantasies,'" p. 64). The same image appears in Fulke Greville's "The Four Foster Children of Desire," where the nursing queen is ambivalently both "Desire" and a fortress under assault from four courtiers, the

> long haple, now hopeful fostered children of Desire; who having bin a great while nourished up with that infective milke, and to too much care of their fiery fosterer, (though full oft that dry nurse Dispaier indevered to wainne them from it) being nowe as strong in that nurture, as they are weake in fortune, incouraged with the valiaunt counsaile of never fainting Desire, and by the same asured, that by right of inheritaunce even from ever, the Fortresse of Beautie doth belong to her fostered children.

As "Desire" suggests the maternalized Venus, here partly internalized, so the fortress figures not only the unattainable goddess, but also the woman's cold will to survival—cf. the fortified self described in Chapter 4—that the foster children cannot penetrate. Fulke Greville, "The Life of the Renowned Sr. Philip Sidney," in *The Works in Verse and Prose of the Right Honourable Fulke Greville . . .* , ed. Alexander B. Grosart (1870; reprint, New York: AMS Press, 1966), pp. 313–14.

16. Perhaps Paphos was the only politic solution open to the poet. Akrigg sees the notoriously elusive *Phoenix and the Turtle* in terms of the Essex rebellion. Expanding on other evidence that one of the lost birds "certainly symbolizes Essex," he contends that "Elizabeth is present . . . in the poem but she, having ordered the deaths of Essex and his friends, is now the Eagle with the 'tyrant wing'" (*Shakespeare and the Earl of Southampton*, pp. 251–52).

17. M. C. Bradbrook, *Shakespeare: The Poet in His World* (London: Methuen, 1980), p. 75. Cf. the poem's voluptuous sacrifice of the hunter/warrior Adonis and Carpaccio's transfigured martyrs (Figure 2), "commissioned by Cardinal Ettore Ottoboni to commemorate a vow made in time of pestilence" (Molmenti and Ludwig, *Vittore Carpaccio*, p. 213).

18. See Muriel C. Bradbrook, "Beasts and Gods: Greene's *Groats-Worth of Witte* and the Social Purpose of *Venus and Adonis*," *Shakespeare Survey* 15 (1962): 68–71; reprinted in *Shakespeare: The Poet in His World*. Bradbrook proposes that Shakespeare wrote his sophisticated epyllion in an effort to transcend his own artistic identity as the "upstart" parvenu Greene had ridiculed.

Chapter 8

1. One justly influential study finds that many of Shakespeare's plays "reveal the high cost of patriarchal values; the men who uphold them atrophy, and the women, whether resistant or acquiescent, die." See *The Woman's Part: Feminist Criticism of Shakespeare*, ed. Carolyn R. S. Lenz, Gayle Greene, and Carol Thomas Neely (Urbana: University of Illinois Press, 1980), pp. 5–6. Also see Kahn, *Man's Estate*, pp. 82–104. Peter Erickson's *Patriarchal Structures* is also primarily concerned with the representation of gender and its political implications. More disposed to see patriarchy as a comprehensive social system is Marianne L. Novy, *Love's Argument: Gender Relations in Shakespeare*

(Chapel Hill: University of North Carolina Press, 1984), esp. chap. 3. Debora Shuger ("Reflections of the Father") persuasively complicates the prevailing stereotypes of the coercive patriarch.

2. Cf. Lenz, Greene, and Neely, *The Woman's Part*: "Although women may strive to resist or correct the perversions of patriarchy, they do not succeed in altering that order nor do they withdraw their allegiance from it" (p. 6).

3. "At the beginning of the world," Machiavelli theorized in the *Discourses*, "the inhabitants were few in number, and lived for a time dispersed like beasts. As the human race increased, the necessity for uniting themselves for defence made itself felt; the better to attain this object, they chose the strongest and most courageous from amongst themselves and placed him at their head, promising to obey him" (Schochet, *Patriarchalism*, p. 29). Schochet surveys patriarchal political theory in the Tudor period, pp. 37–53.

4. Richard Hooker, *The Works of Richard Hooker*, ed. John Keeble, 3 vols. (Oxford, 1888; reprint, New York, 1970), 3: 652 (cited in Shuger, "Reflections of the Father").

5. The chronic instability of patriarchy is implied in the patricidal conflicts of "The Revesby Sword Play," in which the son Pickle Herring's "bad news" for his father is that "We have all concluded to cut off your head" (ll. 135–36). The sons sing, "for your estate we do your body kill" (l. 248). The slain father, however, repeatedly springs to life, offering a communal dance rather than revenge (cf. Old Capulet's ball) even as he goes on to compete sexually with his sons. When Pickle Herring disguises himself as a rich old man to court the maid Cicely, the ploy backfires: Cicely rejects him and his father concludes: "Tis I that carries the lass away" (l. 569). See Adams, *Chief Pre-Shakespearean Dramas*, pp. 357–64. Christopher Martin shows patriarchal anxiety to be a source of mock death and romance-heroism in Sidney. See "Misdoubting His Estate: Dynastic Anxiety in Sidney's *Arcadia*," in *English Literary Renaissance* 18, no. 3 (1988).

6. It is tempting to see the origins of patriarchy in Robin Fox's sketch of the gerontocratic social order that at one stage controlled access to breeding in the prehistoric past. See "The Conditions of Sexual Evolution," in Philippe Ariès and Andre Béjin, *Western Sexuality* (New York & Oxford: Oxford University Press, 1986), pp. 1–13.

7. Gerry Brenner, "Shakespeare's Politically Ambitious Friar," *Shakespeare Studies* 13 (1980): 50.

8. See Brian Gibbon's Arden edition of the play, p. 170n. The allusion to orgasmic dying could be strengthened even further by recalling the Lord's promise to Abraham that his immortality would be in infinite progeny: "Look now toward heaven, and tell the stars, if thou be able to number them: and he said unto him, So shall thy seed be" (Gen. 15.5).

9. Edward A. Snow discriminates two distinct modes of desire in the lovers, "exquisitely fitted to each other, but rarely meeting in the same phenomenological universe" (p. 178). Where Juliet "experiences genesis and gestation, Romeo is haunted by a sense of emptiness and unreality." His love "remains to some extent an attempt to escape from a reality he finds oppressive." See "Language and Sexual Difference in *Romeo and Juliet*," in Erickson and Kahn, *Shakespeare's "Rough Magic,"* p. 179.

10. Juliet's invocation of Phaeton suggests an unconscious appreciation of the perils of the lovers' usurpation of patriarchal reins (3.2.1–4).

11. Since a slave must at least pretend to replace his own extirpated will with his master's, slavery can be seen as a form of playing dead in order to survive. I examine the servants' behavior in *Shakespeare's Creation*, pp. 120–21.

12. Cf. Juliet's "O'ercovered" and "your daughter cover'd with a Barbary horse" in *Othello* (1.1.111).

13. Romeo has mortgaged his life to "Some consequence yet hanging in the stars,"

and the stars themselves are associated with fathers, as Harold C. Goddard says in *The Meaning of Shakespeare* (Chicago: University of Chicago Press, 1951), 1: 119. Cf. the indebtedness to a father associated with mourning in, e.g., *Twelfth Night* and *Love's Labors Lost*. Erickson notes Prince Hal's sense of guilt toward paternal figures (*Patriarchal Structures*, p. 46), and directly links Henry V to Hamlet in their common dilemma of indebtedness to fathers (pp. 63–72).

14. I am assuming that the child has perceived the mother's own identification with the father, although in the earliest years of life the mother must have been experienced as the omnipotent and subsuming force. In an adult's unconscious, in varying ways and degrees, father and mother seem likely to have been fused. In a relevant historical context John Demos provides a useful assessment of infantile fantasies about the mother. See *Entertaining Satan* (New York: Oxford University Press, 1982), pp. 200–206.

15. "Romeo tends to hypostatize feelings. . . . When he does imagine himself in the world rather than 'looking on' [1.4.38], it is usually by picturing himself as an object in space that is 'moved' by external forces. . . . [His] favorite metaphor is the sea-journey, with himself more often the ship than the pilot" (Snow, "Language and Sexual Difference," p. 171).

16. "When Shakespeare makes Romeo wonder whether death keeps Juliet as his paramour . . . his words are a variation on a common notion" (Spencer, *Death and Elizabethan Tragedy*, p. 77). The "monster" Death is based on conventional imagery of the skeleton (pp. 72–77). In the play as well as in the social world from which it derives, however, that imagery is also profoundly patriarchal.

17. A fourteenth-century English poem, "Death and Life," makes Death a devouring woman with "a marvelous mouth full of long tushes, / & the neb of her nose to her navell hanged" (quoted in Spencer, *Death and Elizabethan Tragedy*, p. 29). "Tushes" evoke the boar-as-death in *Venus and Adonis*. The condensation of family relationships in Romeo's fantasy about death prefigures the patterns of incest and intimate strife that shadow the major tragedies and the late romances. The Capulets' monument laden with the bodies of slain suitors may anticipate the opening of *Pericles*, for example, where the palace of the incestuous tyrant Antiochus displays the severed heads of suitors who have failed to release his daughter from his thrall by answering a riddle about a devouring monster.

18. Cf. also Juliet's vision of lying "o'ercovered" by dead men in a charnel house (4.1.85).

19. Their own aggression exposed, the fathers behave like patriarchal sons insofar as they compulsively imagine a debt of mourning—cf. Chapters 3 and 4—that their gold statues can pay or expiate.

20. The criticism of *Romeo and Juliet* readily reveals the compulsion to console for death. In *Coming of Age in Shakespeare* (London: Methuen, 1981) Marjorie Garber vows that "although Juliet will die young, her experiences with love, sex, pain, and loss are enough for a lifetime of adulthood" (p. 37). Cf. this Tennysonian straw ("it is better to have lived and loved than not to have lived at all") with John Lawlor's wishful encomium (cited in Chapter 3): "It is essential . . . that we see [Romeo] grow . . . to a final maturity which outsoars all else in the play" (p. 133). Even Coppélia Kahn tries to give the lovers' force of will a quasireligious vitality: "their love-death is not merely fated; it is willed. It is the lovers' triumphant assertion over the impoverished and destructive world that has kept them apart" (Kahn, *Man's Estate*, p. 103).

Chapter 9

1. G. R. Elton, *Policy and Police* (Cambridge, Eng.: Cambridge University Press, 1972), p. 53.

2. See Gerard H. Cox, "Apocalyptic Projection and the Plot of *The Alchemist*," *English Literary Renaissance* 13, no. 1 (1983): 70–87. In *2 Henry VI* the Duchess of Gloucester falls for a prophetic con game much as Neville did.

3. Elton, *Policy and Police*, p. 50. In his *Diary* Philip Henslowe lists among his theater's props a cloak of invisibility which, in conjunction with Neville's, witnesses the complexly equivocal attitudes toward the supernatural in Shakespeare's England.

4. A. P. Rossiter, *Angel with Horns* (New York: Theatre Arts Books, 1961), p. 20.

5. George A. Kelly, *A Theory of Personality* (New York: Norton, 1963). Because his theory "emphasizes the creative capacity of the living thing to represent the environment" and therefore "do something about it if it doesn't suit him" (p. 8), it is especially suggestive when applied to the theater, where characters must create their worlds.

6. Cf. William Neville's ambivalent fantasies, described earlier in the chapter, in which he wished Henry VIII dead one moment and the next identified with him by imagining himself slaughtering Henry's enemies "of low blood."

7. In *Dream in Shakespeare* (New Haven, Conn.: Yale University Press, 1974), Marjorie B. Garber explores Shakespeare's development of the dream from a "predictive device" to a "way of presenting the mind at work" (p. 15). Her analyses of dreams in *Richard III* explore imaginative modes akin to the prophetic (pp. 15–25).

8. K. V. Thomas, *Religion and the Decline of Magic* (New York: Scribner's, 1971), p. 398.

9. Glendower illustrates the point by attempting to intimidate the skeptical Hotspur with prophecies that supposedly prove him "not in the roll of common men" (*1H4* 3.1.42). For a discussion of the "Mouldwarp" prophecy that engages Glendower (3.1.147), see Thomas, *Religion and the Decline of Magic*, pp. 399–403. In *Shakespeare's History Plays* (London: Chatto & Windus, 1956), E. M. W. Tillyard emphasizes that Richmond himself claimed that he and his heirs were King Arthur reincarnate (p. 30).

10. Calderwood, *Macbeth and Tragic Action*, analyzes Shakespeare's distinction between (perverse) augmentation and (natural) increase, which reflects the taboo against self-aggrandizing seizure of the future. Seeking to be more than what he was, "Macbeth ultimately renders himself and, in his despairing judgment, all of life nothing" (p. 57). See my treatment of the taboo as self-effacement in Chapter 2.

11. Shadow: "An unreal appearance; a delusive semblance or image; a vain and unsubstantial object of pursuit" (*OED* 6a); also "an obscure indication . . . a prefiguration, foreshadowing" (*OED* 6c). "Shadow" is also Elizabethan slang for an actor.

12. The Folio prints "spy my shadow," whereas the first Quarto gives "see my shadow."

13. Cf. the "cloak of invisibility" that would dissolve the mortal body and confer expansive powers. As a projection of the self out of the body, Richard's repudiation is related to Macbeth's summons of his own will to murder in the form of "seeling night" that can "scarf up the tender eye of pitiful day, / And with . . . bloody and invisible hand / Cancel and tear to pieces that great bond / Which keeps me pale" (3.2.46–48).

14. Muriel Bradbrook, *The Living Monument* (Cambridge, Eng.: Cambridge University Press, 1976), p. 19. Richard fulfills a prophecy the first time we see him in battle, killing Somerset in *2 Henry VI* under the sign of the Castle: "Let him shun castles" (1.4.35).

15. Moody E. Prior, *The Drama of Power* (Evanston, Ill.: Northwestern University Press, 1973), p. 43.

16. Dolores M. Burton, "Discourse and Decorum in the First Act of *Richard III*," *Shakespeare Studies* 14 (1981): 59.

17. In *Europe's Inner Demons* (New York: Basic Books, 1975), Norman Cohn traces the history of the fantasies that produced the persecution of witches in Europe, construing the anxious fascination with the devil as "unconscious resentment against Christianity as too strict a religion, against Christ as too stern a taskmaster. Psychologically, it is altogether plausible that such an unconscious hatred would find an outlet in an obsession with the overwhelming power of Christ's great antagonist, Satan" (p. 262).

18. Henry Howard, Earl of Northampton, *A Defensative against the Poyson of Supposed Prophecies* (1583), D4.

19. Norman Cohn, *The Pursuit of the Millennium* (New York: Harper & Row, 1961), p. 69. My analysis of Hal's behavior here draws upon the dynamics of the apocalyptic fantasy Cohn details. The fantasy has echoes in Shakespeare, but without the revolutionary and chiliastic elements that surfaced again soon after in the behavior of the Ranters.

20. Holinshed attributes Satanic qualities to Worcester, whose aim "was ever (as some write) to procure malice and set things in a broil." In *Shakespeare's English Kings* (New York: Oxford University Press, 1977), Peter Saccio calls Worcester "a born agent of chaos, something like a witch out of *Macbeth*" (p. 50).

21. Ernst Kris, "Prince Hal's Conflict," *The Psychoanalytic Quarterly* 17 (1948): 487–506.

22. See Gilles Quispel's analysis of Augustine's Jerusalem in "Time and History in Patristic Christianity," in *Man and Time*, ed. Joseph Campbell (Princeton, N.J.: Princeton University Press, 1957), p. 106.

23. In *Shakespeare's Creation*, I have tried to show in detail how Shakespeare himself will often grossly conventionalize his art in order to violate those conventions and induce in the audience a sense of wonder or tragic awe.

24. William Carroll, *The Metamorphoses of Shakespeare's Comedy*, implicitly recognizes the radical nature of the play-death figured in this speech: "Hal's claim to have achieved a total transformation, in which his former self is annihilated and the 'is not' triumphs, sounds chilling" (p. 180).

25. James L. Calderwood, *Metadrama in Shakespeare's Henriad* (Berkeley: University of California Press, 1979), p. 83.

26. Andrew Gurr, "'Henry V' and the Bees' Commonwealth," *Shakespeare Survey* 30 (1977): 67.

27. See Norman Rabkin's account of these interpretive possibilities in *Shakespeare and the Problem of Meaning* (Chicago: University of Chicago Press, 1981), pp. 33–62, esp. p. 58. In *A Kingdom for a Stage* (Cambridge, Mass.: Harvard University Press, 1972), Robert Ornstein notes apocalyptic images in *Henry V* (pp. 177–78).

28. Ornstein contends that *Richard II* "describes an ideal cosmological scheme in its poetry and mocks it in its dramatic action" (*A Kingdom for a Stage*, p. 105).

29. Barber *Shakespeare's Festive Comedy*, pp. 219–21.

30. Newspapers described the 1984 presidential campaign, as is customary, in terms of military assault. One candidate spoke of being criticized as "taking incoming" (= artillery). A governor's press secretary was quoted as saying that another candidate for president "hit this state so fast and exploded like an atom bomb." The metaphor naively expresses the dynamics of the fantasy I have been tracing in the histories, in which a leader may be felt capable of annihilating opponents and dominating the collective consciousness with a superhuman power.

31. See Ernst H. Kantorowicz, *The King's Two Bodies* (Princeton, N.J.: Princeton University Press, 1957), esp. his chapter on *Richard II*, pp. 24–41. Kantorowicz appreci-

ates that Renaissance minds could recognize the fictional nature of the royal ideology without altogether demystifying it.

32. Cf. Hamlet's sense of his own intuition as foreknowledge: "O my prophetic soul!" (1.5.40).

33. In *The Pursuit of the Millennium*, Norman Cohn demonstrates that especially in their early stages the Nazi and Communist movements endowed "social conflicts and aspirations with a transcendental significance—in fact with all the mystery and majesty of the final, eschatalogical drama" (p. 308). Both movements "have been inspired by phantasies which are downright archaic" and "heavily endebted to that very ancient body of beliefs which constituted the popular apocalyptic lore of Europe" (p. 309). But striving for transcendence is by no means limited to these totalitarian movements. Witness the 1912 campaign in which Theodore Roosevelt declared that "we fight in honorable fashion for the good of mankind . . . we stand at Armageddon, and we battle for the Lord." In the early 1980s, drawing on the prophecies of Ezekiel, the American president likewise invoked Armageddon, representing the Soviet Union as an "evil empire" bent upon world conquest and the extirpation of all freedom, while characterizing his own ideology, as he did on the evening of his reelection in 1984, as a "prairie fire" that has swept across America from sea to sea. The apocalyptic violence dissociated in the presidential rhetoric is projected onto the demonized rival, the Soviet Union. At the time 37 percent of Americans reportedly believed the Russians were their enemies "because they are atheists" (*Harper's Magazine*, March 1985). See Grace Halsell, *Militant Evangelists on the Road to Nuclear War* (Westport, Conn.: Lawrence Hill, 1986).

34. Prior, *The Drama of Power*, p. 338.

Chapter 10

1. Marsilio Ficino, "Commentary on Plato's Symposium," trans. Sears Reynolds Jane, *University of Missouri Studies*, vol. 19, no. 1 (1944), p. 145.

2. Irving Singer, *The Nature of Love* (Chicago: University of Chicago Press, 1984), 2:174. Ficino restricts love to masculine friendship so that it can be understood as a solution to the potentially lethal conflicts in hero worship as described earlier in Chapter 4.

3. Erik H. Erikson, *Childhood and Society*, 2d ed. (New York: Norton, 1974), p. 250.

4. Richard Wheeler, "'Since first we were dissevered': Trust and Autonomy in Shakespearean Tragedy and Romance," in Schwartz and Kahn, *Representing Shakespeare*, pp. 154–55.

5. Sigmund Freud, *The Standard Edition of the Complete Psychological Works of Sigmund Freud*, ed. and trans. J. Strachey, 24 vols. (London: Hogarth Press, 1953–74), 14:94.

6. Melanie Klein, "Some Theoretical Conclusions Regarding the Emotional Life of the Infant," in *The Writings of Melanie Klein, 1946–1963*, ed. R. E. Money-Kyrle (New York: Free Press, 1984), 3:62.

7. D. W. Winnicott believes that objects gain stability in the external world for the child only after the child has attempted to destroy them within the omnipotent imagination. "It is the destructive drive that creates the quality of externality" and objects that, surviving attack, can then be used. Richard Wheeler observes that this process "is crucial to the establishment of both trust and autonomy: it makes possible relations to others that can unite persons who acknowledge the separateness of one another" (Schwartz and Kahn, *Representing Shakespeare*, p. 161).

8. Cf. masques in which "wild men" abduct the courtly ladies and hold them captive

until their heroic courtiers edifyingly rescue them. See, e.g., Roy Strong, *Splendour at Court: Renaissance Spectacle and the Theatre of Power* (Boston: Houghton Mifflin, 1973), pp. 106–7.

9. A comprehensive treatment of projective relationships in the play is Murray M. Schwartz's, "Between Fantasy and Imagination: A Psychological Exploration of *Cymbeline*," in *Psychoanalysis and Literary Process*, ed. Frederick Crews (Cambridge, Mass.: Winthrop, 1970), p. 225. See also Meredith Skura, "Interpreting Families from Above and Below: Families, Psychoanalysts, and Literary Critics," in Schwartz and Kahn, *Representing Shakespeare*, pp. 203–16.

10. Schwartz, "Between Fantasy and Imagination," summarizes: "Posthumus moves in his psychic disintegration and partial reintegration from reaction-formation (which fails) to violent ambivalence (which releases the wish for the death of the sexual mother-wife) to mother-identification (which restores original purity and denies castration fears by assuming a castrated position) and finally to the restoration of the father's care for his impotent child" (pp. 277–78).

11. Cf. Jachimo's plaint, "The guilt within my bosom / Takes off my manhood" (5.2.1–2): i.e., the part *he* came with. The introjected guilt is reminiscent of Romeo in his suicidal moments.

12. In the play's iconographical allusions "Fidele's" resurrection implies Christ's. See Peggy Munoz Simonds, "The Marriage Topos in *Cymbeline*: Shakespeare's Variations on a Classical Theme," *English Literary Renaissance* 19, no. 1 (1989).

13. The omnipotent Oberon and Jupiter are both displacements of the weak father insofar as they are philanderers and not above rape.

14. Spying, Jachimo reduces Imogen to a rich "inventory" of furnishings he can steal to convince Posthumus of his conquest (2.2.25–30). On the one hand, this is the envious greed of a parvenu dazzled by privilege. On the other, it suggests an infantile fragmentation of the unobtainable mother into fetishistic parts, even as his desire substitutes the necrophiliac passivity of a "monument" for dangerous intimacy (31–33).

15. In "'I Wooed Thee with My Sword': Shakespeare's Tragic Paradigms," in Lenz, Greene, and Neely, *The Woman's Part*, Madelon Gohlke (Sprengnether) gives this doubleness a cogent analytical basis, pp. 161–62.

16. *Dominance and Defiance*, Diane Elizabeth Dreher's study of father-daughter relations in the plays (Lexington: University of Kentucky Press, 1986), sees Prospero as Erikson's exemplum of "the mastered self."

17. David Sundelson, *Shakespeare's Restorations of the Father*, (New Brunswick, N.J.: Rutgers University Press, 1983), whose title reflects themes of play-death, develops Prospero's acceptance of his own sonship.

18. Caliban thus reenacts the usurpation of the treacherous brother. See Stephen Orgel, "Prospero's Wife," in Ferguson, Quilligan, and Vickers, *Rewriting the Renaissance*, p. 51.

19. Orgel, "Prospero's Wife," p. 62.

20. Orgel comments, "At moments in his public utterances, James sounds like a gloss on Prospero: 'I am the husband and the whole island is my lawful wife; I am the head, and it is my body.' Here the incorporation of the wife has become literal and explicit" (p. 59).

21. Harry Berger, Jr., "Miraculous Harp: A Reading of Shakespeare's Tempest," *Shakespeare's Studies* 5 (1969): 279.

22. Douglas L. Peterson, *Time, Tide and Tempest* (San Marino, Calif.: Huntington Library, 1973), p. 248.

23. Akrigg, *Jacobean Pageant*, pp. 136–37.

Chapter 11

1. Otto Wagener, *Hitler—Memoirs of a Confidant*, ed. Henry Ashby Turner, Jr. (New Haven, Conn.: Yale University Press, 1985). Cf. the final chapter of Norman Cohn's *The Pursuit of the Millennium*.

2. "Hampshire Life," *The Daily Hampshire Gazette*, March 11, 1988, p. 39.

3. Associated Press story, February 13, 1985.

4. *Weekly World News*, November 11, 1986, p. 5.

5. Martin Gardner, "Giving God a Hand," *The New York Review of Books*, August 13, 1987, p. 18.

6. Fergus M. Bordewich, "Mortal Fears: Courses in 'Death Education' Get Mixed Reviews," *The Atlantic*, February 1988, pp. 30–34.

7. Jim Jones was obsessed with play-death. On one occasion he knocked out a defiant child with drugs, then "resurrected" the boy from this punitive death in an effort to oversway his will and impress the congregation. As a magical healer (cf. Cerimon) he regularly caused gullible believers to expel "cancers"—actually rotten chicken parts manipulated by a confederate—and feel reborn. In an imagination charged with apocalyptic hopes and fears, Jones's obsession with rescues from doom became part of a tragic pattern of paranoid victimization and megalomania. See, e.g., Jeannie Mills, *Six Years with God* (New York: A & W Publishers, 1979).

Appendix

1. A. L. Rowse, *The Case Books of Simon Forman* (London, 1974), p. 31.

2. Louis Adrian Montrose, "'Shaping Fantasies': Figurations of Gender and Power in Elizabethan Culture," *Representations* 1:2 (1983): 63.

3. See A. L. Rowse's *Sex and Society in Shakespeare's Age* (New York: Scribner's, 1974), pp. 45–47.

Index

Abraham, 90, 91, 110
Adelman, Janet, 210 (n. 30), 216 (n. 18), 217 (n. 21)
Aeneas, 3, 5, 52, 75, 78
Akrigg, G. P. V., 127, 190, 207 (n. 4), 221 (n. 14), 222 (n. 16), 228 (n. 23)
Alexander the Great, 87, 96
All's Well That Ends Well, 4, 15, 16
Alvarez, A., 208 (n. 3)
Andrewes, Lancelot, 209 (n. 20)
Antony and Cleopatra, 4, 5, 9–11, 17, 18, 34, 42–48, 94, 117, 124, 143, 176
Apology for Actors, An, 215 (n. 8)
Ariès, Philippe, 212 (n. 9)
Aristotle, 25, 44, 48
Armstrong, John, 219 (n. 10)
Aronson, Alex, 219 (n. 10)
Ashanti, 9
As You Like It, 16, 21, 30, 32, 66, 92, 97, 99, 104–5, 112–13, 149, 150, 189
Atlas, 37
Auerbach, Erich, 218 (n. 13)
Augustine Novello, Saint, 38, 39, 41, 42, 76
Augustine of Hippo, Saint, 21, 27, 164, 207 (n. 4), 209 (n. 24), 221 (n. 8); *City of God*, 92; *Confessions*, 164

"Ballet of a father, A," 220 (n. 17)
Barber, C. L., 34, 54, 77, 78, 167–69, 209 (n. 19), 211 (n. 36), 214 (n. 29), 217 (n. 10), 226 (n. 29)
Batman upon Bartoleme, 210 (n. 32)
Battenhouse, Roy, 217 (n. 7)
Batty, Bartholomew, 209 (n. 22)
Beaty, Nancy Lee, 212 (n. 9)
Beaumont, Francis, vi
Becker, Ernest: *The Denial of Death*, ix, 11, 36, 39, 40–42, 58–61, 63, 129, 211 (n. 1), 213 (n. 20), 216 (n. 20), 217 (n. 8), 221 (n. 5)
Becon, Thomas, 30, 210 (n. 28)
Beltz, Walter, 218 (n. 13)
Berger, Harry, Jr., 211 (n. 35), 228 (n. 21)
Bergeron, David M., 84, 89, 214 (n. 26), 218 (n. 18)

Blanpied, John, 215 (n. 5)
Bloch, Maurice, 217 (n. 2), 218 (n. 22)
Bodkin, Maud, 217 (n. 4)
Book of Common Prayer, 91
Booth, Stephen, 212 (n. 12)
Bordewich, Fergus M., 229 (n. 6)
Bradbrook, Muriel C., 132, 156, 222 (nn. 17, 18), 225 (n. 14)
Bradley, A. C., 30, 210 (n. 31)
Brenner, Gerry, 142, 223 (n. 7)
Bridenbaugh, Carl, 162, 209 (nn. 13, 16), 210 (n. 30)
Brooke, Arthur: *Romeus*, 146
Brower, Reuben, 212 (n. 10)
Brueghel, Pieter, 217 (n. 5)
Bullein, William, 8, 9, 207 (n. 9)
Burckhardt, Sigurd, 212 (n. 12)
Burke, Kenneth, 110–11, 221 (n. 19)
Burton, Dolores M., 226 (n. 16)

Caesar, Augustus, 138, 140
Caesar, Julius, 54, 56
Calderwood, James L., 211 (nn. 37, 38), 220 (n. 12), 225 (n. 10), 226 (n. 25)
Calvin, John, 91, 210 (n. 28); Calvinism, 125
Campbell, Joseph, 74, 105, 217 (n. 2)
Canetti, Elias, 119, 216 (n. 20), 221 (n. 3)
Cantor, Paul A., 213 (n. 22)
Carpaccio, Vittore, 52, 53
Carroll, William, 207 (n. 4), 226 (n. 24)
Cassirer, Ernst, 212 (n. 15)
Castiglione, Conte Baldassare, 23
Ceres, 100
Chambers, R. W., 18, 208 (n. 4)
Charles I (king of England), 191
Charlemagne, 60
Choron, Jacques, 213 (n. 16)
Christianity, 9, 15, 19–21, 27–30, 39, 52–57, 70, 74, 78–83, 85, 87, 90,91, 96, 102–3, 106, 108, 110, 125, 132, 135–37, 157–58, 160–71 passim, 180, 185–86, 188, 193–95, 198–99, 203–5, 226 (n. 17)
Cleopatra, 96, 151
Cohen, Norman, 161, 226 (nn. 17, 19), 227 (n. 33)